Shifting Production to Southeast Asia

Shifting Production to Southeast Asia

Electronics Transnational Corporations Moving to Vietnam since the 2000s

David Yuen Tung Chan
Chun Yang

LEXINGTON BOOKS
Lanham • Boulder • New York • London

Published by Lexington Books
An imprint of The Rowman & Littlefield Publishing Group, Inc.
4501 Forbes Boulevard, Suite 200, Lanham, Maryland 20706
www.rowman.com

86-90 Paul Street, London EC2A 4NE, United Kingdom

British Library Cataloguing in Publication Information Available

Library of Congress Cataloging-in-Publication Data

Names: Chan, David Yuen Tung, 1992 – author. | Yang, Chun (Economic geographer), author.
Title: Shifting production to Southeast Asia: electronics transnational corporations moving to Vietnam since the 2000s / David Yuen Tung Chan and Chun Yang.
Description: Lanham [Maryland]: Lexington Books, [2025] | Includes bibliographical references and index. | Summary: "This book investigates Vietnam's integration into the changing global and regional electronics production networks since the 2000s. It reveals that instead of driving only by the traditional lead firms and the lower costs, this complex production reconfiguration has been co-led by various firms and non-firm actors under different emerging dynamics"—Provided by publisher.
Identifiers: LCCN 2024037191 (print) | LCCN 2024037192 (ebook) | ISBN 9781666931464 (cloth) | ISBN 9781666931471 (epub)
Subjects: LCSH: International business enterprises—China. | International business enterprises—Vietnam. | Electronic industries—Location—China. | Electronic industries—Location—Vietnam. | Regional economics—China. | Regional economics—Vietnam.
Classification: LCC HD2891.85 .C43 2025 (print) | LCC HD2891.85 (ebook) | DDC 338.8/8859—dc23/eng/20241101
LC record available at https://lccn.loc.gov/2024037191
LC ebook record available at https://lccn.loc.gov/2024037192

∞™ The paper used in this publication meets the minimum requirements of American National Standard for Information Sciences—Permanence of Paper for Printed Library Materials, ANSI/NISO Z39.48-1992.

Contents

List of Tables

List of Figures

Abbreviations

ADB	Asian Development Bank
AFTA	ASEAN Free Trade Area
APEC	Asia-Pacific Economic Cooperation
ASEAN	Association of Southeast Asian Nations
ATP	Assembly, Testing, and Packaging
BRICS	Brazil, Russia, India, China, and South Africa
CAFTA	China-ASEAN Free Trade Agreement
CFO	Chief Financial Officer
CM	Contact Manufacture
CPTPP	Comprehensive and Progressive Agreement for Trans-Pacific Partnership
EDZ	Economic Development Zone
EPZ	Export-Processing Zone
ETNC	Emerging Transnational Corporation
EU	European Union
EZ	Economic Zone
FDI	Foreign Direct Investment
FGP	Flying Geese Paradigm
FIE	Foreign-Invested Enterprise
GCC	Global Commodity Chain
GDP	Gross Domestic Product
GPN	Global Production Network
GSP	Generalized System of Preferences
GVC	Global Value Chain
HKTDC	Hong Kong Trade Development Council
HTZ	High-Tech Zone
IB	International Business

IC	Integrated Circuit
IDM	Integrated Device Manufacturer
IMF	International Monetary Fund
IP	Industrial Park
IT	Information Technology
IZ	Industrial Zone
LLL	Link-Leverage-Learn
M&A	Mergers and Acquisitions
MIT	Middle-Income Trap
NGO	Nongovernmental Organization
NIE	Newly Industrialized Economy
OBM	Own Brand Manufacturer
OBOR	One Belt and One Road
OECD	Organization for Economic Co-operation and Development
OEM/ODM	Original Equipment Manufacturing/Own Designing and Manufacturing
OFDI	Outward Foreign Direct Investment
OLI	Ownership Advantages, Location Advantages, and Internalization Advantages
PCI	Provincial Competitiveness Index
PRD	Pearl River Delta
RBV	Resource-Based View
R&D	Research and Development
RPN	Regional Production Networks
RRD	Red River Delta
SEZ	Special Economic Zone
SITC	Standard International Trade Classification
SME	Small and Medium Enterprise
SOE	State-Owned Enterprise
TiVA	Trade in Value-Added
TNC	Transnational Corporation
TPP	Trans-Pacific Partnership
UNCTAD	United Nations Conference on Trade and Development
UNIDO	United Nations Industrial Development Organization
USBTA	US Bilateral Trade Agreement
VCCI	Vietnam Chamber of Commerce and Industry
VCP	Vietnamese Communist Party
WTO	World Trade Organization
YRD	Yangtze River Delta

Preface and Acknowledgments

This book starts from the successful award of the National Natural Science Foundation of China (NSFC) project entitled "China–ASEAN Industrial Relocation and Restructuring of Regional Production Networks: Evidence from Vietnam and Cambodia" by the second author—Chun Yang—for four years (2016–2019). The work was born in the time and space contingency. After the global financial crisis under the post-Washington Consensus, the consumption power of the traditional advanced economies in the West has been shrinking. Together with the increasing pressure on labor-intensive manufacturing in coastal China, the export-oriented industrialization in the Pearl River Delta and the Yangtze River Delta has started to transform since the 2010s (Yang, 2012, 2013, 2014, 2016; Yang & He, 2017). On the other hand, the Global Production Network (GPN) 2.0 theory, which is building upon elements of the global value chains (GVCs, Gereffi et al., 2005) and the initial GPN 1.0 framework (Coe et al., 2002), emphasizing, both organizationally and geographically, the complex firm networks and territorial institutions involved in all economic activity, was developed in the mid-2010s aiming to address parts of the criticism of the GPN 1.0 and to have a greater analytical precision and explanatory power in a theory of GPNs (Coe & Yeung, 2015). Seeing the potential of the GPN 2.0 theory, and the compelling need to update the empirical literature on production relocations out of China, and with the fiscal support from NSFC as well as the University Grants Committee (UGC) and Hong Kong Baptist University, the first author, David Yuen Tung CHAN, was recruited in 2016 as the second author's PhD student and participated in the project.

In retrospect, the journey of this book-length research was composed of sweat and tears. Without established connections in Vietnam back then, we started our project by extensively giving out name cards during Vietnam investment promotion talks held in Hong Kong. After hundreds of declines upon our interview invitations, we then started to gradually connect with a few concerned actors. With limited budgets and not knowing Vietnamese, the field investigations were never smooth. Having an interview in a backward village in the middle of nowhere when there was a heavy rainstorm followed by an electricity cutout and then flooding is surely one adventure to be memorized. Thankfully, with help from different parties, especially the Chinese investors and businessmen in Vietnam, we have eventually met different tiers of firms and levels of government and institutions as we originally planned. We cannot thank them enough for their warm welcome, introduction, and hospitality for the fluent carrying out of this project.

Not only from the first author's PhD study that ended in 2020, but this book also came from our continuous research afterwards, especially chapter 8 in which we tried to summarize the impacts of the Sino-US trade war and the COVID-19 pandemic. Some original chapters of this monograph have been published in the *Journal of Contemporary China* (Chan & Yang, 2022a), *Applied Geography* (Yang & Chan, 2023), and a book chapter on the transformation of Asian electronics production networks edited by J. Bryson, C. Billing, W. Graves, and G. Yeung (2022) and published by Edward Elgar. With the rising attention from different scholars toward the GPN studies as well as the production network restructuring and relocation from China to Southeast Asia, our works benefited from many constructive comments from a broad community of scholars, both within economic geography and beyond. We thank (and apologize for any omissions): Neil Coe, Henry Yeung, Robert Hassink, Martin Hess, Fenghua Pan, Yehua Dennis Wei, Ingo Liefner, Danny MacKinnon, Kean Fan Lim, Jianfa Shen, Godfrey Yeung, Suisheng Zhao, Xiaohui Hu, Tianlan Fu, and Huiwen Gong, and so on. Special thanks need to be given to Canfei He for his constructive comments on the first draft of the book. We would also like to thank Alexandra Rallo, Bay Pang, Zichang Li, Ruopu Yang, Jingyi Chen, Jianqiu Liang, Lanyan Yang, Rongxuan Zhao, Shuyan Wang, Xue Zhang, and other helpers for assisting us in putting our work into one piece.

The first author gives his sincere gratitude (in alphabetical order) to David Wong, Harry Lee, Helen Du, James Lenzer, Jianfeng Li, Ka Ho Mok, Kar Ming Yu, Lachlan Barber, Siming Li, Simon Zhao, Tianlan Fu, Yung Yau, as well as all the teachers, peers, and colleagues at the University of Hong Kong, Hong Kong Baptist University, and Lingnan University for the continuous support throughout his academic and career path. He also thanks Donghui Li and the members of Lingnan's Jockey Club Hall for providing a congenial living environment throughout the writing of this book. Of course, the first author is forever indebted to Prof. Chun Yang not just for seeing his potential and patiently guiding his doctoral project but, more importantly, for transmitting the attitudes and inner values of how one scholar should be like. Lastly, the first author would like to express a heartfelt acknowledgment to his family members, loved ones, and friends, for their love and care that helped to get through all the ups and downs in his academic journey and have made it even more colorful and memorable. No words can literally express this thankfulness.

The second author is indebted to the funding of the NSFC (Project No.: 41571119 & 4207114) and support from the co-investigators of the project, namely Canfei He at Peking University, Serey Sok at Royal University of Phnom Penh, Cambodia, and Nam Hoang Nguyen at National Economics University, Vietnam, as well as the PhD students and postdoctoral fellows who participated in and contributed to the undertaking of the project. Appreciations go to the anonymous interviewees and organizations that shared their valuable viewpoints in the interviews and focus group meetings conducted in Vietnam and Cambodia. Last but not least, grateful thanks extend to Yang's family members, colleagues, and friends for their enduring love and support, without which the book could hardly be generated as presented.

Hong Kong SAR,
May 2024

Chapter 1

Introduction

WHY SHOULD ONE CARE ABOUT PRODUCTION RELOCATION TO AND IN THE GLOBAL SOUTH?

In the second half of the twentieth century, the advanced economies of North America and Western Europe—the "Global North"—started to shift to a more spatially and organizationally flexible mode of production from the previous Fordist production system due to the increasingly competitive pressures at the global scale, the advancing technologies, the decline in mass markets, and the rapidly changing consumer tastes (Coe & Yeung, 2015; Dicken, 2007; Gereffi, 2014; Gereffi et al., 2005; Schoenberger, 1988). As the large, vertically integrated plants struggled to cope with the changing economic environment by shedding employment with the decline of the Fordist production system, a structural shift in Atlantic capitalism in which networks of small producers knitted together through input and output linkages started to appear by the late 1970s. The "flexible specialization" based on "flexible—multi-use—equipment; skilled workers; and the creation, through politics, of an industrial community" (Piore & Sabel, 1984: 17) soon took place with the popularity of offshoring and outsourcing strategies to look for lower cost, higher flexibility, and speed. Hence, the production systems, with more firms involved, have rapidly emerged and developed across different developed and developing countries serving the advanced economies in the North (see, e.g., Ernst, 2005; Gereffi, 1994, 1996).

However, as Kenney (2004) pointed out, the world economy's spatial and organizational configurations differed from one of the 1990s mentioned earlier at the turn of the millennium. According to Coe and Yeung (2015: 3),

> (o)rganizational shifts have been accompanied by profound geographic shifts relating to the rise of emerging market transnational corporations and shifts in global patterns of demand towards the Global South, both in terms of the burgeoning level of so-called South-South trade and as a focus for firms from the Global North.

As the rapid rise and changes of the developing and emerging economies in the "Global South" where not only lower costs and higher capabilities in manufacturing have been increasingly unleashed but also the market power (Yeung, 2022b), we should, on the one hand, update our understanding of the changing configurations of the global production system as well as their regional operations empirically given the changing dynamics and, on the other hand, renew our understanding of the original conceptual frameworks of the global production systems, that is, the Global Commodity Chain (GCC), Global Value Chain (GVC), and the Global Production Network (GPN), which were relatively "Northern lead-firm centric" (Horner & Nadvi, 2018: 231) in nature as they are presumed to be coordinated by the firms from the advanced economies and to serve the developed markets in the "Global North." What about the rising "Global South"? Are these conceptualizations still valid to understand the world economic landscape in the 2000s, particularly in the aftermath of the global financial crisis and the most recently heightened geopolitical tensions, and the COVID-19 pandemic?

With the work of the "new international division of labor" and its impacts, Gereffi (1994) grasped the reality of the "new" forms of industrial organization related to the post-Fordism and flexible specialization by developing the framework of GCC and later into the GVC to look into the cross-border firm-based transactions and the governance and dynamics along the input-output commodity/value chains of the production. The focus has been placed on the organization of firms, the inter-firm networks, and, to a lesser extent, the related socioeconomic developments (see, e.g., Gereffi et al., 2005). Yet, different shortcomings have been pointed out using this framework to understand the global production systems and the regional developments under economic globalization (e.g., Coe et al., 2008; Coe & Yeung, 2015; Henderson et al., 2002; Neilson et al., 2015). For example, the lack of geographical sense and ignoring of the role of nonfirm actors, institutions, and "multi-scalarity" have been repeatedly criticized. To overcome the theoretical limitations in the literature for a more sophisticated framework to analyze the territorial formation and economic development in the global economy, Henderson et al. (2002) constructed one better-integrated framework, that is, the GPN, to understand the uneven spatiality of production and consumption, the different roles of structural and institutional conditions at different scales, and the strategies and responses of both firms and nonfirm organizations, including government bodies, shaping the global economy across space and time. However, one of the main drawbacks of this framework is that it is relatively fragmented and lacks explanatory strength as it does not link various ideas into a causal mechanism so as to establish a relatively connected and comprehensive framework. The "GPN 2.0" framework recently developed by Coe and Yeung (2015) thus tried to offer a more complete framework with a causal mechanism to increase the explanatory strength to explain "from the structural capitalist dynamics that underpin global production network formation and operation to the on-the-ground development outcomes for regional economies" (Coe & Yeung, 2015: 22). Despite the aforementioned efforts, various theoretical and empirical research gaps in the GPN 2.0 framework for a better understanding of the changing dynamics in the global production system and the related regional developmental outcomes still appear and will be spotted later in this book.

Since the 2000s, particularly in the aftermath of the global financial crisis in 2008–2009, the changing competitive cost pressure in the "World Factory"—China—has led to a new round of "spatial fix" (Harvey, 1995) through which the firms have to seek for lower-cost production bases. Due to the increasing wages and land rents, shortage of labor, strengthening environmental laws, and so on, the export-oriented industrialization in coastal China has been challenged, and apart from "going up" to upgrade the production and product itself, two relocation patterns for the labor-intensive industries have been observed by Zhu and Pickles (2014). Besides "going in" by relocating to the inland provinces of China, "going out" to relocate the labor-intensive activities overseas is also a resort encouraged by the central government of China, particularly since 2001 when "going out" was included officially in the national development plan. Notably, the current trade war between China and the United States imposing extra tariffs on China's exports has intensified the "going out" relocation motives for the manufacturing firms located in China to the nearby countries in developing Southeast Asia to avoid the extra tariff and turbulence. Moreover, the "Belt and Road Initiative" launched by the Chinese central government could also accelerate the exit of manufacturing activities from China to the developing countries nearby, such as Vietnam and India (Lee & Zhou, 2019). With the popularity of the "China Plus One" strategy to diversify the risk, an increasing number of manufacturing factories invested by different tiers of transnational corporations (TNCs) from different sources of origins, including the ones from China, have seemed to expand, if not completely relocate to the developing economies in developing Southeast Asia. Under the transformation of the "World Factory," although an increasing number of firms going out of China to the nearby countries have been increasingly witnessed, the recent focus has still concentrated on the notion of "going in" (Yang, 2016, 2017).

Under the changing dynamics aforementioned in both GPNs and Asian regional production networks (RPNs), this book focuses on better understanding the recent wave of production relocations from China to developing Southeast Asia. While previous studies primarily focused on the roles of the lead firms originating from the relatively advanced economies in the "North" as well as the ones from the newly industrialized economies (NIEs), the emerging roles of the firms from the emerging and developing countries, including China, have been overlooked (Azmeh & Nadvi, 2014; Henderson & Nadvi, 2011; Horner & Nadvi, 2018). Questions related to the participation and the changing role of these economies, such as China and Vietnam, in restructuring the GPNs and RPNs should also be studied. As shown by Yeung and Liu (2008), although Chinese firms have continuously been globalized, the case studies on the internationalization of Chinese firms tended to focus mainly on a few "celebrated" cases and the state-owned enterprises (SOEs), and this ignores a wide range of relatively small and medium-sized privately owned emerging transnational corporations (ETNCs), which have been found to be increasingly important, particularly to the regional economy (Yeung, 2017), in restructuring the production landscape. Besides, in studying the current production expansions from China to the developing countries, the increasing role of the lower-tier suppliers has so far received little attention, despite the fact that a few empirical studies have showcased their growing abilities to manage the geographical and organizational restructuring of GVCs and GPNs, particularly the Asian transnational contract manufacturers (Azmeh & Nadvi, 2014; Lee & Gereffi, 2015; Yang, 2017). In short, how different tiers of the firms from different origins have expanded and reorganized their cross-border production networks using different strategies and coupled with the institutions of various levels to settle in the host regions deserves more attention as the current changing economy has been driven not only by the leading TNCs from the "Global North" but also the actors of different tiers and scales originated from all economies.

In developing Southeast Asia, Vietnam, which joined the World Trade Organization (WTO) in 2007 and recently signed various multilateral trade partnerships, such as the Comprehensive and Progressive Agreement for Trans-Pacific Partnership (CPTPP) in 2018, should be studied as it has rapidly participated in the global production systems over the past two decades. Due to various push and pull factors at multiple scales, foreign direct investment (FDI) inflow to Vietnam increased from 8 billion USD in 2010 to 14.1 billion USD in 2017, ranking third among the Association of Southeast Asian Nations (ASEAN). Notably, most FDIs in Vietnam went into the manufacturing sector (UNCTAD, 2018). However, although the FDI inflows and the production relocations to Vietnam have been increasingly witnessed and studied (e.g., Anwar & Nguyen, 2010, 2011a, 2011b; Meyer & Nguyen,

2005; Oh & Mah, 2017), the majority of the studies focused on the drivers and impacts of FDIs. Whereas insufficient attention has been paid to unpack the cross-border production expansions into Vietnam and the related reconfiguration of the production networks in detail, as well as the coupling process between Vietnam and different production networks, to better grasp the reality of how Southeast Asian countries have articulated into the shifting GPNs/RPNs in such a short span.

Last but not least, as the world has currently entered the "slowbalization" age, which is termed by *The Economist* (2019) to represent the slowing down of intensive globalization after the global financial crisis, sluggishness has been increasingly seen and exacerbated by some unprecedented global dynamics emerged in the late 2010s, such as the heightened geopolitical tensions, the outbreak of COVID-19 pandemic, and the accelerating global environmental protection agenda (Titievskaia et al., 2020). Economic globalization is now at a critical conjuncture as a more finely-grained, multiscale, territorial patchwork of production activities has been witnessed, leading to more fragmented global production systems (Coe & Yeung, 2019; Martin et al., 2018). Despite being claimed as the "final" winner in the Sino-US trade war (Davis & Wei, 2022), the pro-reshoring policies seeking to domesticize the supply chains due to the recent rise of economic nationalism in the "Global North" (Elia et al., 2021) are likely to set back Vietnam's internationalization efforts made in the past several decades. Although the "slowbalization" has currently started to take place and hence it would be too early now to jump to a conclusion of how it reconfigures the global production systems, in a later chapter of this book, we will explore the nature and the logic behind the curtain to try to forecast its impacts on the future picture of the manufacturing activities in the developing Southeast Asia, particularly Vietnam standing at a crossroads under the uncertainties and risks.

In a nutshell, starting from the 2000s, the "Northern lead-firm centric" (Horner & Nadvi, 2018: 231) globalization theories have not been enough to capture the current restructuring of global production systems with the rise of the "Global South" both as an increasingly important production base with the low production costs and an emerging end market. The actors in these emerging and developing economies have been now playing a more critical role, particularly in the recent trend of "slowbalization." Apart from the existing studies, which pay most of the attention to the overall changing patterns of the international trade and investment flow (e.g., Lee, 2016), a comprehensive exploration of the process and mechanism of the recent wave of cross-border production relocations to developing Southeast Asia with solid and rich empirical evidence is a much-needed update on understanding the settings and changes of the global/regional production systems entering the 2020s.

RESEARCH OBJECTIVES AND HYPOTHESES OF THE RESEARCH

To study the labor-intensive production relocations and the restructuring of the RPNs and GPNs, the electronics industry, and to be exact the consumer electronics manufacturing industry, is an ideal sector. It has dominated the international intermediate goods and final goods trade, forming the "backbone" of the global production system, which significantly impacts different countries' economies (Sturgeon & Memedović, 2011). As aforementioned, the rise of Vietnam in developing Southeast Asia deserves more attention. In particular, the rapid participation of Vietnam in the global electronics value chain/production network has attracted increasing academic awareness (e.g., Sturgeon & Zylberberg, 2017). Therefore, to be explicit, the central research question we would like to answer in this book is: Driven by different tiers of firms from different origins under the changing dynamics of the RPNs and GPNs, how electronics production has been relocated from China to Vietnam? The main objectives are to examine how the electronics production networks, particularly at the regional scale, have been restructured and to explore the way Vietnam has engaged in and the role Vietnam has taken in the global and regional electronics production networks orchestrated by different tiers of TNCs from different origins. The reasons behind why and how different TNCs have expanded and organized their production networks in Vietnam using unique sets of firm-specific strategies will also be explored.

To systematically dive in and answer the central questions mentioned earlier, three further sets of subquestions have been set:

1. How did the global and regional electronics networks change, and how did Vietnam participate in the networks? What are the evolving roles of China and Vietnam, as well as other relatively developed economies nearby, such as Japan and the NIEs, in the changing landscape of international trade and investment?
2. Why and how did different tiers of leading electronics TNCs, especially the ones from the NIEs, use different firm-specific strategies to relocate and organize their production networks in Vietnam with various firms and nonfirm actors? What are the roles of different levels of host governments in Vietnam? How is the multi-scalar strategic coupling process?
3. Why and how did ETNCs, with different attributes compared to the established TNCs, from the emerging and developing economies, for example, China, expand and coordinate their cross-border production networks in Vietnam, spatially and organizationally? And in particular, how did the inherent legacies embedded in these firms affect the

process? What about the roles of the institutions both at home and in the host region?

These questions will be analyzed in detail accordingly in chapters 5, 6, and 7. Apart from answering these questions relying on in-depth field investigations, chapter 8 is a relatively introductory outlook to the recent changes in the global economic landscape. The authors will attempt to elucidate the drivers and the logic behind followed by the consequences that could be expected in terms of the reconfigurations of the production networks, particularly toward the electronics industry in Vietnam. Based on our continuous updates amid the COVID-19 pandemic until the first quarter of 2023, this chapter provides some hints on how different firms have treated and reacted to these uncertainties and risks. In addition to the forecasts on the empirical impacts, this chapter will also discuss how one should better capture these newly emerged dynamics in the late 2010s in conceptualizing and applying the global production network framework and the potential future research arenas.

To study the earlier questions, several primary hypotheses or presumptions have to be fulfilled. Yet, before doing so, three specific key terms must be defined for better clarity of the research questions and further interpretations: developing and emerging economies, the "Global South/North," as well as the ETNCs. Although there are no widely accepted definitions for the terms "developing economies" and "emerging economies" and many studies have used these two terms interchangeably, there are indeed slight differences among them. According to Roztocki and Weistroffer (2008: 1),

> (t)he term "developing" is often used as a synonym for "poor" or "economically underperforming" . . . (C)ountries specified as developing are not locked into a state of poverty, but rather they are in control of their economic future and able to advance by developing an industrial and commercial base.

Compared to developing economies, such as Vietnam, emerging economies are countries or regions that are gradually migrating or emerging from developing to developed status (Arnold & Quelch, 1998) so that they generally have a higher and faster-growing per capita income as well as a higher market potential. An ideal case of an emerging economy would be China. In relation, there are various understandings of the term "Global South/North" under different contexts. While many differentiate them from the angles of political economy, we do it in a rather intuitive way in terms of the economic development level as Horner and Nadvi (2018) did so as to easily highlight the gap between the developing and the developed world where global production systems connect and are built upon. ETNCs are the TNCs that originated from emerging economies. As implied by Dunning et al. (2008), as the countries under the category of emerging economies change constantly, what the term "ETNC" refers to changes over time. And in this book, "ETNCs" refer to the firms that originate from emerging economies at present, such as BRICS (Brazil, Russia, India, China, and South Africa). More specifically, among different types of firms that emerged from the emerging economies, the term "ETNCs" largely referred to the relatively small and medium-sized firms with limited internationalization experience and resources instead of the emerging "giants" like Huawei and Xiaomi from China.

And here come the hypotheses or presumptions. First, as this book explores how production networks across different countries in the international region, that is, Asia, and the world have been organized by the TNCs, the authors assume that the actors both in the TNCs' home economies and in host regions will be explicitly involved in the networks. Indeed, as pointed out by Yeung and Liu (2008), some of the firms, especially the relatively smaller ones in terms of capital, would become "suitcase TNCs," which means that the entrepreneurs take the money and set up a new business in the host countries, in their internationalization process. These so-called "TNCs" usually do not have clear and official relationships, rather than a personal connection, with their previous partners as well as other nonfirm actors at home. And thus, this "guerrilla-style" strategy makes observing the relationships within the networks hard and unsound. The authors will hence try to avoid this kind of firm in the field investigation. Second and most importantly, it is assumed that different tiers of firms and levels of government have different actor-specific strategies even under the same set of competitive dynamics in the networks. As different actors have their own attributes, responses, and strategies adopted to maximize their value captures/benefits, different power dynamics, relationships within the production networks, and different strategic coupling results will thus be caused. By looking closely into a wide range of different firms and nonfirm actors, a comprehensive understanding of the situations and the configurations of the production networks could be hopefully achieved. In connection, one of the main rationales that separated chapters 6 and 7 in this book is because of the third presumption. It is assumed that the TNCs from relatively developed economies, for example, Japan and the NIEs in Asia, and the ETNCs from emerging economies, such as China, will adopt different strategies to coordinate their production networks due to their unique attributes, e.g., resources, experiences, and origins. These differences, driven by various sets of competitive dynamics, will lead to distinct spatial and organizational configurations of their production networks and result in different developmental outcomes for the regions involved. Fourth, and we will further elaborate in chapter 8, it is assumed that, rather than a rational calculation, firms sometimes react to uncertainties subjectively. Even in a perfectly open market without information bias, firms of various origins, corporate cultures, managing structures, organizations, and of various locations, even under the same parent company, are likely to respond very differently. How these firms faced the Sino-US trade war and the COVID-19 pandemic is, therefore, a fascinating question to peek at. In sum, by taking these underlying assumptions mentioned earlier, the current monograph wishes to investigate how electronics production has been relocated from China to Vietnam, driven by different tiers and levels of firms and nonfirm actors from different origins under the changing dynamics in the GPNs and RPNs since the 2000s.

RESEARCH SIGNIFICANCE AND BOOK ORGANIZATION

By studying the production relocations of the electronics industry from China to Vietnam since the 2000s, this monograph comprehensively looks into the current restructuring of the GPNs and RPNs through three different empirical chapters, along with a few chapters to introduce the backgrounds of research, conceptual frameworks we adopted, and a most updated outlook on the changing global dynamics based upon our updated investigations amid the COVID-19 pandemic. The conceptual and empirical research significances are briefly listed below.

As aforementioned, the conceptualization of the global production systems, that is, GVC and GPN, has been relatively "Northern lead-firm centric" (Horner & Nadvi, 2018: 231). Yet, this study shows that the global production systems are no longer dominated solely by the TNCs originating from the advanced economies in the "North" offshoring and outsourcing production activities to developing countries. The actors outside the "Global North," which have been increasingly influential in reconfiguring the production networks, particularly the regional ones, and their roles in this wave of production relocations have been thoroughly studied. In chapter 6, we pay more attention to different tiers of TNCs that are mainly originated from the NIEs in Asia as well as their ways to relocate and organize their production networks. While chapter 7 focuses on the ETNCs from emerging economies, such as China, to see how these ETNCs expand and coordinate their cross-border production networks. Through these two chapters, we are able to go beyond the conventional conceptualization of the GPNs and better understand how different firm actors outside the traditional advanced economies, such as the United States and the European countries, have changed the landscape and settings of the global production systems.

In relation, one of the features of the "Northern lead-firm centric" conceptualization of the GPN is that the end markets are always the advanced economies. TNCs from developed countries relocate their production activities to different developing countries merely to cut down the production costs, and the goods are eventually exported "back" to the advanced economies. Yet, this study showcases that the emerging markets outside the "North" can also be a reason for the production relocations. Chapter 5 reflects on the situation of the emerging domestic market in Vietnam as well as the regional market in Southeast Asia and of course the vast consumer market in China. And in chapter 7, it is pointed out that one of the main reasons for the ETNCs originated from China, particularly the own brand manufacturers (OBMs), to expand and organize the cross-border production networks is hoping to tap into the domestic market in Vietnam.

Third, although the newly developed GPN 2.0 has placed particular attention to the extra-firm bargaining strategies (Fuller & Phelps, 2018), the in-depth conceptualization of the firm-state bargaining relationships and the exact interactions between the firms and the states can still be further elucidated as will be discussed later in the specific chapter. Combining the notions from international business (IB) literature, chapter 6 gives a better understanding of the firm-state bargaining process using the cases of the multi-scalar strategic couplings between different tiers of firms in the network and different levels of the host governments.

Fourth, despite the fact that the "multi-scalarity" has been one of the advantages of the GPN framework over other theorizations of the global production systems, such as the GVC, it is pointed out that

> the understanding of regional institutions . . . has tended to suppress the agency of national states, with empirical research focusing largely on regional-level strategies for the promotion of strategic coupling. (Dawley et al., 2019: 856)

Therefore, in later chapters of the current book, we have paid attention not only to the firms but also to the institutions at different levels as well as the relationships between these institutions of different levels, that is, the national-level government and the provincial-level government, to understand the multi-scalar strategic coupling process, rather than simply focusing on one single level.

Fifth, in the conventional "Northern lead-firm centric" (Horner & Nadvi, 2018) GPN framework, the traditional lead firms are defined as the ones that have significant firm-specific power and organizational capacity in exercising the market control through product and market definition (Coe & Yeung, 2015: 40) or have enough

> power given their size and control over key corporate assets (such as investment capital, technology, managerial expertise and marketing channels) to orchestrate

> the activities of the dispersed networks of firms that make up their global supply chains. (Gereffi, 2019: 197)

Yet, as aforementioned, the emerging "lead firms" from the emerging and developing countries, which have increasing power in coordinating particularly the spatial and organizational configurations of the RPNs, should also be incorporated into the GPN framework. Thus, in chapter 7, how these "power-rising" firms from emerging economies have relocated and organized their cross-border production networks would be interrogated, given their unique attributes and inherent legacies.

Sixth, not only the privately owned and relatively small and medium-sized enterprises from emerging economies, such as China, which have an increasing role in the current restructuring of the production networks, have been largely ignored in the literature, but the important role of the institutional contexts in shaping the nature of firm strategic choices in and out of emerging markets has also been overlooked (Tang et al., 2008). Taking Chinese firms as an example, the institutional environments co-constructed by various levels of government both at home and in the host region encountered by these privately owned and relatively small and medium-sized enterprises compared to the state-owned enterprises (SOEs) and the emerging "giants" (Wu & Deng, 2020) are different, and this affects the ways these firms internationalize. Besides, the inherent legacies embedded in these ETNCs with little internationalization experience may also affect how they coordinate their cross-border production networks. Unlike the previous studies, which focus mostly on the SOEs and the "giants," chapter 7 adopted the notions from the institutional perspective to see why and how these ETNCs relocated and coordinated their cross-border production networks spatially and organizationally.

Last but not least, apart from the conceptual breakthroughs and enrichments, one of the most significant contributions of the current monograph is the empirical insights it provides. According to Yang (2016), the recent research on the transformation of the "World Factory" has primarily focused on upgrading the firms and the "going in" interregional relocations within China. Even though labor-intensive industries have been increasingly moving away from China and to the countries nearby in developing Southeast Asia, not enough effort has been placed into this wave of international production relocations. On the other hand, so far, the research looking into Vietnam's internationalization (see, e.g., Anwar & Nguyen, 2010, 2011b; Hollweg et al., 2017; Jandl, 2013; Meyer & Nguyen, 2005; Oh & Mah, 2017; Sturgeon & Zylberberg, 2016) mainly focuses on the reform history, economic integration of Vietnam from the economic perspective, as well as the impacts of FDIs on Vietnam's socioeconomic development, and on the position and function of Vietnam in different value chains, and so on. Nevertheless, to the best of our knowledge, there are rare comprehensive studies to examine how firms from different origins have expanded their production networks in Vietnam. Hence, this book not only updates the restructuring of the GPNs and RPNs in the "Global South" and the current wave of production relocation away from China to the developing countries nearby, but it also thoroughly studies the ways different firms have expanded to Vietnam as well as the articulation of Vietnam into the production networks of different scales with different firms and nonfirm actors involved. Of no doubt, this book, especially chapter 8, also contributes to the conceptualization and applicability of the GPN framework in the late 2010s. On the one hand, rarely have empirical studies so far had the most-updated investigations on the detailed impacts of the current uncertainties and risks in the late 2010s on the production relocations and the network reconfigurations apart from the observations based on the statistics. On the other hand, established in the early 2010s when global trade of both goods, parts, and components peaked, while the GPN framework hitherto has been adopted mostly to study the global production system in the aftermath of the 2008 financial crisis, in the current "slowbalization," some scholars have recently questioned the "global" element of the GPN as some of them assume the production systems will become more regionalized and even nationalized. Besides, the conceptualization of the notion of uncertainty in GPN has faced new challenges due to the unprecedentedly changing global risk environment. Hence, our timely updates not only could reveal some preliminary insights on the current changing dynamics of the production network reconfigurations but also could enrich the GPN framework accordingly by applying it in such a special temporal context.

By and large, this monograph aims to push forward the understanding of the current dynamics in and the restructuring of the GPNs and RPNs under the rise of the emerging and developing economies in the "Global South" by the case studies of the production relocations of the electronics firms to Vietnam. Theoretically speaking, on the one hand, this study contributes to the GPN framework by moving away from the "Northern lead-firm centric" conceptualization of globalization. While on the other hand, it also enriches the GPN 2.0 theories by rethinking the firm-state relationships and extra-firm bargaining strategies as well as uncertainties and risks in a broad capitalist environment and adding back some neglected elements, such as the multi-scalar home and host institutions, the ETNCs, and the notion of institutional escape and legacy into the network analysis. Furthermore, as some references are taken from other disciplines, that is, IB literature and institutional studies, the concepts and studies in those fields could be, in turn, testified and applied in the network analysis. Lastly, entering the era of "slowbalization" with some newly emerged forces since the 2010s, where have they come from and how will these forces impact the global production systems, and in return, how the conceptualization of the global production systems, that is, GVC and GPN, should be revamped to better capture these dynamics, will be also talked through.

The empirical studies in this book also generate several practical policy suggestions. First and foremost, this book provides a relatively comprehensive overview regarding the reorganizations of production networks of the traditional labor-intensive industry, that is, the consumer electronics manufacturing industry, particularly at the regional level. This reorganization has provided ample opportunities for the firms and governments, both in the home and host countries of the emerging and developing economies, to participate in the network, benefit from the spillovers and upgrade themselves so as to achieve socioeconomic developments, and even break free from passively following the shepherd from the Northern lead firms and institutions. More specifically, this study provides valuable insights for various levels of government in developing countries, such as Vietnam and the nearby countries, regarding how they can leverage their regional assets and the domestic firms as a bargaining chip in the extra-firm bargaining process with the TNCs to achieve a better regional development result from the strategic coupling and how they can utilize the building of institutional environments at different scales to attract the overseas investors and to anchor to the global production systems. For example, to "escape" from the structural coupling, helping domestic suppliers and producers to increase their core competitiveness and to couple with the emerging domestic market are two possible policy recommendations for these emerging and developing economies. For another example, to speed up the industrial upgrading process, this study points out that apart from the SOEs and some relatively established firms, governments in both the host, that is, Vietnam, and the home countries, such as China, should also pay attention to the small and medium privately owned ETNCs. While in chapter 8, we also disclosed that the different firms perceived the risks from the Sino-US trade war and the COVID-19 pandemic differently, but generally, the firms expected a longer and more severe impact from the former than the latter. Because of the industrial upgrading and the "Belt and Road" initiatives pushed by China, on the one hand, the popularity of the "China Plus One" diversification strategy, and the recently heightened global geopolitical tensions, on the other hand, it is foreseeable that more firms of different scales in the labor-intensive industries in China will relocate to the developing countries inside or even outside developing Southeast Asia, such as India and countries in South Africa. And this context further enhances the value of the current book's case studies for future applications.

To achieve the study goals as aforementioned, nine chapters, including the current one, are organized as follows. After introducing the study background, objectives, hypotheses, significances and contributions of the current monograph in this chapter, the second chapter critically surveys the conceptual and empirical literature relevant to the production relocations. First, different ways that economic geographers conceptualize global production systems will be revisited, and the limitations of the current conceptualizations will be pointed out. Apart from the literature on economic geography, insightful literature in other disciplines, such as business and economics, will also be reviewed. Second, the empirical studies of different waves of production relocations, particularly regarding the electronics industry, will be studied, and the empirical research gaps will be spotted. To provide a more comprehensive understanding of the dynamics of the broadly defined electronics industry as well as the shifting production to Southeast Asia, the situations of the semiconductor sector and the textile and garment industry will also be surveyed. The history of Vietnam's opening up and reform process will be briefly dissected in chapter 3 to contextualize the temporal and spatial settings of the current study. In particular, the industrial policies and their regional variances will be delineated. The following chapter will describe and justify the detailed research area, design, and methodology adopted throughout this monograph. In chapter 5, the big picture of Vietnam's articulation into the electronics production networks in the recent changing landscape of global and regional investment and trade will be analyzed to grasp the idea of how Vietnam has become a "new" destination for TNC's investment and electronics manufacturing. Not only the changing global and regional electronics production networks can be captured, but the changing role of different countries, including China, in the current restructuring networks will also be analyzed. Further firm-level studies will be presented in chapters 6 and 7 to better look into the details of the relocations and the reconfigurations of the production networks. Chapter 6 focuses on the different tiers of electronics TNCs, particularly the ones from the NIEs, which have been Vietnam's most prominent investors, and how they have used different firm-specific strategies to relocate and reorganize their production networks in Vietnam, with particular attention to the extra-firm bargaining with the multi-scalar host institutions. Chapter 7 pays particular attention to the ETNCs from emerging economies, that is, China, as they have increasingly invested and expanded overseas to other nearby developing countries, including Vietnam, to see how they relocated their productions and how the institutions, as well as the inherent legacies from their home region, have impacted the process. Before the final chapter, which includes a summary of the major findings and contributions, as well as the limitations of the current study and the possible future research agenda, chapter 8 will try to outline the most recent dynamics that emerged in the late 2010s/early 2020s and speculate their impacts both on the configurations of the production activities and on the theoretical conceptualization of the global production systems.

Chapter 2

The Changing Electronics Production Landscape

A Brief Review

> The ever-deepening spatial and organizational fragmentation of production has produced a global economy that is profoundly different from the one of 1990. Organizational shifts have been accompanied by profound geographic shifts relating to the rise of emerging market transnational corporations and shifts in global patterns of demand towards the Global South, both in terms of burgeoning levels of so-called South-South trade and as a focus for firms from the Global North. (Coe & Yeung, 2015: 2–3)

This quotation captures precisely the changes in the global economy in recent decades, at least before the latter half of the 2010s (refer to chapter 8). After the turn of the new millennium, particularly the global recession that happened in 2008, the geographical and organizational shifts of production have arguably accelerated toward the "Global South," which, as aforementioned refers in general to the low- and middle-income countries located in Asia, Africa, Latin America, and the Caribbean, in contrast to the high-income nations in the "Global North" (Hollington et al., 2015). As the pattern of increasingly "poly-centric" trade (Horner & Nadvi, 2018) has been witnessed, the scale of "South-South" trade goes beyond the trade in intermediate goods, and the value chains and production networks increasingly consolidated yet reconfigured within Asia do not only end up serving the Northern end markets (Horner & Murphy, 2018). Horner and Nadvi (2018) concluded that the contemporary global economy had changed dramatically after the 2000s from the original conceptualization of global production systems. Two differences have been spotted. First, the lead firms that dominate the orchestration of production systems are not limited to those from the Northern developed economies. Second, besides the global capital flows between the "North" and the "South," the value chains and production networks are not necessarily globalized but seem increasingly regionalized as global consumption shifts. Although their observations have been somewhat general, as the authors will review and explore the ongoing dynamics in the production networks more deeply in the coming sections and chapters, these two are still good observations to remind us that we must update the understanding and conceptual developments of the global production systems before better looking into the current wave of production relocations and the rise and changing roles of the actors, in particular those in developing Asia, which has received increasing business and academic attention, under the changing world economic landscape. On the other hand, apart from the conceptual challenges, compared to those that investigate the offshoring of production activities from the "North" to the "South," the empirical literature regarding the recent rounds of production relocation within Asia, particularly from the "World Factory"—China to nearby countries in developing Southeast Asia—is still in a relatively beginning stage. Although more research attention has been recently directed to developing Southeast Asia to see how the countries inside have articulated into the global value chains/production networks, hitherto, there are insufficient comprehensive studies to explore how exactly the production relocations and production network reorganizations have been conducted and governed.

However, before investigating the recent round of production relocations to developing Southeast Asia, this chapter needs to review the literature about the temporal, spatial, and organizational configurations of the TNC production activities as well as the flow of FDIs and trades. This helps not only to understand the contributions of previous literature and to learn from it but, more importantly, to help spot both theoretical and empirical knowledge gaps, which is necessary to better understand the current changing global economic landscape. This chapter is divided into two sections. In the first section, attention will be paid to the conceptual development concerning transnational production activities and their changing organizations to understand how economic geography scholars conceptualized TNCs, their transnational production activities, as well as the rationales and impacts on regional development. Not limited to the studies in the field of economic geography, the literature in international business studies will also be briefly reviewed as they have doubtlessly improved our understanding of the ideas of production relocation and (re)organization of production activities. In the second section, empirical literature regarding the temporal, spatial, and organizational reconfigurations of the labor-intensive production network, in particular the electronics manufacturing industry, driven by different changing dynamics in global production systems, will be reviewed. Apart from the labor-intensive segment, which the authors primarily focus on in this monograph, to provide a more comprehensive outlook of the changing organizations of the electronics industry, the situations of the rather capital-intensive segment, that is, the semiconductor manufacturing, will also be briefly summarized in the section. In addition, in the last part of the second section, the authors will also survey the situations of another labor-intensive manufacturing industry that has been relocated to Vietnam to draw a bigger picture of the dynamics in the global production landscape. After identifying both conceptual and empirical research gaps, the overall analytical framework of the book and the research questions will be developed accordingly in the final part of this chapter, hoping to fill the knowledge gaps identified from the literature survey.

FRAMING THE PRODUCTION ORGANIZATIONS OF TNCS

In this section, attention will be paid to the theoretical development of the spatial and structural production organization of TNCs and the flow of FDIs and trade to see how different scholars in economic geography and other study fields conceptualize this topic. Four subparts are divided here. Different leading conventional theoretical perspectives in economic geography, which have laid the geographical foundation of the production systems, including the post-Fordist flexible specialization and network analysis, will be very briefly reviewed in the first part. In the second and third parts, attention will be paid to the currently widely adopted global commodity chain, the global value chain, and the recently developed global production network perspectives to see how they have conceptualized the global production systems. Last but not least, dominant theories in international business and development study, which provide insightful ideas related to the internationalization of firms and their productions, such as Dunning's eclectic framework and Akamatsu's flying geese paradigm (FGP), will be reviewed in the fourth part. In fact, besides the ones mentioned earlier, there are so many more meaningful pieces of work in the field that have paved the road for our understanding of global production after the crisis of Fordism, and it is out of the scope of this chapter to take into account all the previous contributions. Hence, in the following sections, including both theoretical and empirical reviews, we will only selectively include the ones that we subjectively think have the strongest linkages with the production (re)location and (re)organization and help to establish our overall analytical framework of the current book.

Insights from the Conventional Perspectives

Different from the traditional research that focuses on the Weberian and the location theory as well as the behavioral location model that was prominent in the field before the 1980s, in the post-Fordist era since the 1970s, economic geographers have started to focus on capital structures and relations of production (e.g., Harvey, 1982) since flexible production systems, vertical disintegration, and agglomeration economies have been witnessed. Compared to the mass production system searching for international economies of scale in which firms are vertically and horizontally integrated, the post-Fordist production system, which seeks external economies of scale and scope, looks at firms in a vertical disintegration mode where firms are specialized in only parts of the production process. Through inter-firm interdependence, networks of firms are formed in the production process. The "spatial switching," which is led by new technologies, linkages, and labor demands, and the sequential "social switching," which leads to changes between labor and social relations, together lead to the emergence of new industrialized spaces (Scott, 1988, 1992). These new industrial space territorial tendencies, in terms of industrial complexes, industrial linkages, and industrial districts, were largely attractive to scholars until the mid-1990s (Yeung, 1994). Although post-Fordist flexible specialization has presented changes in the structures of capitalism as well as the relations of production and the related spatial and social manifestations, due to its shortcomings in methodology and theoretical foundation, it is not good enough to capture the production systems nowadays. Briefly speaking, the literature tends to see the growth of industrial districts as capital accumulation of endogenous factors, which overlooks the interdependence at the regional and global levels between economic actors (Sunley, 1992). More importantly, among different theoretical shortcomings that have been identified (e.g., see Sunley, 1992; Yeung, 1994), the missing role of states, the unclear business organizational forms, and the limited spatial implications of flexible production systems are three particularly crucial pitfalls particularly crucial, which hinder the understanding of international business and production organization of firms.

The earliest geographical works using network analysis started in the mid-1970s (e.g., Taylor, 1975). However, they tend to concentrate solely on the complex inter-firm linkages, and thus, the scope and scale of research are limited (Yeung, 1994). The reemerging interest in the notion of the "network" of industrial organization was witnessed in the late 1980s (e.g., Christensen et al., 1990; Dicken, 1994). The spatial organization of the network is one of the important aspects of economic geography literature. It is inevitably complicated as substituting spaces of points with spaces of relations. According to Christensen et al. (1990), a firm's spatial and network ties are affected by the strategic positioning of the firm. Because of the differences in technological and organizational capabilities, the spatial proximity of the firms is important as the distances between firms affect their interactions (Green, 1993). Although this network approach provides insightful ideas about the spatial locations and connections of the firms as it moves away from the relatively single and limited notion of a representative firm in the neoclassical behavioral geography, a critical pitfall has been found. According to Camagni (1992), the embeddedness of the institutional and sociocultural elements in the network is overlooked as the focus is mostly on the economic costs. On the other hand, as it focuses on the external relationships and interactions among the firms, the intra-firm relations are ignored in the literature. Hence, this network analysis still needs to be upgraded to become more geographically informed and to better capture the internal dynamics within the multinational corporates whose overseas branches have already been forming a global "network" themselves.

Insights from the Global Value Chain and Global Production Network Perspectives

As the economy and production have become increasingly globalized, different contributions to studying the cross-border activities of firms have been made since the 1980s by various scholars in social science. In the following paragraphs, we will briefly review the conceptual development of the GCC/GVC and the GPN, two of the arguably most popular analytical frameworks to analyze global production systems so far. After justifying the use of GPN as the main theoretical framework in this book, the most recent theoretical development of the GPN will be reviewed, and the knowledge gap that can be enriched by our work will be explored in the next part.

With the work of the "new international division of labor" and its impacts, Gereffi (1995) grasped the reality of the "new" forms of industrial organization, related to post-Fordism and flexible specialization, by developing the framework of the GCC and later the GVC to examine cross-border firm-based transactions and their related developmental results. The GCC/GVC has included a wide range of actors and elements relevant to the organization of firms and inter-firm networks and the possibilities for socioeconomic development. Even though four analytical dimensions have been identified, attention has mostly concentrated on the notion of the governance structure of the chains (Gereffi, 1995). Gereffi (1994) identified two governance structures: the producer-driven chain and the buyer-driven chain. The former is characterized by the integrated production systems of TNCs in which corporate power is exercised vertically from the headquarters down through different layers of subsidiaries, while the value generated in dispersed subsidiaries flows upward back to the headquarters. The latter chain is characterized by horizontally exercised corporate power originating with the retailers or brand holders to the firms incorporated into the chain, and the value generated is mostly added at the stages of branding and marketing, which are controlled by the retailers or brand holders. Renewed in 2005, Gereffi, Humphrey, and Sturgeon identified three variables that govern the GVCs. Due to different degrees of "complexity of transactions," "ability to codify transactions," and "capability in the supply-base," five different types of highly dynamic and overlapping GVC governance structures have been identified, namely the hierarchy, captive, relational, modular, and market value chain in which the dual spectrums of explicit coordination and power asymmetry are descending.

Although the GCC/GVC framework has provided enormously important insights into the recognition of different complex and dynamic governance relations and coordination forms within global production systems, as well as on how firms and localities plugged into the chains and with what consequences, including upgrading, a few shortcomings have been pointed out (e.g., Coe & Yeung, 2015; Henderson et al., 2002; Hess & Yeung, 2006). First, despite the effort to deepen inter-firm governance, for example, from the two- to fivefold typologies of governance, as the framework focuses primarily on firm actors, the place-specific institutional conditions, as well as the intra- and extra-firm dynamics that can also sharpen the governance, have been somehow overlooked. Hence, the on-the-ground complexity and variation in the governance structure cannot be fully captured by these typologies. Second, and in relation, as the GVC was originally built upon knowledge from development studies, industry studies, and economic sociology, the lagged development of the geographical conceptualization and territorial component limited not only the consideration of the ways societies with different characteristics constitute the firm networks but also the unit of analysis that is mostly at the national scale. Third, the GVC analysis generally failed to take into account the firm's originality and ownership structure, which are argued to be decisive to its organizational strategies (Yeung, 2004). Last but not least, although the GCC/GVC serves as a powerful framework to unpack the production structures behind certain commodities, one of its pitfalls, according to Coe and Yeung (2015), is that the spotlight on the products instead of the leading actors could hamper the ability to explain the dynamics of competition within overlapping multiproduct and multiservice worlds. That said, the rather complex interindustry dynamics in highly interconnected contemporary capitalism could likely be overlooked.

To overcome the theoretical limitations mentioned earlier for a sophisticated framework of the business and production organizations of firms, Henderson et al. (2002) constructed an integrated framework, that is, the GPN, to understand the uneven spatiality of production, the roles of structural and institutional environments at different scales, and the responses of both firms and nonfirm organizations and government bodies shaping the global economy across space and time. Briefly, the development of the GPN framework has been influenced by four antecedents, namely, the value chain framework, the networks and embeddedness perspectives, the actor-network analysis, and the GCC/GVC framework (Hess & Yeung, 2006). The production networks have become more complex organizationally with a more global geographical extent cutting through different "state boundaries" over the years. Not only do they consist of the firms and their dynamic relations, but these networks also include the national economies in which the firms are embedded and produced, and the nonfirm actors, which could impact the sociopolitical contexts, thereby adding back the "geography." In a nutshell, the GPN framework, which can help to grasp the multi-scalar economic and social dimensions of the processes involved in different and changing forms of business globalization, is more comprehensive for one to understand the global production systems driven by TNCs as well as their impacts on socioeconomic development at various scales. Consequently, we will adopt the GPN as the major analytical framework for the current monograph. The framework for GPN analysis is shown in figure 2.1.

As pointed out by Henderson et al. (2002), GPN analysis focuses on four main aspects: the network of firms of a given product and its organization, the distribution of corporate power inside the network, the institutions that influence firms' strategies, and the implications for the actors and economies. In relation to the last objective, the notion of strategic coupling, in which the advantages of regions match the strategic needs of the actors in the global production networks, has been developed to represent regional developments through the coupling process (Yeung, 2016). Through three different modes of strategic coupling with the global production networks, according to different GPN dynamics and coupling mechanisms, different regional

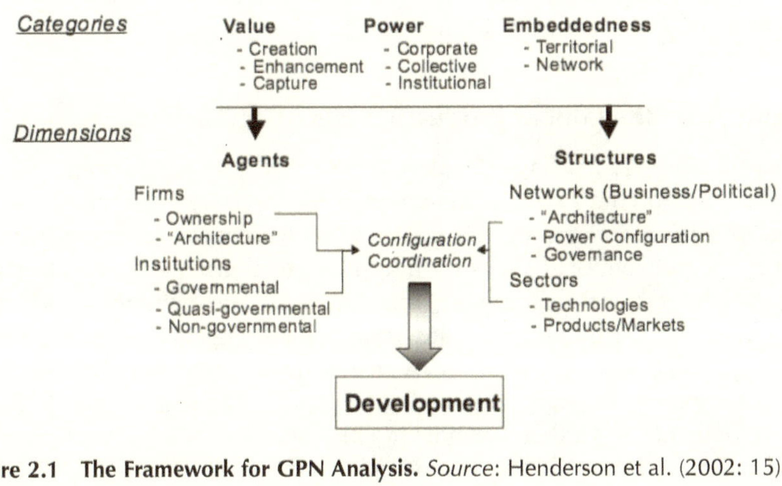

Figure 2.1 The Framework for GPN Analysis. *Source*: Henderson et al. (2002: 15).

development trajectories and regional development results, both positive and negative, can be caused (Yeung, 2015).

Although the GPN perspective has been arguably a more comprehensive framework for understanding the global economy and regional development, different shortcomings of the so-called GPN 1.0 framework (refer to figure 2.1) have been pointed out. Sunley (2008) has criticized the "selective ontology" of GPN 1.0 and pointed out its vague analytical boundaries and weak causal explanations:

> (N)etwork here (in the GPN) . . . includes just about everything and lacks analytical boundaries and clarity. Networks are defined vaguely as "relational processes" and are used to mean a whole range of things at different levels of abstraction . . . Networks are defined in such an elastic manner that they can include virtually anything. One cannot escape the conclusion that such a loose and ubiquitous idea explains everything and nothing. (Sunley, 2008: 8)

Besides, as admitted by Coe et al. (2008), practically, the attention to the GPN 1.0 framework, similar to the GVC literature, still focuses mainly on the inter-firm relationships to the extent that the intra-firm relationships, such as the internalization and externalization of functions and the power relationships within firms, have been ignored. Indeed, both the intra-firm relationships and the nonfirm actors that have different spatialities should have been integrated into the GPN studies more seriously. For instance, the institutional factors in the host and home environments that affect and are affected by the operation and governance of the production networks have not been examined thoroughly. Furthermore, the literature failed to connect the production, distribution, and consumption processes, and thus, the role of consumers and the consumption spaces need to integrate fully into the GVC and GPN literature (Jackson, 2002; Leslie & Reimer, 1999).

Insights from the Global Production Network 2.0 Framework

Coe and Yeung (2015) have developed the GPN 2.0 framework, trying to improve parts of the earlier shortcomings by stepping back and offering greater precision concerning the constituent elements and actors; backing up from the conventional focus on inter-firm relationships to reveal underlying forces or dynamics driving the strategies and actions of different types of firms; and moving forward from considering firm-level outcomes to conceptualize their intersections with territorial regional economies and their development impacts therein. It understands the firm-centric concept of development by further establishing the social, cultural, and environmental aspects (Yeung, 2016). By identifying the lines of causality between global production networks and territorial economic development, the GPN 2.0 framework aims to "connect through conceptually, from the structural capitalist dynamics that underpin global production network formation and operation to the on-the-ground development outcomes for regional economies" (Coe & Yeung, 2015: 22). Three competitive dynamics, including the "cost-capability ratio," "market imperatives," and "financial discipline," and the broader "risk environment" have been used to elaborate four different actor-specific strategies for the firms, particularly the lead firms, to organize their global production networks (refer to figure 2.2).

To achieve higher efficiencies and exert tight control over their activities, lead firms can internalize their activities through an intra-firm coordination strategy. Internationalization through greenfield FDI directly by lead firms or through mergers and acquisitions (M&A) with different strategic partners or specialized suppliers is a common way for them to expand their production networks overseas. Besides intra-firm coordination, lead firms can externalize their risk by outsourcing the production activities while at the same time still maintaining tight control over the production by developing a highly captive relationship with their suppliers (the inter-firm control strategy). These two strategies have been found frequently in the lead firm-centric organizational configuration of production networks. Besides internalizing or outsourcing their activities with a tight grasp, to increase their competitiveness, lead firms can also choose to build inter-firm partnerships to collaborate with their strategic partners and specialized suppliers. In doing so, lead firms and their suppliers can benefit mutually. Apart from the matching of the lead firm and their partners in terms of assets and knowledge, industrial standards are also needed to govern the relationships between the lead firms and their partners.

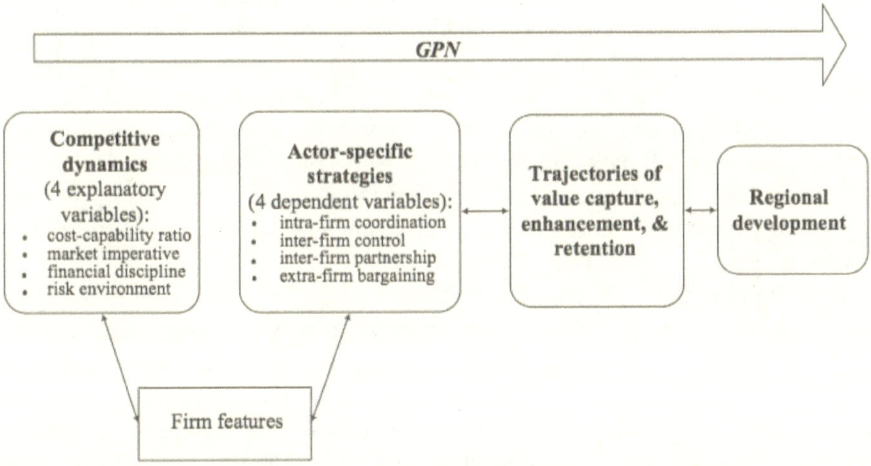

Figure 2.2 The Framework for GPN 2.0 Analysis. *Source*: Yeung (2016: 267).

This relationship is commonly found in the strategic partnership organizational configuration model. Besides interacting with the firm actors to better capture the value in the production networks, a two-way extra-firm bargaining strategy has been inevitably deployed by firms to negotiate with and accommodate the nonfirm actors involved in the production networks, such as the state and consumers, which can actively affect the coupling process between the local actors in the host regions and the production networks of the TNCs by providing the critical regional assets that fit the strategic needs of the TNCs. Apart from the facilitator, it was later proven that these actors, such as the state, have multiple and crucial roles in connecting and regulating the on-the-ground operations of the global production systems (Horner, 2017).

The global production networks are articulated on the formations of vertical and horizontal relations, which can be broken down into different forms of strategic coupling between the lead firms, their branches, and their strategic partners and suppliers in different locations. In the GPN 2.0 framework, three types of strategic coupling have been identified: indigenous coupling, functional coupling, and structural coupling. Different types of strategic coupling are critical for value capture, enhancement, and retention paths in different regional economies, and they are dynamic in nature. Although regional strategic coupling with the global production network has a strong and direct effect on regional development, positive outcomes, however, are not guaranteed (Christopherson & Clark, 2007). A region may lock into a lower value-added development path through structural coupling, acting as the assembly hub in the global production networks. In this scenario, the strategic coupling process may shift toward decoupling with the current production networks and recoupling with other production networks initiated by regional or other actors in the production networks. Seeing the decoupling and recoupling of a process as the outcomes of the regional selection and abandonment processes, MacKinnon (2012) added that it is crucial to understand the dynamic coupling, decoupling, and recoupling process with the evolutionary approaches and the concept of path dependence. Besides, updated studies have also shown that the mechanisms and interactions that constitute the strategic coupling could have been more diverse as different actors are involved in driving the processes (Coe & Yeung, 2019).

Although the GPN 2.0 framework has broadened our understanding of the organization of the global production networks that are constructed by the TNCs and the regional development outcomes with different social, cultural, political, and environmental elements included in the analytical framework, as admitted by Coe and Yeung (2019), many conceptual and empirical studies remain to be done when trying to chart and explain the restless geographies of the global economy. To help better frame and understand the production relocations to Vietnam, among different theoretical research gaps, four major knowledge gaps in the GPN 2.0 framework that we attempted to enrich in this book are identified later. Besides generally pointing out the gaps, in each respective empirical chapter, these research gaps, as well as other related ones, both conceptual and empirical, will be further elaborated on so as to have an even more in-depth understanding of these knowledge gaps found in the GPN framework and how they could have possibly been filled in.

The first relates to the capitalist dynamics for the relocation and reorganization of the production network. The existing literature on the GVC/GPN has been criticized as it has been overwhelmingly "productionist" as it ignores consumption (Coe et al., 2008). After the 2000s, indeed, not only the intermediate goods but also the trade of final products among the emerging and developing economies, especially within Asia, has expanded rapidly (Horner & Murphy, 2018; Horner & Nadvi, 2018). This implies that the trade flow of the final goods has been no longer dominated by the unidirectional South-North flow, in which the goods are manufactured in the developing economies and exported to the developed Northern countries. Besides the developed economies, the emerging and developing countries in the "Global South" have emerged as new destinations for production chains and networks. While the GPN framework assumes there is a "significant" role of the lead firms dominating the market in the "Global North," the rise of the final market in the "Global South" does pose a threat to the dominating role of these lead firms as they may not have the power and capacity in exercising market control in these emerging developing markets. It is not uncommon to see that TNCs from advanced economies have increasingly set up research and development (R&D) facilities in these emerging markets (e.g., Ivarsson & Alvstam, 2010) to understand these markets better. Different from the consumer demands of the Western markets, say the United States, consumers in developing and emerging economies have lower concerns about product standards and quality levels (Yeung & Coe, 2015). For example, according to Kaplinsky and Farooki (2010), unlike the standards-intensity of GVCs going into Northern economies that have increased remarkably and have become more and more complex in recent decades, the ones feeding into Southern markets have lower levels of standards mainly due to the low levels of per capita incomes of the consumers in these emerging markets. And this has created new opportunities for new actors to enter the national and regional markets as Brandt and Thun (2011) have shown that domestic firms could have an advantage over their foreign counterparts in tapping into the home markets due to a better understanding of the consumers' needs. A case in point is the popularity of *shanzhai* handsets with "good-enough" innovation in China (Chen et al., 2013). Although the consumer demands and standards, as well as the associated upgrading and downgrading opportunities by tapping into these emerging markets in the "Global South," are still under debate (e.g., Barrientos et al., 2016; Kadarusman & Nadvi, 2013; Nadvi, 2014; Navas-Alemán, 2011; Pickles et al., 2016), these markets, without a doubt, have been an emerging driver affecting the trade flow, the relocation, as well as the reorganization of global and regional production networks. Therefore, since the rise of the "Global South," as not only a manufacturing center but also an emerging final market after the 2000s, especially after the 2008–2009 global financial crisis when the demand from the Western market has been shrinking, one should remember that the production relocation has not solely been driven by seeking lower cost-capability ratios but also the emerging final markets. Hence, to understand the current changing dynamics of the global production networks, besides the cost capabilities, one has to also pay attention to other competitive dynamics in the GPN 2.0 framework (refer to figure 2.2), especially the changing market imperatives.

The second theoretical shortfall of the GPN framework relates to the "new" firm actors in the production networks. Indeed, these firm actors are not "new" at all. The term "new" here is used to describe their newly emerging roles in the production networks. As mentioned earlier, the rise of the final markets in the emerging and developing economies in the "Global South" has provided more chances for the domestic and regional firms in those economies to couple by reorganizing their production networks to serve the burgeoning middle class in addition to the end markets in the developed Western economies. More attention should be paid to these firms, particularly at the national and regional levels, under the changing global economy. As concluded by Horner and Nadvi (2018), it is increasingly rare to see production systems that only involve firms from relatively developed economies, for example, the United States, Western Europe, Japan, and recently East Asia, offshoring to a set of developing countries to solely serve the markets in the developed economies. Thus, apart from the "lead firms" from the advanced economies, the roles of different firm actors in the networks at various levels and scales deserve more attention. For example, Yang and He's (2017) study implied that by leveraging exports and the emerging domestic market in China in the reorganization of the laptop computer production networks, the contract manufacturer of the lead firm has gained more power and become the strategic partner of the lead firm. Besides, emerging transnational corporations (ETNCs) originating mainly from emerging and developing economies are another arena to be studied as they have increasingly expanded their production networks overseas to different developing and even developed countries around the world seeking different resources, including cheap costs, advanced technologies, and natural resources, as well as for market and upgrading opportunities. Not solely limited to the leading firms from the "Global South" looking for resources as well as markets across borders, this also includes the suppliers, particularly the power-rising first-tier suppliers, that is, contract manufacturers (CMs), as mentioned, from these economies as they have also been found critical to the restructuring of the value chains and production networks (see, e.g., Azmeh & Nadvi, 2014). Although these ETNCs are now able to direct or affect the reconfiguration of the production chains and networks at global, regional, and national levels, insufficient effort has been paid to these "new" actors. As urged by Dohse et al. (2012), more comprehensive research has to be done to better understand these ETNCs, as well as their roles and functions in the global production systems, since the conventional concepts explaining OFDI from the traditional TNCs in the "Global North" do not fit well to explain the logic and impacts of Outward Foreign Direct Investment (OFDI) from ETNCs.

The third limitation relates to the agency of the nonfirm actors, for example, the governments, as well as their interactions with the firm actors in the GPN framework. As commented by Coe and Yeung (2019), over the last decade, many studies have tried to broaden the understanding of the intersections between the GPNs and the states. They have explored the changing and diverse roles of the state in underpinning the activities of the networks. For example, they have looked into how the changing politics of the state has helped East Asian firms to plug into and upgrade within the global production networks (e.g., Yeung, 2014). They have also looked into the multiple roles of the state (e.g., Horner, 2017). Besides a facilitating actor that catalyzes the coupling process through different incentives, the state could also take the role of a regulator, producer, buyer, and investor. Although the roles of the state in the organization of production network and strategic coupling have been frequently explored, the "multi-scalarity," which has been emphasized in the earliest formulations of GPN (e.g., Coe et al., 2004), has been neglected in recent studies. As pointed out by Dawley et al. (2019), the GPN 2.0 framework offered little analysis of the relational and scalar interactions between different levels of actors. In practice, the agency of the national states has been suppressed as the understanding of regional institutions, rather than incorporating, separates the national actors. As the roles assigned to different levels of government and their effectiveness in performing them differ, in GVC/GPN research, it is crucial for us to understand what responsibilities are assigned to different tiers of government and how they interact (Gao et al., 2019). Hence, echoed by Gong and Hassink (2019), in studying the development and organization of an industry in a region, the roles of multi-scalar institutions have to be taken fully into account. Besides the agency of multi-scalar institutions, the detailed interactions between these nonfirm actors and the firm actors in the extra-firm bargaining under the coupling process are also somewhat unclear in the GPN 2.0 framework (Fuller & Phelps, 2018). Although the prominence of the "extra-firm bargaining" has been placed in the GPN 2.0 framework as a response to the criticism of the GPN

1.0 framework, for example, Smith et al. (2014), the GPN 2.0 framework is focused more on explicating the overarching outcomes rather than the actual practices. The processes of deliberation in the extra-firm bargaining between the TNCs and the host governments have also been overlooked. Using three types of micropolitical behaviors identified by Dunning and Lundan (2010), Fuller and Phelps (2018) illustrated three choices of how a TNC responds to the institutional settings in the host regions according to different degrees and natures of embeddedness with the host localities. Yet, the interactions within the firm-state bargaining process, how firms come up with certain strategies and choices, and how exactly the bargaining agent of the firms has been exerted to turn the institution of the host region conducive to the firms' aims and vice versa are still largely unclear and deserve more attention.

The fourth conceptual challenge has appeared very recently in the aftermath of the Sino-US trade war and the COVID-19 pandemic. As shown in figure 2.2, besides the three capitalist drivers, risk is also another causal driver at the structural level. According to Coe and Yeung (2015), five types of risk, economic, regulatory, environmental, product, and labor—have been identified. They urge a deeper consideration of both the actor and the structural level of risk analysis, focusing on the organization-environment interaction to unlock the explanatory potential of GPN risk in a highly interconnected economy. The case of the COVID-19 pandemic has showcased that risk can be transmitted and amplified across actors and geographies through the network itself (Coe, 2021). Although particular risk manifestations can be seen as specific to certain industries, Vietnam being the "winner" of the Sino-US trade war (Davis & Wei, 2022) and the electronics industry being the "backbone" of the global production system (Sturgeon & Memedović, 2011) are worthwhile to pay attention to. As pointed out by Völlers et al. (2023), the underlying premise notion of risk applied in the GPN 2.0 framework dates to Knight's (1921) dichotomy of uncertainty and economic risk, in which the risks can be assigned a measurable probability of occurrence, which can be used as a basis for strategic decisions and managerial actions (Coe & Yeung, 2015). They have diagnosed that the dominant Knightian understanding of risk understates the decision-maker-based sensemaking of reality and the strategic decision-making processes based on risk beyond the rationale of cost and benefit under conditions of rational choice. Although a multi-scalar framework based on a performative risk narrative perspective to see how the production and constitution of risk are caused by the organization-environment interaction has been insightfully constructed to display how GPN risk causally matters (Völlers et al., 2023), the puzzle of how exactly does the context environment in which organizational decision-makers are embedded constitutes a source of perceived uncertainty about a value at stake is still somewhat vague, especially regarding the active roles of different nonfirm actors in altering the risk narratives under the uncertainties. Hence, in the following chapters, we hope to enrich these aforementioned literature gaps in GPN 2.0 by looking into the relocation and development of the electronics industry in Vietnam.

Insights of TNC Organizations Outside Economic Geography

Besides the economic geography literature on understanding the production organization of TNCs, studies in other fields, for example, international business (IB) and economic studies, as well as those in the broader social science field, have also made insightful contributions in various aspects. In this part, some of the major contributions from these fields will be selectively reviewed to further comprehend our understanding of the cross-border expansions of TNCs and the industries.

Although many IB theories on TNCs are valid until now, they have been criticized by economic geographers. For example, as pointed out by Henderson et al. (2002), as the TNC literature mostly deals with their roles, little effort has been made to understand the changing organizations of TNC subsidiaries as they emerge, evolve, and impact the host economies and the related firms. The studies, as a whole, also tend to be confined only to companies in developed economies while ignoring the developing world. In addition, the literature has been criticized for the ignorance of the "relational entrepreneurial space" as the studies have primarily focused on the physical space in explaining the entrepreneurial emergence and operation of TNCs by some standard spatial variables, such as distance and location (Yeung, 2005, 2009a). Indeed, the entrepreneurial space cannot be solely quantified by the physical space as it is bound by the organizational capabilities of the firms/entrepreneurs rather than the territorial boundaries; as the concepts, for example, proximity, are highly relational and subject to social relations among the actors; and as the entrepreneurial space may have nothing to do with economic reasons of a physical location, for example, the untraded interdependencies (Jones, 2008; Yeung, 1998).

Although the IB literature has been criticized, it contributes substantially to the explanations of the operation and management of TNCs (see, e.g., McCann, 2010), which have been seen as the central agencies of global production systems (Dicken, 2011). As the primary IB research focuses on the competitive advantages, entry modes, decision-makings, operations, and impacts of the TNCs, by reviewing the related literature, one can gain some ideas about transnational entrepreneurship and its activities. For instance, one of the main strands in the IB literature is the ownership advantages and the entry mode of the TNCs. Based on the assumption that firms face costs of doing business abroad and need advantages to overcome the costs (Hymer,

1960), Dunning (1977) proposed the eclectic paradigm to justify the investments of TNCs abroad rather than at home. Despite revisions that have been made later (e.g., Dunning, 1988, 1995, 2003), the core of the paradigm is that three conditions have to be fulfilled prior to the existence of the TNCs (Eden & Dai, 2010). First, a firm has to have a net ownership advantage in serving an overseas market over other firms (O advantage). Second, rather than selling or leasing, it should be more beneficial for the firms to internalize these advantages even across national boundaries (I advantage). Third, the advantages should be more profitably exploited when used with the factor inputs in the host country (L advantage). These three sets of advantages also affect a firm's entry mode decision, and it is suggested that when the OLI advantages are higher, more integrated modes of entry will be preferred as the entrepreneurs have high perceptions of the asset power and market attractiveness (Brouthers et al., 1999; Dunning, 1993). In short, compared to the reasoning in the economic geography literature, the OLI framework in the IB studies provides a more concrete, organized, and integrated idea about why and how the firm would rationally calculate and decide to internationalize its operations besides the competitive dynamics in the GPN framework. While the OLI theory is rather inward-looking, it is indeed helpful for better understanding the organizational settings of the TNCs and the global production networks.

Apart from the IB studies, to understand the spatial and temporal production relocation pattern, particularly in relation to Asia, the FGP in economic studies has been insightful. Originally developed by Akamatsu (1962), the FGP was used to describe the industrialization of Japan, which favored facilitating comparative advantage of progressively more cutting-edge and value-added industries. It has since been extended to explain the dynamic shift of industries from one country to another. FGP predicts a staged sequence of spatial and temporal expansion for lead industries from Japan to the NIEs, followed by ASEAN, China, and then Southeast Asian countries. Driven by the primary motive to maintain comparative advantage and competitive edge, these "lead" industries, with mature products, "fly" through different stages of import, domestic production, and export and are replaced by another "lead" industry. The electronics industry is a central consideration of the FGP as it is one of the most sophisticated and highest value-added industries (e.g., Edgington & Hayter, 2000; Ginzburg & Simonazzi, 2005; Milelli, 1997; Tung, 2003). Despite the fact that the highly generalized spatial and temporal relocation patterns of the electronics industry within Asia somewhat fit the FGP, four different shortcomings of the FGP in understanding the dynamic production relocation in Asia have been pointed out (e.g., Edgington & Hayter, 2000; Kasahara, 2004; Lin, 2012; Ozawa, 2011; Tung, 2003). First and foremost, instead of the traditional division of labor among different economies, international production fragmentation has been increasingly important in recent decades (Tung, 2003). It was argued that rather than the production relocation described by the FGP, a production network expansion in Asia has been witnessed as there have been mainly the lower value-added products and production processes, that is, assembly, being relocated to the host countries; while the higher value-added processes, as well as the parts and components of higher value-added products, still stayed in Japan and other relatively developed economies, such as Korea and Taiwan (Edgington & Hayter, 2000; Tung, 2003). Second, the unit of analysis of the FGP is primarily at the national level (Kasahara, 2004). Yet, the production of a particular product could be at the "subnational" stage of development. For example, the technology level of firms in coastal China has generally been higher than the ones in the inland regions. Hence, instead of a "national" stage level, a multi-scalar level analysis of production relocation of the electronics industry within China will be more insightful. Third, the FGP, in general, ignores the expansion of the domestic market as a driver since traditional production systems have primarily assumed to serve the Western markets (Ginzburg & Simonazzi, 2005). Fourth, and more importantly, the FGP does not appreciate the bottom-up heterogeneous forces of economic development. As pointed out by Edgington and Hayter (2000), the FGP underplays the roles of policies in the host region as well as the local capital. Despite the fact that different shortcomings of the FGP have been pointed out, and despite the fact that the FGP does not give a precise prediction about the timing, scale, and location of investments, the generalized spatial, temporal, and sectoral industrial production relocation pattern within Asia does fit the FGP overall. Therefore, it can, to a certain level, help us forecast the big picture of the coming rounds of production relocation within Asia.

To sum up, in this section, theoretical developments related to the internationalization and organization of TNCs have been briefly and selectively reviewed. Although IB and economics studies both contribute significantly to the conceptualization of the overseas operation and management of TNCs and the sectoral, spatial, and temporal production relocation patterns, the geographical elements, such as the ideas of spatial scale, are relatively weak in the foundations of these studies. Be that as it may, they are still insightful in explaining production expansions and relocations. Conventional economic geography literature that was prominent before the 1990s, such as the post-Fordist flexible specialization and network analysis, to conceptualize the business and production organization of firms, as well as two popular frameworks that have been developed since the 1990s, that is, GVC and GPN, to conceptualize the global production systems mainly driven by lead firms from developed countries serving consumers primarily in Western markets, have been reviewed in this section. Various conceptual limitations under the current changing global economy have been pointed out. More importantly, the newly developed GPN 2.0 framework aims to provide a more comprehensive and better overall understanding of the causal mechanism of the capitalist dynamics, the operations of the TNCs, and the impacts from and on different firm and nonfirm actors as well as on the regions that have also been surveyed. It is out of the scope of the current chapter to include all works related to the relocations and organizations of TNCs or to appraise various concepts from different literature, mainly within the broader social science and business fields, that could possibly enrich the GPN 2.0 conceptualization. Specific theories will be introduced and examined in each following empirical chapter.

Before addressing the theoretical gaps, particularly in connection with the GPN 2.0 framework that this book greatly relies on, it is worth reviewing the substantial spatial, temporal, and organizational reconfigurations of production activities in the past decades to have a better understanding of the changing trends and landscape of the real-world global manufacturing economy. Hence, in the next section of this chapter, empirical literature regarding different rounds of production relocation of the electronics manufacturing industry, one of the most geographically dispersed industries having a central role in global production systems (Sturgeon & Kawakami, 2011), will be reviewed. The questions of "why" and "how" the TNCs have relocated and reorganized their production networks will be focused on. The following section is not only to revisit the changing dynamics in and of the electronics production networks, but by reviewing the empirical studies done previously by scholars, we can also better explore the insightful empirical knowledge gaps regarding the current round of production relocations from China to developing Southeast Asia.

PRODUCTION RELOCATIONS AND RECONFIGURATIONS OF THE GLOBAL PRODUCTION NETWORKS

In the previous section, the conceptualization of the organization of TNCs and the global production systems, as well as the theoretical shortcomings, has been reviewed in brief. In this section, the on-the-ground empirical literature related to production relocations and the reconfigurations of the networks will be surveyed to set the background story of this book. Given its geographically extensive and fast-growing nature, the electronics production system is having a greater impact on the global economy and regional development nowadays (Kawakami & Sturgeon, 2010; Sturgeon & Memedović, 2011). Compared to other global industries, such as the textile and garment industry, the electronics industry has better market development potential and possibilities for technological advancement given its high value-added nature. Hence, in this section (as well as this monograph), attention will be primarily focused on the consumer electronics manufacturing industry, especially the labor-intensive manufacturing segment that has been increasingly offshored to developing Southeast Asia. To systematically revisit different rounds of production relocations and reconfigurations of the electronics production networks, in the following section, we will first review the temporal and spatial restructurings of the electronics production landscape and then the related organizational reconfigurations. In addition, the capital-intensive segment of the industry, that is, the semiconductor sector, will be briefly revisited in the third subsection as a comparison case to help us better grasp the whole picture of the electronics industry. Last but not least, relocating to Southeast Asia is not only limited to the electronics industry. To offer a broader picture for the readers to better understand the recent dynamics of the globally changing production landscape and the basic conditions of other industries on the "move," the authors will also briefly survey and discuss the situation of the textile and garment industry, which has been the second-largest exporting product of Vietnam according to table 5.3, in the final part of the current section.

Temporal and Spatial Restructuring of the Electronics Production Networks

Before the 1960s, electronics production was concentrated mainly in the Western economies, that is, North America and Western Europe. Since the 1960s, the globalization of electronics production has expanded to Asia. In fact, at that time, only a few manufacturers in Asia had been plugged into the global production networks since the production structure was rather vertically integrated. The leading manufacturers from America, Europe, and later Japan established their production facilities in the NIEs in Asia to enjoy cheaper production costs, such as lower labor and infrastructure costs (Yeung, 2007). As the capabilities of the domestic suppliers in the NIEs were weak at that time, they could only act as low-tier suppliers of these leading manufacturers.

The capabilities of these Asian suppliers have increased through different channels of spillover from the lead firms during the process (e.g., Saxenian, 2006). As pointed out by Gereffi et al. (2005), in the late 1980s, as the global electronics industry became more and more competitive, to maintain high-cost efficiency as well as to shorten the time-to-market, the majority of the electronics lead firms outsourced their production activities in order to focus on the R&D and marketing and sales processes. Thanks to this shift, as the lead firms outsourced their production activities, it provided a chance for the emergence and growth of domestic firms in Asian NIEs, that is, South Korea, Taiwan, and Singapore (Borrus et al., 2000). This resulted in an increase in the number of manufacturing service providers and specialized component suppliers in the NIEs, such as Compal and Quanta, which originated in Taiwan (Yang & Hsia, 2007; Yeung, 2006, 2007). Later, some of the firms in the NIEs even become the brand-name lead firms themselves, such as Samsung and LG.

In the late 1990s, as pointed out by Sturgeon (2002), contract manufacturing has been a popular mode of industrial organization. Not only could the global lead firms focus on the higher value-added activities, but outsourcing to contract manufacturers (CMs) also helped to lower the production costs by achieving economies of scale. For example, many leading brand-name companies, such as Apple, Dell, HP, IBM, and NEC, have outsourced a high percentage of their production to the CMs originating from the NIEs, especially Taiwan (Yang & Hsia, 2007). At that time, besides R&D and marketing and sales, the electronics production process was mainly conducted in Asian NIEs.

Starting from the 1990s, the firms in these Asian NIEs began to move to the Pearl River Delta (PRD) in China mainly due to price pressure and the growing competition from firms in other Asian countries (Yeung, 2001). Since the late 1990s, Asian firms, particularly the Taiwanese ones, have initiated another round of production relocation to the Yangtze River Delta (YRD). Yet, the scale of this wave of relocation was bigger than the previous one, as, in comparison, fewer CMs moved to the PRD region (Yang, 2009). Taiwanese electronics and information technology (IT) manufacturers started to relocate and develop the new industrial cluster by expanding from Taiwan and the PRD region to the YRD region. The lion's share of investments from Taiwanese firms has been recorded in the cities in the YRD region, such as Suzhou, Wujiang, and Kunshan. Starting from the 2000s, mainly due to the rise of production costs in coastal China, interregional production relocation has been increasingly witnessed as the labor-intensive manufacturing industries have been "going west" (Zhu & Pickles, 2014). Besides cutting down the production costs, as pointed out by Yang (2013), one of the reasons for the production relocation from the coastal region to inland China is the emergence of China's domestic market-oriented production networks. Particularly in the aftermath of the global financial crisis in 2008–2009, when the external demand from advanced economies decreased, the growing domestic market became one of the dynamics driving the production relocations within China.

From a broader spatial scale, according to Baldwin and Lopez-Gonzalez (2015), over the past decades, countries in East Asia, including China, have engaged in global production networks, and after analyzing the trade pattern, a "triangular trade" pattern has been described. While the intermediate goods have been imported from the Asian NIEs and Japan, China has been an assembly base to assemble the parts and components and export the final goods to the Western developed economies in the United States and the EU. This pattern is still, for the most part, valid for the electronics industry nowadays. In his reports, Yeung (2019) pointed out that there are obvious geographical concentrations of the manufacturing of parts and components of higher value added, such as camera modules, in East Asia, the United States, and Western Europe, and all other rather lower value-added electronics manufacturing has been mainly shifted and concentrated in China. And although there have been some manufacturing activities in Southeast Asia, the firms in China are still reluctant to move out from China to other nearby countries, such as Vietnam, the Philippines, and Indonesia, even though the labor costs are lower on average (see, e.g., Yeung, 2019). Despite the fact that the "triangular trade" pattern still dominates and China is still the "World Factory," the "transformation" of the "World Factory" has been increasingly witnessed in three directions: "go up," "go west," and "go out" (Zhang, 2014; Zhu & Pickles, 2014). As pointed out by Yang (2016), the existing literature has primarily focused on the internal production relocation within the "World Factory" running the risk of overlooking the emerging cross-border production expansion from China to developing Southeast Asia. The detailed relocation process, the restructuring of global and regional production networks, as well as its impacts on regional developments, urgently need an updated and comprehensive study.

In relation to the need to update the recent round of production relocations from China to Southeast Asia, besides the competitive dynamics to lower the cost-capability ratio, other drivers of the production relocation should not be ignored. As shown in the empirical studies earlier, the changing market imperatives have been one of the drivers of the current wave of production relocations and the restructuring of the production networks (e.g., Horner, 2014; Horner & Nadvi, 2018; Kaplinsky & Farooki, 2011; Yang & Fu, 2017; Yang & He, 2017). Besides the changing market imperatives, although the risk environment has been added to the GPN 2.0 framework as one of the competitive dynamics, its importance has been overlooked hitherto. Besides a better conceptualization of the risk in production systems, the empirical studies are far from enough. Even if it is included in the empirical studies, it is analyzed mostly in a relatively endogenous way at the national level. For example, in the report by Yeung (2019), although mitigating environmental risks and dealing with unfavorable government regulations and policies were listed as the drivers for the electronics firms to relocate their productions, these risk environments mainly referred to the home and host countries' regulations and rules, such as environmental risks, local content requirements, and import/export restrictions. The risk environment on a broader scale is somehow missing, especially in the current era of tense geopolitical relationships. Although some updated economic studies have pointed out that the trade war between China and the United States happened since 2018 has impacted the FDI inflow and trade patterns of some Southeast Asian countries, for example, Malaysia (see, e.g., Yean et al., 2019) and of course Vietnam, few studies have been conducted to see how this global-level risk environment has impacted the organizations of the production networks at different scales. A more detailed look into the case of Vietnam, which has been identified as the winner in the Sino-US trade war (Davis & Wei, 2022), is needed to better capture the current global dynamics as well as the implications on the changing economic landscape. Apart from the tightened environmental regulation and enforcement as well as the more intense geopolitical situation, the outbreak of COVID-19 has undoubtedly induced another unprecedented global risk atmosphere that affects not only the production networks of electronics but all other related products and productions up and down the stream. Apart from the risk-related research gaps mentioned earlier, while the updated literature has so far focused on how firms reacted to and recovered from the current risk environment, the active roles of institutions in managing the risk expectations and subsequent performative risk narratives (Völlers et al., 2023) have been understudied.

In short, in updating the recent rounds of production relocations from the "World Factory" to Vietnam, particularly after 2008, the drivers apart from the traditional cost capabilities deserve more attention as, on the one hand, the market imperative has been changing and, on the other hand, the situation of the international political economy and the overall risk environment that pose both opportunities and risks in the global production systems has also been changing. Last but not least, it was realized that in the study of production relocations, the situations and institutions in the home regions, which could help better grasp the "push factors," have been often ignored in the expanse of the attention paid to the host regions (Chan & Yang, 2022a, 2022b).

Organizational Reconfigurations of the Electronics Production Networks

Besides the temporal and spatial restructuring of the electronics production network, since the physical setting of a network can never be delinked from its organizational structure, empirical literature related to the organizational reconfigurations of the network will be reviewed in this part to look at how the production network has been structured and governed over time and what the roles of different actors in the network are so as to identify the related research gaps.

The first wave of large-scale production relocations of electronics manufacturing in the 1980s from the United States and Western Europe, and later Japan, was primarily led by the leading brand-name manufacturers themselves as they sought to offshore their productions to Asian NIEs to reduce production costs. The second wave of production relocations since the 1990s from Asian NIEs to coastal China was mainly propelled by the "factory-less" brand-name lead firms (Yang & Hsia, 2007) instead of the manufacturers themselves. Despite the fact that the productions of these lead firms have mostly been outsourced to firms from Asian NIEs, particularly from Taiwan, under the business model of original equipment manufacturing/own designing and manufacturing (OEM/ODM), these OEM/ODM firms had to follow the orders from the lead firms as the latter held the "systemic power" in the global electronics production networks (Yang & Hsia, 2007). As argued by Sturgeon (2002), the governing structure of the electronics value chains has been in a modular mode, and this means that the lead firms are able to switch among their suppliers relatively easily in theory. This creates a power asymmetry that the former can leverage. Therefore, this wave of production relocation and network reorganization was said to be actually pushed by the brand-name lead firms behind the scenes.

The organizational structure of the electronics industry, especially between the lead firms and the CMs, has been changing as the specifications of the electronics products have become more complex over time. As pointed out by Yang and Chen (2013), the increasing dependence on certain CMs by the lead firms has been observed. Not only have these tier 1 suppliers become the strategic partners of the lead firms, but they have also played an increasing role in reconstructing the GVCs (Lee & Gereffi, 2015). Unlike previous rounds of production relocations, updated research has found that the recent round of production relocation from coastal China to inland China, for example, Chongqing, has been coordinated by these tier 1 suppliers, rather than the brand-name lead firms, leading to the organizational transformation of the production network changing from the lead firm-centric model in coastal China to the strategic partner firm-coordinated model (Yang, 2017; Yang & He, 2017). Reflected by these recent empirical studies, in the study of production relocation and the organizational reconfiguration of the production networks, apart from the lead firms, one should also pay more attention to other firm actors. Besides the tier 1 suppliers, as mentioned, other ETNCs of a relatively small scale from the emerging and developing economies, as aforementioned, should not be overlooked as they have started to attract the spotlight recently due to their increasing importance in the production networks, particularly at the regional level (Yeung, 2017).

In addition, apart from the roles of different firm actors, the nonfirm actors, particularly the host governments, have been important in the strategic coupling process as they not only determine whether the strategic coupling can take place, but also affect which kinds of strategic coupling and how the strategic coupling would be taking place by their abilities to shape the regional resources. For example, in the previous empirical studies, Yeung (2006) studied how Asian NIEs have articulated into the global electronics production networks and played different roles and how the processes have been influenced by their home governments; Lee et al. (2016) also compared how four East Asian countries have joined the global mobile phone value chain with different positions and the relationships between their different development paths and positions and the states' policies. Besides the positions and roles of the domestic industries in the global value chains and production networks, the importance of the government also reflects in the production relocation process (MacKinnon, 2012). According to the empirical study by Yang (2009), the efforts of different levels of regional and local institutions marked a big difference between the results of the spatial restructuring of the Taiwanese investments in the PRD and the YRD region in China and later inland China (Yang & He, 2017): unlike the "implicit" coupling initiative in the PRD's case, the production relocations of Taiwanese firms to the YRD and inland China have been driven by the "explicitly coupling" initiated by the top-down governmental intervention. The ways in which the productions were moved and settled were very different in these two rounds of relocations. That said, in studying the latest round of production relocations from China to Vietnam, the role of the nonfirm actors, especially the institutions of different scales, should not be overlooked. And as mentioned in the theoretical literature review earlier as well as the address by Dawley et al. (2015) in their empirical study, the "multi-scalarity" and the multiple roles of the state deserve more attention. Last but not least, under the current era of uncertainties and risks, the role of government has clearly emerged as an even more interesting research object in the GPN literature. The strategies and policies they made have been crucial in determining the leave or stay for the TNCs as well as the production network configurations over the latest trend of "slowbalization." Relevant updated investigations conducted amid the pandemic will be, therefore, presented in chapter 8 to have an outlook on the electronics production network in the post-COVID-19 time.

The High-End Segment: Organizations of the Semiconductor-Making Industry

To provide a more comprehensive survey of the electronics industry and its production network, the authors will single out and summarize the changing organizations of the semiconductor sector, referred to hereafter as "chip," in this subsection. While it might seem to be under the same umbrella as the electronics industry, the nature of the chip-making industry and the general electronics manufacturing sectors, such as personal computers, mobile phones, and other consumer electronics, which the current monograph primarily focuses on, vary. Although one could see the former as an intermediary stage of the latter, the semiconductors made could be used outside the electronics industry, such as in the automotive sector, where the final products need to process information. The impacts of the chip shortage of chip since 2020 have been tremendous, affecting over 169 sectors and consumer lines (Mohammad et al., 2022). According to Yeung (2019), the global revenue of the chip segment alone in 2018 surpassed that of the consumer electronics segment and was almost half of the personal computer segment with less than one-third of the number of firms. That said, the value added per firm in the chip-making segment is much higher than in other electronics firms. The strategies used by chip makers in organizing their production activities structurally and spatially are different. While the authors have briefly reviewed the overall changing picture of the general electronics industry in two previous subsections, compared to the rather low value-added and labor-intensive manufacturing segments, the organizational logic and hence the outcomes of the chip production landscape differ and will be highlighted in this subsection.

By excluding the software service, simply speaking, chip making could be broadly divided into three stages: the design of the chip integrated circuit (IC), the fabrication of the chip wafer, and the assembly, testing, and packaging (ATP). While the first two stages are more capital intensive and the last stage is more labor intensive, all three stages are relatively technologically sophisticated. Unlike the general electronics firms in the United States, which started their offshoring in the 1960s with the advancement of manufacturing technology, the design and the fabrication of the chip remained, while only some labor-intensive ATP tasks were offshored. According to the US Government Accountability Office (2006), to reduce financial risk, chip makers started to move some wafer fabrication activities in the 1980s to Asian contract manufacturers, and Taiwan was one key offshore location for US chip makers initially for ATP tasks and later for fabrication. Later in the 1990s, as China started to open its market, some Taiwanese firms then expanded parts of their fabrication plants there. Yet, before the 2000s, the offshoring activities were mainly limited to ATP and wafer fabrication.

The geographical expansion of chip making is highly associated with structural changes in its business model. Apart from the integrated device manufacturers (IDMs), which are vertically integrated by internalizing the production stages from R&D to chip design and fabrication to facilitate innovation for faster time-to-market and better risk management (Yeung, 2019), since the 1980s, foundries specializing in capital-intensive wafer fabrication started to emerge in Asia, particularly Taiwan, to serve the fabless design firms that specialize only in chip design. Since then, with the support of their national governments, rather than simply doing the manufacturing and ATP tasks, East Asian countries, such as Japan, Korea, Taiwan, and later China, have emerged to become big players in the industry. More recently, in the late 2010s, according to Yeung (2019), chip fabrication was highly concentrated in Northeast Asia, especially Taiwan, while Southeast Asia, Europe, and the United States also shared a significant percentage in wafer fabs. The picture of the overall chip manufacturing, including ATP, remained largely the same with increased shares of Northeast and Southeast Asia, especially China. In terms of R&D, similar to what the US Government Accountability Office (2006) pointed out, chip design, which comprised more than 50 percent of the R&D facilities in the electronics industry, was primarily concentrated in Europe and North America as well as in Northeast Asia, although to a slightly smaller portion. That said, this implies that while Northeast Asia has increasingly become an important location for chip design and fabrication recently, on one hand, Europe and North America have remained in their dominant position in the chip design tasks, and, on the other hand, the rather labor-intensive tasks, such as ATP, have been largely moved to China.

One thing worthwhile to note is that, rather than solely benefiting from the cross-border relocation of leading firms from the Global North like other end-product industries, the growth of the chip fabrication capacity in East Asia was said to be due to the heavy investments of domestic firms, that is, this is argued to be the changing relative shares of chips from different macro regions instead of a geographical shift (Yeung, 2022a). In the literature on economic geography, development, and innovation studies, supply-side factors, such as the strong and constitutive roles of states like Taiwan and Korea, and the related national policies, regional innovation systems, and global linkages, have been accounted for to explain the above shift (e.g., Fuller, 2019; Grimes & Du, 2020; Hsu, 2017; Shin, 2017). While these studies emphasize the importance of supply-side drivers, especially the state, Yeung (2022a) emphasized the significance of demand-led market dynamics as a codriver for the chip-making capacity growth in East Asia. He argued that the fabless firms and the device manufacturers create a huge intermediate market demand for chips to serve their end markets and that the overwhelming role of China as the key site for the final assembly of major electronics products influences the geography of fab location and capacity growth. Customer intimacy in intermediate markets and demand responsiveness in end markets are two critical dimensions of market dynamics in semiconductor production networks.

Apart from offering a fuller picture of the electronics industry's configuration, the short survey on chip making earlier in the text does provide some insights that enlighten the authors in studying the electronics production location in the coming chapters. First, regarding the spatial configuration, the higher value-added activities of chip-making, such as R&D, have still been dominated by the Western developed economies and firms. While Northeast Asia has been increasingly catching up, China and other Southeast Asian countries have remained stuck at the lower value-added activities, such as ATP tasks. Second, unlike general labor-intensive electronics manufacturing, the nonfirm actors, particularly the state, are too big to be ignored in the reconfigurations of this rather knowledge- and capital-intensive sector requiring heavy initial investments, not to mention the fact that chip making has become one crucial battlefield in the current Sino-US "tech war." In relation, the priorities of the capitalist dynamics driving the organizational strategies of firms in the chip-making sector will be different from other sectors and industries. Third and perhaps most importantly, the arguments by Yeung (2022a) remind us of the importance of the often-neglected demand-led market dynamics in explaining geographic shifts of production networks in complementing supply-side explanations.

Insights from Another Labor-Intensive Industry on the "Move": The Textile and Garment Industry

To provide a more comprehensive survey of the changing global production landscape, this subsection aims to grasp the recent dynamics of the international relocations of labor-intensive manufacturing activities to Southeast Asia by looking into the textile and garment industry (including the apparel industry) as a comparative case. While it is not possible to fit the detailed conditions of the industry's changing configurations in a subsection, we intend to spotlight some major ones to flesh out the story.

Compared to the boom of electronics manufacturing in China around the 1990s, as aforementioned, the emergence of the textile and garment industry in China was a bit earlier, around the late 1970s (Fu, 2017; Chen & Li, 2019). The industry was primarily concentrated in coastal regions, such as the PRD and the YRD. Owing to the low wages, abundant supply of labor, poor environmental standards, and weak enforcement of national and local laws, along with the export quota removal after China's WTO accession, this export-oriented industry grew rapidly in the 1980s. Apart from providing low-wage labor and low-end technology, the industry has been integrated into the global value chain more deeply since the 1990s, as the manufacturers shifted their comparative advantages to medium technology and higher-quality goods through the learning-by-doing effect (Zhu & Pickles, 2014).

Yet, entering the 2000s, the limits of this labor-intensive, export-led growth model have started to be witnessed not only in the electronics industry but more so in the textile and garment industry of even lower value-added. On one hand, the production costs in China increased with stricter labor and environmental protection regulations. On the other hand, the global financial crisis-driven shrinking demand in the markets of developed countries, as well as the more intense competition from the low-income economies, has heavily hurt the industry along the coastline. Apart from turning to explore the domestic market, relocating to inner regions to cut down production costs, and upgrading to engage in production activities of higher value-added (Zhu & Pickles, 2014; Butollo, 2015), cross-border delocalization of production activities in the industry has been seen. Particularly since the late 2000s, an increasing number of Chinese apparel enterprises have set up and/or outsourced low-wage assembly tasks to factories in low-cost producing centers like Southeast Asian countries such as Cambodia, Vietnam, and Bangladesh.

The motivations and the ways of "going out" of the firms in the current wave are indeed highly diversified (Zhu & He, 2013; Zhu & Pickles, 2014; Fu, 2017; Chen & Li, 2019). By distinguishing four types of firm relocation, namely complete relocation, partial relocation, acquisition or expansion, and outsourcing or subcontracting, and constructing a tripolar analytical framework interpreting industrial relocation through systematic interrelationships and ongoing interaction between globalization, regionalization, and localization, Zhu and He (2013) emphasized that the rising production costs cannot explain the whole picture of the relocation, but one needs to be aware of a firm's characteristics and the complex balance in relocation processes between a range of forces derived from regionalization and localization, as well as globalization, to explain the underlying mechanisms driving a firm's decision on relocation and geographical restructuring. For example, Shenzhou International (an OEM located in YRD) and Biaomei (an OEM and ODM located in PRD) relocated in different ways; while the former was expanding to Vietnam and Cambodia to increase its production capacity with the operations in China unchanged, the latter was relocating its manufacturing to Myanmar with only the higher value-added activities, such as design, innovation, and procurement of raw materials, in China (Chen & Li, 2019). Besides the "low road" delocalization mainly to cut down production costs, the "high road delocalization" has been also increasingly witnessed recently in the case of Bosideng, China's largest down clothing manufacturer, which moved its R&D and marketing activities to the United Kingdom for better access to overseas markets (Zhu & Pickles, 2014).

In alignment with the aforementioned observations from the chip sector, the supply-side factors are clearly no longer enough to explain the full story of the changing dynamics in the production networks of the textile and garment industry, as well as the diversified ways of delocalization and the rationales behind them, not to mention the tribulations that would be caused by the current global geopolitical tensions and the specter of economic nationalism that follows. "(I)t is too early to conclude that a return to protectionism and the dismantling of GPNs will become the 'new normal' of geopolitics and global economic organization" (Hess, 2021: 32). Yet, it is undeniable that the Sino-US trade friction has greatly affected the industry in China and benefited many developing economies nearby, such as Vietnam (Dhar et al., 2023). Although some recent studies have measured the impacts on the production chain/network, that is, Ye et al. (2022) pointed out that the trade friction had a gradually decreasing effect on the Chinese textile and apparel companies, and the firms in midstream and downstream production stages of the industry chain were more negatively affected, similar to the situations of the electronics industry, how exactly the firms have the firms responded and reconfigured their production activities spatially and structurally in different ways, as well as the reasons and the mechanisms behind them, are still yet to be fully unboxed.

CONCLUSION AND OVERALL RESEARCH FRAMEWORK OF THE BOOK

As mentioned and pointed out by Horner and Nadvi (2018) and Horner and Murphy (2018), since the "South-South" trade goes beyond the trade in intermediate goods, and the value chains and production networks are increasingly consolidating yet reconfiguring within Asia, not only end up serving the Northern end markets, the contemporary global economy has changed dramatically after the 2000s from the original conceptualization of global production systems. First, the lead firms that dominate the orchestration of production systems are no longer limited to those from the Northern developed economies. Second, besides the global capital flows between the "North" and the "South," the value chains and production networks are not necessarily globalized but increasingly regionalized due to shifting global consumption as well as the more specialized modular mode of production, not to mention that the recent challenges of the global production systems in which they could potentially "reverse" the globalization. Their works have reminded us of the unprecedented and continuous changes in the global economic landscape and, thus, both spatial and organizational configurations of production networks today. Although this stream of work has been a bit vague hitherto and maybe overly general in dividing the world into "Global South" and "Global North," they have paved the road for further concrete explorations into the restructuring of global and regional production networks, particularly in Asia, and has somehow inspired us to conduct the current research.

To wrap up, this chapter aims to understand the production relocation and organization of TNCs from both theoretical and empirical lenses. In the first half, conceptual literature, that is, from conventional economic geography literature to the GCC/GVC, and the GPN framework, as well as the literature from some other related study fields regarding the framing of production activities of TNCs, has been briefly reviewed. To reiterate, since numerous theories and concepts have emerged in the past several decades and enlightened the ways we understand global production systems, it is certainly out of this book's scope, as well as our abilities, to revisit all relevant contributions. Thus, we have narrowed down to selectively focus on the GVC and GPN frameworks, which have been recently widely adopted both inside and outside the economic geography field. Indeed, each following chapter in this book, apart from the theoretical contributions mentioned earlier, will provide more relevant literature to better frame the chapter's particular research questions. In brief, the conventional economic geography approaches are not comprehensive enough to capture the business and production organization of TNCs and the factors, including social and the cultural ones, which affect the organizations nowadays. On the other hand, even though the GCC/GVC can better capture the governance of the global production chains, we reckon that the GPN framework is arguably a more comprehensive approach to analyzing the organization of production activities and their impacts on different actors and physical places in the network, as it includes different firms and nonfirm actors and works across multi-scalar levels. Advanced from the "GPN 1.0," the "GPN 2.0" heuristic, still, has its own "black boxes" waiting to unpack. By pointing out the "black boxes" of the GPN 2.0 framework, this monograph hopes to enrich the GPN literature through the following conceptual-based empirical studies. Besides, although the literature from IB and economics studies, as well as the broader social sciences, does not have many "geographical" elements, as they provide useful insights regarding the detailed decision-making rationales of TNCs, the overall temporal and spatial pattern and mechanism of production relocations, and the relational thinking among the actors involved, their contributions should not be overlooked. In the second half, empirical studies related to the restructurings of the electronics production networks and the related organizational reconfigurations were reviewed. While the current monograph focuses primarily on the rather lower value-added, labor-intensive electronics manufacturing, the changing configurations of chip making, the highest value-added segment of the electronics industry, were summarized as a supplement to provide an overview and a comparison of two very different sectors in the broadly defined electronics industry. In addition, in the last part of the preceding section, the studies of the recent reconfigurations of the textile and garment industry have been highlighted for a better grasp of the common conditions encountered by another labor-intensive manufacturing industry previously located in China's coastal regions as well as their possible ways out. To better understand the current changing dynamics in global production systems, the recent wave of production relocations from China to developing Southeast Asia, for example, Vietnam, serves as a good case in point to see how the global/regional production network and the "triangular trade" pattern have been restructured amid the geopolitical risks and the pandemic. In doing so, after reviewing the previous empirical studies, one has to pay more attention to the drivers apart from the cost capability, the changing roles of the actors in the networks, and the nonfirm actor at multiple scales.

In a nutshell, the current book hopes to enrich both theoretical and empirical research gaps by providing a better understanding of the current wave of production relocations. To be explicit, the main research task of this monograph is to understand the current wave of electronics production relocations to Vietnam by asking the central questions of why and how various kinds and tiers of electronics firms from different origins have expanded from China to Vietnam and how the production networks at both global and regional scales have been restructured. Figure 2.3 illustrates the analytical framework of the current study. Under the rapidly restructuring world economy, changing capitalist dynamics appear at different scales. To stay competitive, firms of different tiers and origins in various locations, such as coastal China, respond with different firm-specific strategies due to various firm-specific motivations and attributes, such as different ownership structures, home imprints, and market powers, to reconfigure their networks via altering their intra-firm, inter-firm, and extra-firm relationships. This results in the reconfigurations

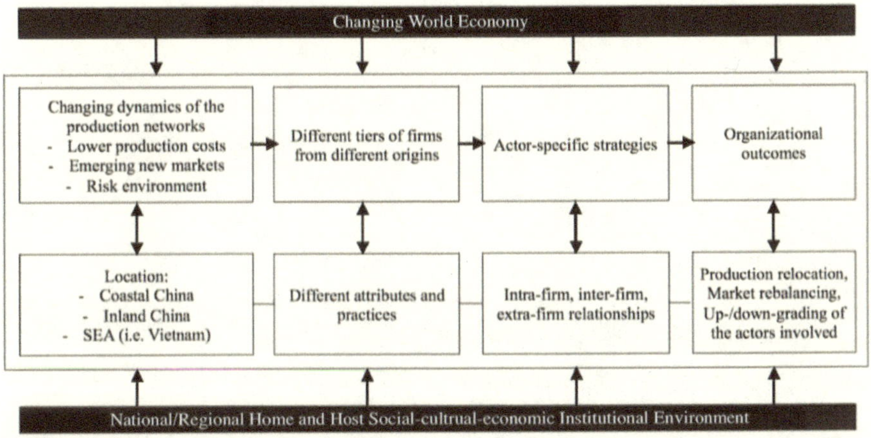

Figure 2.3 The Analytical Framework of the Current Book. *Source*: Compiled by the author.

of the regional and global production networks witnessed by the production relocation, market rebalancing, up/downgrading in the network, and so on. Although this causal process happens under the changing world economy, as the firm is situated and embedded in certain home and host regions with different sociocultural, economic, and institutional contexts, the environments of these two places where the causal process happens have to be considered as well. Without a doubt, rather than simply placing the nonfirm actors in the background, our research highlights their multi-scalar roles in the strategic coupling and hence the reconfigurations of the networks. Our main attention will be placed on exploring how electronics firms have reconfigured their productions spatially and organizationally using different firm-specific strategies as well as the sequential impacts on the actors and the places involved. To this end, three research questions have been designed. First, how exactly did Vietnam articulate into the electronics production networks? Second, how did different tiers of TNCs of different origins expand to Vietnam and reorganize their networks using different firm-specific strategies with the multilevel host institutions? Third, apart from the established TNCs, why and how did ETNCs from emerging economies expand to Vietnam? By looking into these three questions accordingly in chapters 5, 6, and 7, this book could hopefully bring a more comprehensive understanding of the current wave of electronics production relocation under the changing global economic landscape. Lastly, in chapter 8, we will try to reveal how these actors as well as the production network configuration responded to the latest GPN dynamics, that is, the Sino-US trade war and COVID-19, based on our continuous investigations not only to update the literature but also to point to some conceptual arenas worthwhile for further explorations in the post-pandemic era.

Chapter 3

From Backward to Developing

A Brief Introduction to Vietnam's Reform and Regional Development

HIGHLIGHTS OF VIETNAM'S *DOI MOI* REFORM AND THE CURRENT STATUS

After understanding different conceptualizations of the global production systems, the organizations and roles of TNCs, and various rounds of electronics production relocations and reorganizations, as well as some relevant conceptual and empirical gaps that this book aimed to enrich in the previous chapter, this chapter serves to provide a general outlook of Vietnam's situation not only to justify why one should care about the development of the electronics industry, particularly in Vietnam and after the 2000s, but also to demonstrate the rapid development of Vietnam to hopefully draw more attention to other Southeast Asian countries that are likely to be the next coupling anchor points in the global production network.

Before the start of the *doi moi* reform in the 1980s, Vietnam was an underdeveloped agricultural country. At that time, the poor performance of the economic system had led to poor living standards, like in many other planned economies. With a per capita income of less than 200 USD, Vietnam was one of the poorest countries in the world. It ran a socialist economic system based on the allocation of resources via direct central administrative measures. The country encountered food shortages and had to import rice, even though at that time, most of the workers were already engaged in agricultural production. The productivity of the industries was low, and the vast population was stuck in poverty. Starting from the late 1970s, when the failures of the central planning attempt were clearly witnessed, different constraints were relaxed (McCarty & Steley, 2004). For example, a contract system was set up in the agriculture sector in 1981; the plan to emphasize light industry, agriculture, and exports was passed in 1982. Preceded by these partial reforms, the *doi moi* reform program was inaugurated at the 6th Party Congress in December 1986, aiming to move the country to a rather open market economy from the import-substituting industrialization. The term "doi moi" in the *doi moi* reform means "renovation," and by introducing market economic elements gradually, the *doi moi* reform became the turning point of the transition to a relatively "socialist market" economy from a planned economy. Important reform policies include price reform to replace the planned prices with market prices for most nonessential consumer goods as well as economic stabilization to reduce inflation and so on. One core strategy in the reform since the early 1990s is to rapidly integrate into the world economy. Therefore, the breakthroughs made by Vietnam in terms of trade, export, and FDI ought to be highlighted.

Vietnam's trade reform was not an import liberalization (Jenkins & Thoburn, 2003). Like many East Asian countries, which on one hand developed their exports and on the other hand protected their domestic markets, Vietnam did the same in the early reform until the end of the 1990s when increasing trade agreements were signed. Before entering the World Trade Organization (WTO) in 2007, various bilateral trade agreements helped the development of Vietnam's export sector. For instance, a bilateral trade agreement was signed with the European Union (EU) in 1992 and granted Vietnam access to the generalized system of preferences (GSP). The US Bilateral Trade Agreement (USBTA) signed in 2000 also led to a rapid export surge from Vietnam to the United States. Apart from the international agreements, joining the Association of Southeast Asian Nations (ASEAN) Free Trade Area (AFTA) in 1995 helped link Vietnam to the rapidly growing Asian market. The China-ASEAN Free Trade Agreement (CAFTA) since 2004 also brought Vietnam and China closer in terms of trade. After participating in the WTO, different trade agreements were continuously signed between Vietnam and other regions and countries to further continue its export-led growth, such as the Trans-Pacific Partnership (TPP) in 2016 and the updated Comprehensive and Progressive Agreement for Trans-Pacific Partnership (CPTPP) in 2018.

The reform and opening up of Vietnam, as well as its increasingly signed trade agreements, have reflected in its rapid export growth. Counting only 31 percent in 1990, the share of exports of goods and services in Vietnam's gross domestic product (GDP) increased to 70 percent in 2008 after joining the WTO and before the financial crisis, and then further went up to 84 percent in 2020, which was much higher than most surrounding countries, according to the World Bank Database. As pointed out by Thoburn (2009), compared with other low-income developing countries in Southeast Asia that have a much more concentrated and vulnerable export pattern, such as the garment sector alone accounting for 84 percent of Cambodia's, 76 percent of Bangladesh's, and 42 percent of Laos's export earnings, Vietnam has a rather wide range of its exports with successive diversification from textiles and garments to footwear, and now into electronics. As one of the most open economies in terms of the trade-to-GDP ratio, that is, the merchandise trade value has accounted for over 100 percent of Vietnam's GDP since 2002, according to the World Bank Database, through integrating into the global production systems via international trade, Vietnam has grown its competitive advantages in industrial performance. For instance, according to the UN Industrial Development Report 2018, the competitive industrial performance world ranking of Vietnam increased from fifty-ninth to forty-first within just five years, from 2010 to 2015.

Closely linked to export growth are inward foreign direct investments (FDIs), particularly from global buyers and suppliers that have offshored their productions. After more than three decades of reform, Vietnam has achieved many achievements in socioeconomic development, with inward FDI playing an essential role in this process (Revilla Diez, 2016). Not only serving as an "insurance" against relying too heavily on China—a "China Plus One" policy—Vietnam has been an attractive investment destination since the reform due to its increasingly signed trade agreements, relatively cheap production inputs, and increasingly competitive policies to attract FDIs. In the 6th Party Congress in December 1986, Vietnam's government decided to launch economic reform, and the first Foreign Direct Investment Law was implemented one year later. Since then, a number of legal frameworks for businesses have been developed. After the initial promulgation of the Foreign Investment Law in 1987, various amendments were made, such as in 1990, 1992, 1996, and 2000, to open up more sectors and further loosen constraints so as to embrace better the FDIs as Vietnam's government realized the positive effects of FDI inflow. In 2005, the Law on Incentives for Domestic Investment and the Foreign Investment Law of 2000 was replaced by the Investment Law to ensure that the investment activities of both domestic and foreign investors were treated relatively fairly. This law eliminates discrimination between investors from different origins and emphasizes the freedom of business (Asian Development Bank, 2005).

Mainly due to the advantageous endogenous factors for the labor-intensive industries in Vietnam, such as low labor costs (see figure 3.1), Vietnam integrated very rapidly with the world economy. In 2015, the trade openness as a percentage of GDP reached around 200 percent. The number was very high even compared to other export countries, such as Germany (70 percent), the United States (23 percent), and China (42 percent), meaning that international trade has been crucial for Vietnam in recent years and the economy of Vietnam depends on the world market development to a great extent. Indeed, since the Foreign Investment Law took effect in 1987, Vietnam has

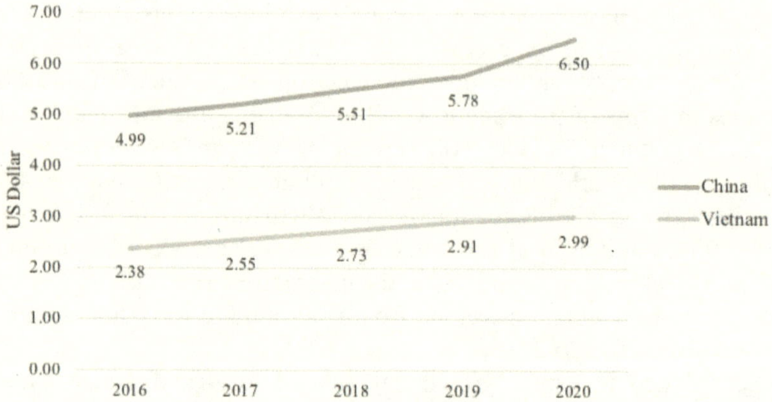

Figure 3.1 Average Manufacturing Labor Costs in China and Vietnam (2016–2020). *Source*: Compiled by the authors according to data from the Statista database.

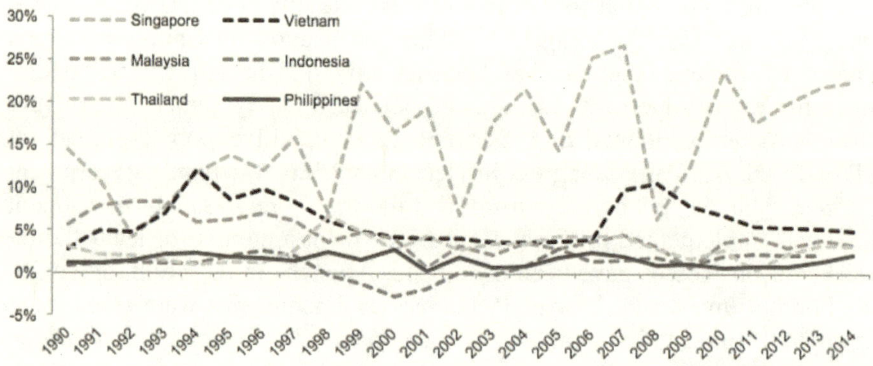

Figure 3.2 Net FDI as Percentages of GDP of ASEAN 6 (1990–2014). *Source*: UNCTAD (2015).

successfully received substantial FDI inflows. As a percentage of GDP, two peaks of Vietnam's FDI inflows were in 1996, before the Asian financial crisis in 1997, and after joining the WTO in 2008. Despite the negative impact of the global financial crisis in 2008–2009, Vietnam's net FDI inflow has still remained higher than 5 percent of the GDP (figure 3.2). Besides, according to figure 3.2, except for Singapore, which belongs to the relatively developed NIEs, Vietnam's net FDI inflow as a percentage of GDP has been the highest compared to other countries in the ASEAN 6, such as Thailand and Malaysia.

From table 3.1, one can see that, firstly, the total FDI registered capital has increased rapidly in the recent decade and the top investors in Vietnam have been Asian countries, particularly those from the NIEs; secondly and interestingly, the FDI capital from the "World Factory" China has increased

Table 3.1 Growth of the Total FDI Registered Capital by Vietnam's Top Partners (2011–2020)

Accumulated Until:	*Dec 2011 (Bil. USD)*	*Dec 2020 (Bil. USD)*	*Growth (2011–2020)*
Korea	23.7	78.5	231%
Japan	24.4	64.3	164%
Singapore	23	66.9	191%
Taiwan	23.6	35.6	51%
British Virgin Islands	15.5	22.1	43%
Hong Kong	11.3	28.4	151%
Malaysia	11.1	12.8	15%
China	4.3	21.6	402%
Others	62.3	89.7	44%

Source: Compiled by the authors according to data from the General Statistics Office of Vietnam.

most rapidly. To the best of our knowledge, China's outward FDI to Vietnam should have started in 1991 with a Guangxi joint venture enterprise with a Vietnamese group in Hanoi. After three decades from the first project, China's FDI in Vietnam has constantly risen in size, investment forms, sectors, and geographical expansion. China alone (excluding Taiwan and Hong Kong) accounted for 2.2 percent of the total registered FDI stock in Vietnam from 2011 to 5.1 percent in 2020. According to Liem (2015), China's investment in Vietnam has entered the third phase of the most dramatic changes since 2011. From table 3.1, one can see that after 2011, the growth rate of China's FDI inflow (402%) has outpaced other top investors, such as Korea (231 percent) and Singapore (191 percent), in terms of total registered capital. As pointed out by the previous chapter, that is, chapter 2 of the current book, and Yang (2016), production relocation has started to expand from China to the nearby developing Southeast Asian countries currently. Among these economies, due to the rapid emergence of Vietnam in both global and regional economies as just shown earlier, Vietnam certainly deserves more attention in the current wave of production relocation. In the study of Vietnam's development and internationalization, the roles of these Asian economies, that is, the NIEs and China, are critical and should have the major spotlight. Not only pushing away the lower value-added electronics manufacturing industry to Vietnam, but China's changing roles in the regional and global production systems and its emerging relationships with Vietnam are also worthwhile to pay attention to and will be further explored in chapter 5.

"(L)iberalization without neoliberalism, development without a developmental state" (Masina, 2012: 204). As concluded by Masina, in over decades of the *doi moi* reform, the Vietnamese leadership has never presented a consistent project for the reform process, either liberalization or a developmental state. Distant from the neoliberal prescriptions, however, the state was still at the center of economic reform. Both in certain industries and the banking system, the state retained very strong leverage. Yet, the country's developmental stance cannot be inscribed under the heading of the "East Asian developmental state" in the work of Evans (2012). Unlike other countries in East Asia where the state would support the acquisition of new technologies and new capabilities in some potential and strategic sectors rather than a united effort to create competitive advantages and create national champions, Vietnam's definition of strategic sectors depends more on an attempt to defend national sovereignty in important industrial sectors. Therefore, with the admission to the WTO, it was witnessed that some of the nonstrategic sectors, such as electronics manufacturing, have benefited from the inflow of FDIs and integrated with the global and regional production networks in a rather short span as Vietnam's government has been quite open to the FDIs in these sectors and hoped to benefit from it (Masina, 2012). That said, just a side note, without heavy state-led interventions and as it has been open to foreign investments, this shows that to study the developments of nonstrategic labor-intensive industries, that is, the electronics industry, in Vietnam, rather than the developmental state perspective, the actor-centric GPN framework fits well in understanding the development of Vietnam as the growth of the sector has much more to do with the extra-regional actors, that is, the TNCs. Be that as it may, the role of Vietnam's state cannot be ignored. As pointed out by Herr et al. (2016a), although the market has been liberalized to a great extent, the Vietnamese leadership did not combine with the market-oriented reforms. As a result, having a better understanding of the institutional environment of Vietnam is important here to have a fuller view of Vietnam's reform to set the background of the study as well as the nature of the embedding soil for the actors.

And to look into the institutional atmosphere of Vietnam, particularly in relation to economic and business policies, interestingly enough, China is too significant to be ignored. The dominance of the role of the state after the reform and decentralization (Pincus, 2015), such as the top-down governance approach, as well as the pragmatic gradualism strategy and so on seen in Vietnam, is somewhat akin to the features of China's reform. Apart from the emerging and changing role of China mentioned earlier in the regional and global production networks, another reason why one should pay attention to China in the production relocation to Vietnam is because of the importance of China in Vietnam's reform and opening, as it is often said that China indeed inspired the successful reform and opening of Vietnam (e.g., Cheong et al., 2011; Dosch & Vuving, 2008; Jandl, 2013; Womack, 2006). According to Dosch and Vuving (2008), in the mainstream view, Vietnam's impressive economic track record rests on three interconnected pillars: the successful implementation of the *doi moi* reform process since 1986, the country's accession to the WTO in January 2007, and China's role as a model for Vietnam. While the first two can hardly be disputable, the third point is more complex despite Vietnamese leaders having looked for advice and guidance from China, such as an unpublicized lesson on how to reform a socialist economy without losing party control for sixteen of Vietnam's senior-most officials assembled in China in June 2000. However, while it is ultimately impossible to find hard empirical evidence for a direct Chinese impact on Vietnam's economic pathways, there are also obvious limitations to the "China model argument" are clearly visible. Vietnam an "emerging China" or a "second China" nor do the direction, dynamics, and results of its economic reform always resemble China's approaches to and outcomes of economic policies. Be that as it may, Cheong et al. (2011) listed three areas of China's experience that loom large in Vietnam's Socioeconomic Development Strategy for the new decade since the 2010s. Apart from the establishment of large enterprise groups to increase the efficiency and competitiveness of, and reduce state subsidies to, the mostly loss-making state enterprises, the special economic zones as well as the technological and industrial policies should be highlighted to better comprehend the efforts from the Vietnamese government, the extra-firm bargaining processes between the FDI firms and the host institutions in Vietnam, and the similarities and differences between China and Vietnam. As pointed out earlier that the global production network and the strategic coupling do not occur in a vacuum without the influences of local, regional, and national institutions. Therefore, realizing the fact that China has been somehow a role model for Vietnam's opening up and reform, at least in economic and business aspects, facilitates our understanding of Vietnam's changing institutional environments after the *doi moi* reform.

According to the GPN 2.0 framework (Coe & Yeung, 2015), apart from the cost-capability ratio, market imperative and the broader risk environment are also concerns for TNCs making the relocation decisions. One of the reasons electronics production, such as laptop manufacturing, moved from coastal regions to inland China was to leverage emerging China's domestic market (Yang, 2017). Besides different endogenous factors that facilitate the manufacturing sector in Vietnam by driving down production costs, such as the lower labor cost (refer to figure 3.1), the emerging market in Vietnam and nearby Southeast Asian countries could be another reason why Vietnam has become an FDI attraction. Even though, according to figure 3.3, the people in the developed countries, that is, North America and Western Europe, will still consume the most in the coming decades, the consumers in China, as well as the South and Southeast Asia, despite relatively smaller consumption sizes, have been increasing rapidly. Detailed research by Hong Kong Trade Development Council (HKTDC) Research (2020) has pointed out that from 2014 to 2018, the retail

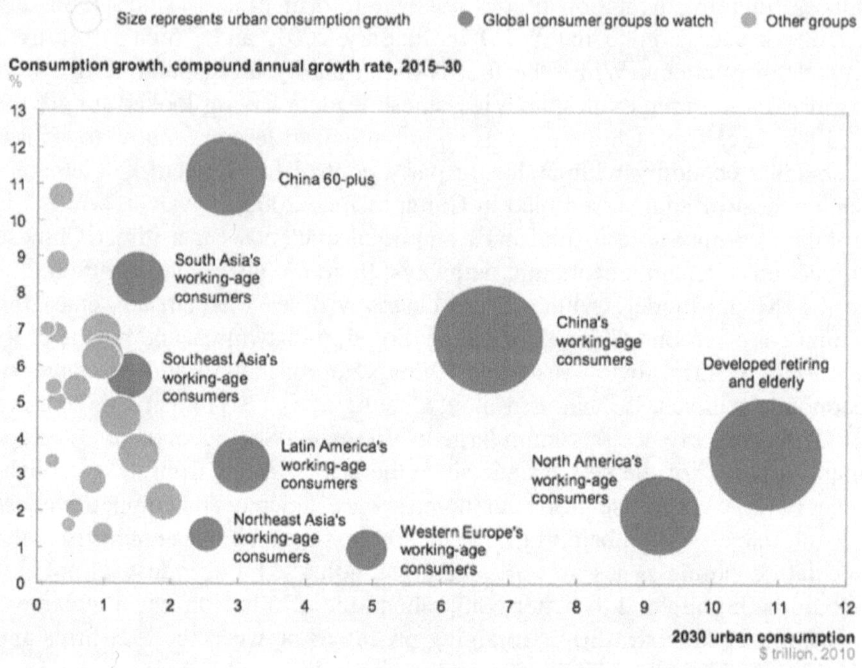

Figure 3.3 Global Urban Consumption Growth (2015–2030). *Source*: McKinsey Global Institute (2016).

sales of consumer electronics in Vietnam expanded by 13.8 percent annually. The sustained rise in disposable incomes is expected to support steady growth in demand for electronics in the coming years, and retail sales were expected to hit 224 thousand billion VND in 2022 from just 820 thousand billion in 2014. In major cities like Hanoi and Ho Chi Minh, it was found that each person has at least one mobile phone and one personal computer. Although the Vietnam market cannot compare with the one in China, according to Euromonitor International (2014), the absolute volume growth and the compound annual growth rate of Vietnam's appliances market from 2008 to 2013 ranked second among other major markets in Southeast Asia, just behind Indonesia. That said, the Vietnamese market has become more attractive recently, especially for smaller firms and ETNCs. Apart from the emerging domestic market, owing to the extensive intra- and interregional trade agreements signed as well as the cheap production costs, Vietnam has been treated as a springboard by large manufacturers to enter major markets in the TPP (Vietnamnet, 2016).

Another reason why Vietnam has received and should continue to receive increasing attention in the global production network has been attributed to the changing risk environment at both regional and global levels. The "China

Plus One" strategy, as aforementioned, has been widely adopted by TNCs to diversify their investments and reduce their reliance on China since the 2000s. This is not to mention the heightened geopolitical conflicts between China and the United States in the late 2010s that have made Vietnam the "winner" as importers would buy from Vietnam instead of China to bypass the higher tariffs imposed on Chinese products (Jamrisko, 2019). Apart from being a "demilitarized zone" and/or "springboard," Vietnam is even more interesting to study as an emerging electronics production base under the pandemic. The COVID-19-induced disruption is another global-level risk affecting the global manufacturing landscape. While it is undoubtedly true that the export-led economies, in particular, would be severely affected, how will the electronics production network be reconfigured? Or put more bluntly, is the idea of the "global production network" still relevant (e.g., Bryson & Vanchan, 2020)? How will Vietnam respond? These are all meaningful questions in facing the recent global dynamics in the GPN. We will have some more discussions in chapter 8.

REGIONAL DIFFERENCES WITHIN VIETNAM: THE RED RIVER DELTA VERSUS THE SOUTH EAST REGION

While a rather general background of Vietnam's reform and current status has been presented earlier and will be further introduced in each empirical chapter later, one important feature of Vietnam, that is, the regional variations, should be noted. Apart from the national and international levels, subnational dynamics are crucial in our multi-scalar study primarily drawing upon the GPN framework. From the partition in 1954, two parallel economic models, that is, the free markets in the South and the Communist command economy in the North, were experienced by Vietnam. The Civil War, lasting for twenty-one years, brought significant impact and damage to the North's economy, which prioritized the development of heavy industries and strictly prohibited private ownership. After Vietnam achieved reunification in 1975, the economy of united Vietnam had to face enormous difficulties in achieving growth, imbalances in payment, inefficiencies in collectivist distribution, hyperinflation, and rising debts. The Fourth Congress of the Vietnamese Communist Party (VCP) in 1976 imposed an immediate "socialist transformation" upon the Southern provinces to turn Vietnam into a socialist country with modern agriculture and industry. Even though free enterprises and the capitalist sector in the South were heavily sanctioned (Fforde, 2019), according to Freeman (1996), these petty entrepreneurs and informal sectors indeed provided the vital goods and services that sustained Vietnam during the bleak years between 1975 and 1986. By serving as both model and stimulus in the *doi moi*, the shadow economy in the South also explained the reason why the commercial expansion of the reform initially bypassed the industrial and political heartland around Hanoi, focusing instead on Ho Chi Minh City and its immediate hinterland.

After the 2000s, Vietnam's economy continued to grow at a rapid pace, with an average annual growth rate of around 7 percent between 2000 and 2019. This growth has been accompanied by a shift in the country's economic structure, with a declining share of agriculture and an increasing share of industry and services. Both northern and southern Vietnam have benefited from these trends, but the southern region has generally been more successful in attracting foreign investment and building a diversified economy. For example, the southern province of Binh Duong has become a major hub for high-tech industries such as electronics, while the southern city of Da Nang has become a center for software development and other IT-related services. One of the main reasons for this is that the southern region has been more open to foreign investment and trade, particularly with the United States and other countries in the Asia-Pacific region. The establishment of export-processing zones, industrial parks, and special economic zones in the southern region has made it a hub for manufacturing and export-oriented industries. The southern region has been able to leverage its proximity to major shipping routes and its well-developed transportation and logistics infrastructure to attract foreign investors. Additionally, the southern region has benefited from its proximity to Ho Chi Minh City, the largest city in Vietnam and a major economic center in Southeast Asia. The city has attracted a large number of foreign investors and businesses, leading to the development of a vibrant start-up ecosystem and a thriving service sector. In contrast, the northern region has traditionally been more focused on heavy industry, such as steel production and mining, which have faced challenges in recent years due to increased competition from other countries and environmental concerns. The region has also been hampered by infrastructure bottlenecks, particularly in the transportation sector, which has made it more difficult to attract investment and develop new industries.

Overall, while the northern and southern regions have attracted significant FDI inflows, the southern region has been more successful, particularly in manufacturing and export-oriented industries. However, the government has been working to promote more balanced regional development, and the northern region has been rapidly catching up. Yet, the variations between the South and the North are still obvious to date. We will focus more on the economic developments of the two major regions later in the chapter.

The Red River Delta

According to the General Statistics Office of Vietnam, except for the oil and gas extracting regions, six different economic regions are defined in Vietnam, namely Red River Delta, Northern Midlands and Mountain areas, North Central and Central Coastal areas, Central Highlands, South East, and Mekong River Delta. As aforementioned, two regions should be particularly highlighted. The Red River Delta (RRD) is one of them. The RRD is a region located in the northern part of Vietnam, encompassing the provinces of Hanoi, Hai Phong, Bac Ninh, Ha Nam, Hung Yen, Hai Duong, Ninh Binh, and Thai Binh. It is named after the Red River, which flows through the region and is a vital source of water for agriculture and industry. It is one of the most densely populated regions in Vietnam, with a population of approximately 27 million people. The region has diverse ethnic groups, including the Kinh (Vietnamese), Muong, and Tay. Socioeconomically, the Red River Delta is a key economic hub in Vietnam, with a well-developed industrial and agricultural base. Over the past few decades, the Red River Delta has experienced significant economic growth and development. The region has benefited from its strategic location, abundant natural resources, and strong industrial base. Key industries in the region include manufacturing, agriculture, and services. It is home to major cities such as Hanoi and Hai Phong, which are important centers of commerce, industry, and culture in Vietnam.

According to figure 3.4, excluding the oil and gas sector, 30 percent of the total FDI received in 2020 flowed into the RRD, and the FDI received

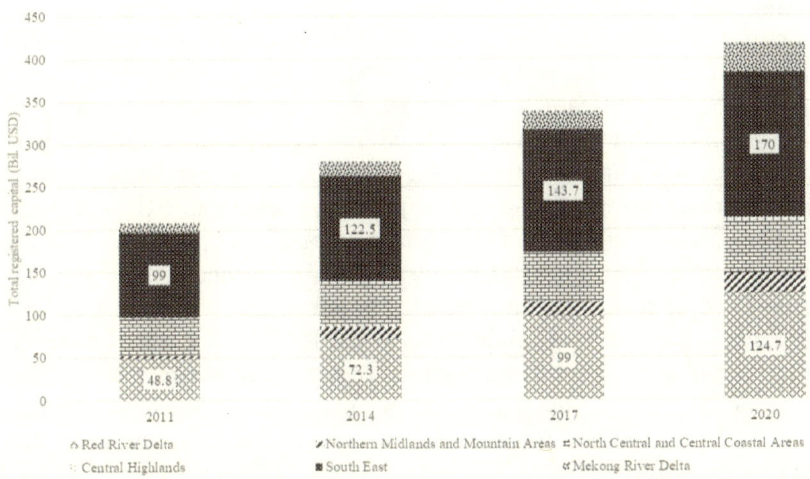

Figure 3.4 FDI Inflow to Different Regions in Vietnam (2011–2020). *Source*: Compiled by the author according to data from the General Statistics Office of Vietnam.

by the RRD grew 156 percent from 2011 to 2020. Although it has only been the second-largest FDI-receiving region, it has been one of the top regions in terms of the growth of FDI inflow. This implies that the region has increasingly caught up and become more attractive to FDIs and TNCs in recent years.

From table 3.2, although the RRD has the lowest land area among other regions (only accounting for 6 percent of the national total), the percentage of land used for agricultural production and forestry was the lowest at 61 percent, and the average urban population ranked second with around 8.5 million people. The 4.8 percent (the second highest) in-migration rate also guarantees the supply of labor in the region. Being a region that received nearly 30 percent of the national FDI inflow and where local governments have put more resources into labor training in recent years by setting up schools and vocational training institutions, the ratio of trained employees above fourteen years old in the RRD was the highest among other regions in Vietnam at 32.6 percent. This indeed implies an abundant supply of human capital of a certain standard, particularly for the labor-intensive manufacturing industries in the region. Apart from the production input, the emerging local market, despite being small, could be another attractant for the FDIs. Ranking second, the monthly average expenditure per capita of the RRD was 14.1 percent higher than the national level.

Another possible reason for RRD to catch up in a short span is the overall competitiveness of its business environment. According to the Vietnam Chamber of Commerce and Industry (VCCI), only two out of eleven provinces in RRD were in the low tier of the Provincial Competitiveness Index (PCI), which is weighted by ten sub-indices, such as transparency and access to information, informal charges, and legal institutions. Given its relatively favorable business environment and an abundant supply of labor, 31.7 percent of the firms in Vietnam were concentrated in the RRD. According to Table 3.3, 32.2 percent of the labor-intensive firms with more than a thousand employees were located in the RRD in 2020. Without a doubt, another reason why an increasing amount of FDI has flowed into the RRD and made its secondary and tertiary sectors particularly strong is its physical location. According to figure 3.5, the RRD is geographically connected to China, its biggest importer of parts and components. Therefore, one of the main advantages of investing and setting up factories in the RRD is that it will be more cost-efficient to source intermediate goods from China, not to mention the vast domestic market in China that Vietnam can leverage. That said, to better understand the production relocations from China to Vietnam, the RRD has to be examined closely.

Table 3.2 Selected Indicators of Vietnam by Regions

Selected Indicator	*Total Land Area*	*Share of Agricultural Production Land and Forestry Land*	*Average Urban Population*	*In-migration Rate*	*Percentage of Trained Labor Force at Fifteen Years of Age and Above*	*Monthly Average Income Per Capita by Salary and Wage at Current Prices*	*Monthly Average Expenditure Per Capita at Current Prices*
Unit, time period	Thousand Ha, 2020	%, as of December 31, 2020	Thousand Person, 2020	%, 2020	%, 2020	Thousand Dongs, 2021	Thousand Dongs, 2020
Whole Country	33,123	80	35,867	NA	24.10	2,383	2,890
Red River Delta	2,126	61	8,498	4.80	32.60	3,051	3,297
Northern Midlands and Mountain Areas	9,520	84	2,598	0.70	20.50	1,510	2,095
North Central and Central Coastal Areas	9,565	85	6,409	1	22.70	1,865	2,561
Central Highlands	5,451	92	1,707	1.60	16.90	1,170	2,174
South East	2,352	78	12,172	20.40	29.50	3,804	3,931
Mekong River Delta	4,082	Nil	4,483	1.20	14.90	1,631	2,493

Source: Compiled by the authors according to data from the General Statistics Office of Vietnam.

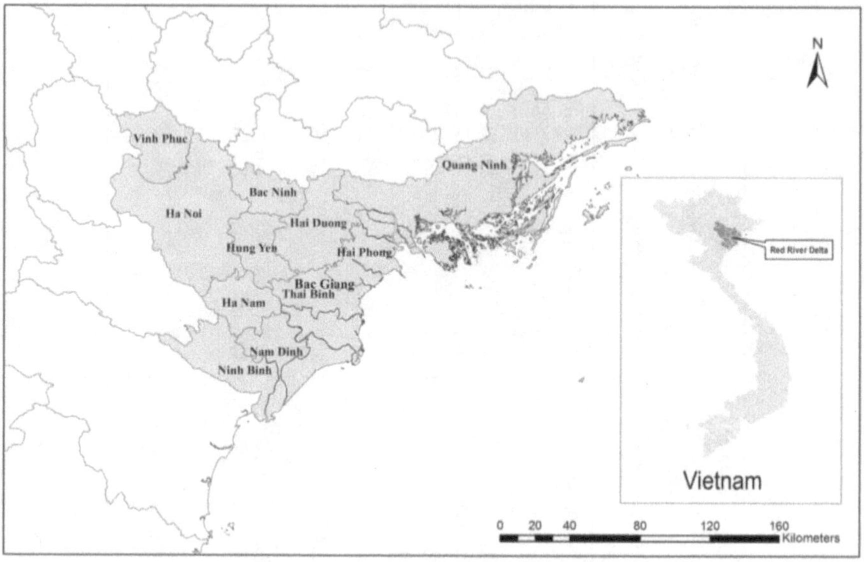

Figure 3.5 Location of the Red River Delta in Vietnam. *Source*: Compiled by the authors.

The South East Region

As pointed out by Freeman (1996), the reform initially bypassed the industrial and political heartland around Hanoi, focusing instead on Ho Chi Minh City and its immediate hinterland. Therefore, under gradualism and the step-by-step economic reform approach, the coastal region in the southern part of Vietnam was opened up first (Jandl, 2013). As such, the South East region (figure 3.6) was the first region in Vietnam to receive FDIs. The South East region of Vietnam is located in the southern part of the country and is comprised of eight provinces and cities, including Ho Chi Minh City, Dong Nai, Ba Ria-Vung Tau, Binh Duong, Binh Phuoc, Tay Ninh, Long An, and Tien Giang. This region is known for its diverse economy, with a mix of industries including manufacturing, agriculture, and tourism. It is the country's economic hub and contributes a significant portion of Vietnam's GDP. Ho Chi Minh City, the largest city in the region and Vietnam's largest city overall, is a major commercial and financial center. Other major cities in the region include Bien Hoa, Vung Tau, and Binh Duong. The South East region has a well-developed infrastructure, including modern highways, airports, seaports, and railways. The region is served by several major airports, including Tan Son Nhat International Airport in Ho Chi Minh City, which is the largest airport in Vietnam. The region also has several major seaports, including the Port of Ho Chi Minh City, which is the busiest port in Vietnam. As of 2021, the South East region has a total population of over 23 million people, making it the most populous region in Vietnam. Most of the population is

Table 3.3 Number of Acting Enterprises Having Business Outcomes as of December 31, 2020, by Regions

	Total	*Less Than 10 Persons*	*10–49 Persons*	*50–199 Persons*	*200–499 Persons*	*500–999 Persons*	*1,000 Persons or Above*
Whole Country	684,260	540,747	109,918	24,046	5,781	2,018	1,750
Red River Delta	216,822	163,747	41,550	8,321	1,933	707	564
Northern Midlands and Mountain Areas	28,118	18,871	6,937	1,724	364	111	111
North Central and Central Coastal Areas	89,246	68,520	16,260	3,421	668	222	155
Central Highlands	17,901	14,511	2,678	568	106	21	17
South East	281,096	235,494	33,774	8,170	2,202	771	685
Mekong River Delta	50,942	39,603	8,715	1,818	479	165	162

Source: Compiled by the authors according to data from the General Statistics Office of Vietnam.

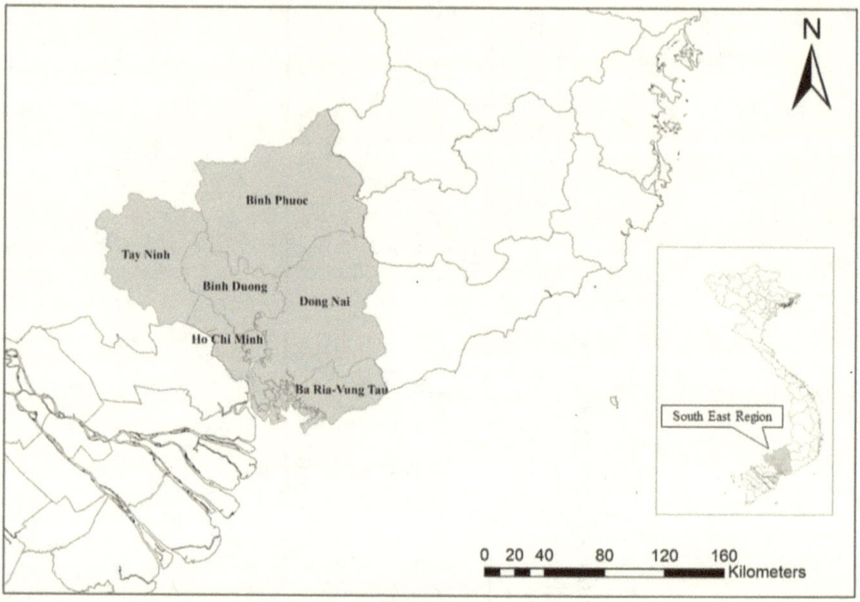

Figure 3.6 The Location of the South East Region in Vietnam. *Source*: Compiled by the authors.

concentrated in urban areas, particularly in Ho Chi Minh City. The region is also home to several ethnic groups, including the Kinh, Cham, and Khmer.

In terms of socioeconomic indicators, the South East region has a relatively high standard of living compared to other regions in Vietnam. It has a higher per capita income, a lower poverty rate, and a higher human development index than the national average. However, there are still significant disparities within the region, particularly between urban and rural areas. The manufacturing sector is a significant contributor to the economy of the South East region in Vietnam. The region is known for its industrial parks, which are home to many large multinational corporations and domestic companies. The manufacturing industry in the region is diverse, with a focus on industries such as textiles and garments, electronics, footwear, and food processing. The electronics industry is a significant contributor to the manufacturing sector in the South East region. The region is home to many electronics factories, which produce a range of products such as mobile phones, laptops, and electronic components. The industry is driven by a skilled workforce and a favorable investment environment.

And the growth of FDI inflow into the South East region has continued in recent years. Within six years from 2010, the growth was 83 percent, and in 2016, it received the highest portion of FDI inflow to Vietnam (40.7 percent) among all other regions in Vietnam. Similar to the RRD, while its land area is limited, its share of agricultural production and forestry land was the second lowest at 78 percent among all regions in Vietnam (refer to table 3.2). Its urban population density is the highest in Vietnam. In 2020, a total of 33.9 percent of the urban population in Vietnam was living in the South East region. According to the General Statistics Office of Vietnam, the in-migration rate of this region has been the highest among all regions at 20.4 percent, guaranteeing an abundant labor supply for the region. One of the reasons why the region is attractive to laborers, as seen in table 3.2. The average monthly earnings of the workers. These have been the highest among all other regions, nearly 60 percent higher than the national average in 2020. In addition, the percentage of trained employees was the second highest (29.5 percent) in the country, after the RRD (32.6 percent). Thanks to a large amount of FDI inflow, the secondary and tertiary economic sectors in the region have been relatively developed. Not only has the top share of enterprises in the country (41 percent), but the South East region also accounts for nearly 40 percent of the country's enterprises of 1,000 persons or above in 2020, implying its attractiveness, especially to labor-intensive industries and firms. Doubtlessly, the PCI is also high in general. Only one province in the region was ranked in the low tier in 2018. Last but not least, in terms of the domestic market, the South East region had the highest consumption level (the monthly average expenditure per capita) at 3,931 thousand dongs in 2020 (36 percent higher than the national average).

Putting historical elements aside, both the South East region and RRD have now become the main FDI attractions in Vietnam mainly because of their competitive endogenous production factors, particularly for the labor-intensive industries. This is due not only to the rather developed infrastructure, strategic locations, and abundant supplies of labor and land but also the supportive business environments and perhaps also the emerging local market. Although the incomes of laborers were the highest in Vietnam, especially in the South East region, the average consumption expenditures of the people in the South East region and RRD were much higher than the national average as aforementioned. Therefore, by paying special attention to these two relatively developed regions, one could also explore whether the rise of the local market impacts the reconfiguration of the production networks. Despite the fact that both the RRD and the South East region have become FDI attractions and the fact that the latter has been catching up rapidly in recent years, regional variations still exist. Unlike the majority of studies looking at Vietnam as a whole, which might run the danger of overlooking the importance of dynamics at the subnational level that is crucial in the coupling process, our study will zoom in to take account of these often-ignored local factors more deeply in the respective chapters later. All in all, in the following empirical chapters, special attention will be placed on these two regions.

Chapter 4

Overall Design of the Current Research Project

As pointed out earlier, the main goal of this book is to dig deep into the shifting production relocation from China to Vietnam, situated in the rising "Global South," and the changing global dynamics, such as the market imperatives, in the past decade. Unlike previous reports and articles, which have mainly relied on statistical models to offer a generalized overview of Vietnam's situation, regional development status, and/or its strategic position in the global supply and value chain, our current project seeks to provide a relatively comprehensive and up-to-date picture of Vietnam's current status and the way it achieved it. Hence, different research designs have been adopted in the coming chapters to achieve the chapter-specific goals. For instance, while chapter 5 focuses more on the reconfigurations of the global electronics production networks and the emergence of the Asian ones, trade, and FDI, data will be largely used to interrogate the national-level dynamics and international interactions to provide a broad sketch of the most recent electronics production landscape; in chapters 6, 7, and 8, by drawing on various conceptual ideas together with the GPN framework, firm-level qualitative investigations will be primarily utilized to find out the coupling dynamics in the relocations. That said, this chapter aims to briefly elucidate the overall design of this entire book-length research project not only to exhibit our thoughts in the very beginning stage of the study but also to rationalize and showcase the research methodology and the scope of our project for a better grasp of the book content.

STUDY PERIOD: SINCE VIETNAM'S INTEGRATION WITH THE WORLD ECONOMY

The study period, in general, covers the period from the early 2000s and continues until today. Despite the fact that the *doi moi* economic reform policy began in 1986 and the Foreign Investment Law took effect in 1987, marking a major shift in Vietnam's economic strategy to encourage foreign investment, promote private enterprise, and reduce the role of the state in the economy, as shown in figure 4.1, Vietnam has achieved substantial FDI inflows since the 1990s. Peaking in 1996 before the 1997 Asian financial crisis, the FDI inflow became substantially lower in the first decade of the twenty-first century. As pointed out by Herr et al. (2016b), the surge of the FDI inflow in the mid-1990s could be seen as the delayed effects of the *doi moi* economic reform. That said, the "true" integration of Vietnam into the world economy should begin with the joining of the WTO in 2007. Not only did the net inflow of the FDI balance of payments triple from 2006 to 2008, but the sum of exports and imports as a percent of GDP reached nearly 150 percent. Hence, it is sound to say that, in reality, Vietnam has integrated with the world, particularly via the FDI inflow and trade, since the mid-2000s. Given the topic of this monograph, the current research time period allows us to capture Vietnam's development trajectory since it connects to the world's supply chain and trading system.

Another reason why we exclude the time period before the 2000s is due to the instability in the early phase of the reform as well as the reliability of the data. Due to the unfamiliarity with the market-oriented economy and the interparty political tensions at the beginning of the reform, learning from

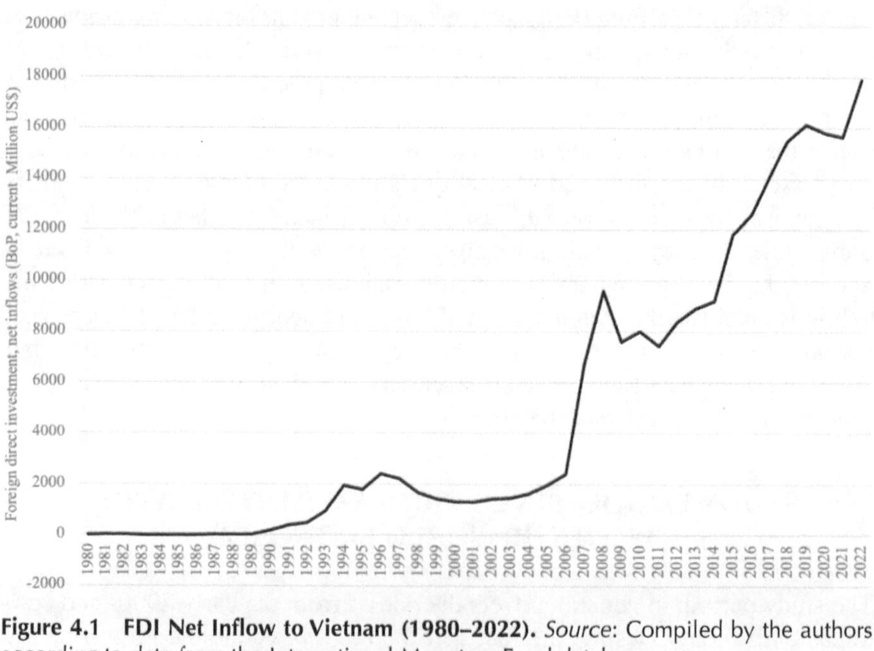

Figure 4.1 FDI Net Inflow to Vietnam (1980–2022). *Source*: Compiled by the authors according to data from the International Monetary Fund database.

China, Vietnam adopted a gradualism approach. Consequently, there have been policy inconsistencies, including the opening strategies, during the experimental stage (Jandl, 2013). Additionally, one very practical concern is data availability. According to Vietnam's General Statistics Office, the annual statistical data has only been readily available since 2000, not to mention the fact that before 2010, some volumes of the statistical yearbook were not been opened to the public.

Besides, from a broader spatial scale, Vietnam's rise and integration with the world economy have been tightly connected with the production relocation out of the "World Factory"—China. According to Yang (2016), due to different push and pull factors, such as the cheaper production costs in Southeast Asia, the shrinking market demand in developed economies particularly after the 2008 global financial crisis, as well as the industrial upgrading plan in China, many relatively low-value-added manufacturing activities, including the electronics sector, have started to move out to the nearby countries since the mid- and late-2000s. Therefore, by focusing on the period since the 2000s, this study can also hopefully cover the entire picture of the current wave of production relocation to better understand the changing competitive dynamics in the networks and how the actors respond, as well as the implications behind it.

Last but not least, while the field investigations have been interrupted by the COVID-19 lockdown and stopped since 2020, continuous observations have been made by us through keeping contact and communications with the previous interviewees in Vietnam via online messaging tools, that is, WeChat and WhatsApp, on the one hand, and through analyzing the secondary resources online, such as the firm's annual reports and the interviews done by the business analysts.

SECTOR SELECTION: THE ELECTRONICS INDUSTRY TOPPING THE WORLD'S INTERMEDIATE TRADE

This study mainly focuses on the labor-intensive manufacturing industry, and the electronics industry is selected as the case study. On the one hand, this industry is important to Asia and both China and Vietnam's economies and trade (see figure 4.2). In 2021, Vietnam and China exported 131 and 899 billion USD worth of electrical and electronic equipment, accounting for 39 percent and 27 percent of the national total export value, respectively. Apart from being an important region of electronics manufacturing and even innovation (mainly referring to East Asia, including Japan, South Korea, and Taiwan), Asia-Pacific, as a whole, has become the world's largest consumer electronics market. Not only limited to Asia, in fact, the electronics hardware

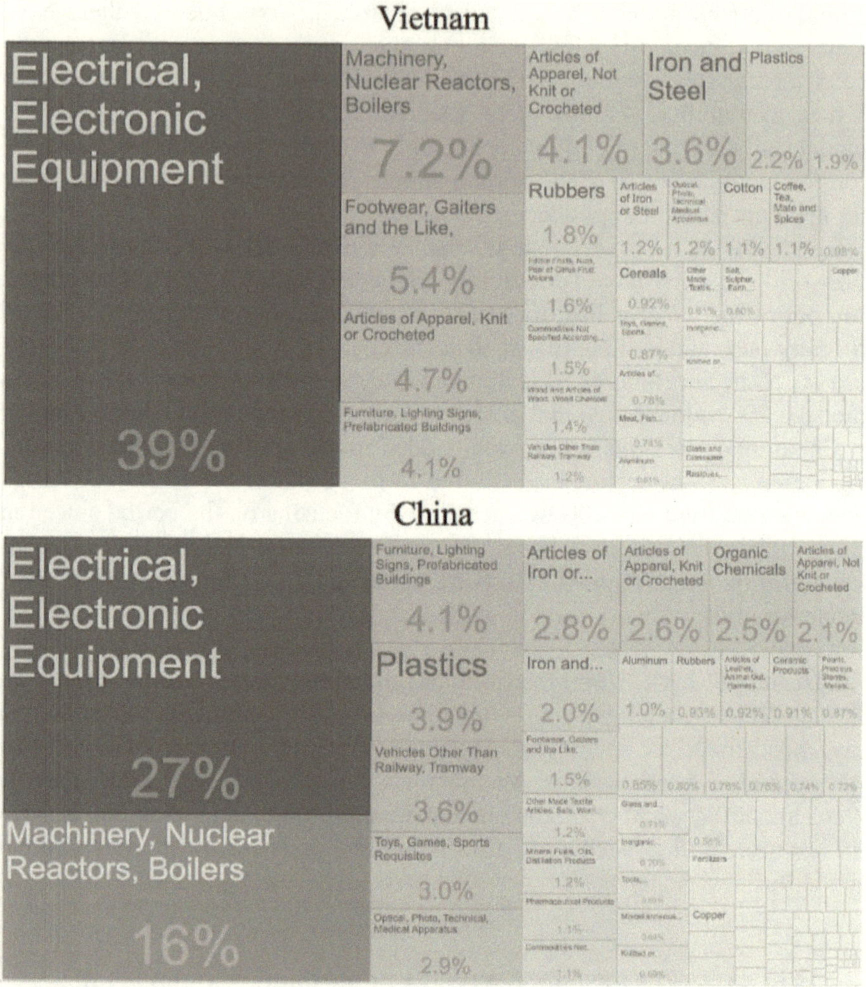

Figure 4.2 Exports by Category of Vietnam and China in 2021. *Source*: Compiled by the authors according to data from the UN Comtrade database.

industry is the world's most important goods-producing sector. Not only does it employ more workers and generate greater revenue than any other sector, but electronics products also enhance productivity in other activities and stimulate innovation across entire economies (Mann & Kirkegaard, 2006). It is what Hirschman (1958) calls a "propulsive sector."

On the other hand, the electronics industry also facilitates the analysis of the changing structures and organizations of production networks as, in general, the production chain of electronics consists of multiple but relatively clear-cut tiers. The study by Grimes and Sun (2016), using the case study of Apple's global value chain, shows that the sourcing and other production activities of electronics products can be highly complex as many different tiers of firms from different countries are involved. Together with the fact that the electronics industry has topped the share of intermediate goods trade, in other words, the reconfigurations of the electronics production networks will have a significant and wide-ranging geographical impact. Due to the advanced technology that enables the standardization of productions and the codification of transactions (Gereffi et al., 2005), instead of vertical integration, firms in the electronics industry are now mainly in a modular governance structure and can be divided into different tiers, such as lead firms, contract manufacturers, platform leaders, specialized suppliers, and some lower-tier generic suppliers (Sturgeon & Kawakami, 2011). As different actors involved will perform different functions along the chain to capture value while at the same time trying to "climb up" the chain, the interactions, powers, and governance inside the electronics production systems are always dynamic and worthwhile to be updated. Besides, as the value-added of and the potential value-added after the upgrade of the electronics industry are comparatively higher than other traditional manufacturing industries, governments of different places have been more proactive and, in some cases, developmental to nurture their domestic firms. Hence, by looking into the industry, one can also explore the roles of nonfirm actors in influencing the configuration of global production systems.

In the past few decades, East Asia in general and China in particular have become increasingly important in the electronics industry, especially the mobile phone sector (Lee & Lim, 2018), both as production locations and end markets; especially after the global financial crisis in 2008, developing Southeast Asia has also engaged in the networks due to its lower production costs and emerging market demand (Horner, 2016; Kawakami & Sturgeon, 2010; Yang, 2016). To understand the current wave of relocations and production network reconfiguration, the mobile phone manufacturing sector is ideal, as it has become increasingly important. According to table 4.1, China was the top mobile phone exporter from 2011 to 2021. In 2021, China alone accounted for more than 50 percent of the total export value of the top ten mobile phone exporters. Vietnam, on the other hand, has risen rapidly from the eighth biggest mobile phone exporter in 2011 to the second in 2016 and 2021. Since the mid-2010s, mobile phones have been the top export item of Vietnam in terms of value (table 5.3), and Vietnam accounted for 12 percent of the total export value of the top ten mobile phone exporters in 2021, up from just 4 percent in 2011. Although its export value was lower than China's, the growth rate has outpaced other top exporters. Compared to the 84 percent and 131 percent growth of China and Hong Kong from 2011 to 2016, the growth of the export value of mobile phones in Vietnam was 377 percent during this period. In the late 2010s, despite global geopolitical unrest and

Table 4.1 Top Ten Exporters of Mobile Phones and Top Ten Importers of the Related Parts and Components (2011–2021)

Export (Million USD)						*Import (Million USD)*					
HS 2007: 851712						*HS 2007: 851770*					
2011		*2016*		*2021*		*2011*		*2016*		*2021*	
China	63,194	China	11,6091	China	14,7056	China	24,245	China	38,203	China	44,962
Korea	15,078	Vietnam	27,155	Vietnam	33,621	Hong Kong	18,144	Hong Kong	31,763	Hong Kong	27,176
Taiwan	10,545	Hong Kong	23,731	Hong Kong	32,232	United States	6,223	Vietnam	9,517	Vietnam	20,649
Hungary	10,349	United States	9,898	United Arab Emirates	21,160	Mexico	5,210	Korea	7,373	India	7,349
Hong Kong	10,288	Korea	8,157	United States	12,637	Hungary	3,914	India	6,376	Korea	4,595
Mexico	7,193	Germany	6,340	Germany	5,685	Japan	3,156	United States	5,356	United States	4,332
United States	6,512	Singapore	5,219	Czechia	5,461	Korea	3,001	Indonesia	2,872	Indonesia	4,044
Vietnam	5,698	Slovakia	3,535	Singapore	5,315	India	2,726	Mexico	2,840	Brazil	2,564
Singapore	4,448	United Arab Emirates	3,480	Korea	4,926	Netherlands	2,665	Japan	2,705	Singapore	2,353
Germany	4,206	Czechia	2,539	India	4,872	Brazil	2,169	Brazil	2,312	Japan	2,037

Source: Compiled by the authors according to data from the UN Comtrade database.

Note: 851712 = Telephones for cellular networks "mobile telephones" or for other wireless networks; 851770 = Parts of telephone sets, telephones for cellular networks or for other wireless networks, and of other apparatus for the transmission or reception of voice, images, or other data, not elsewhere specified n.e.s.

the impacts of the COVID-19 pandemic, the growth rate of Vietnam's mobile phone export value was 24 percent from 2016 to 2021. Besides exporting, the increasing degree of international integration and articulation of Vietnam into the global mobile phone production system can also be reflected by its imports. The growth rate of Vietnam's import value of phone-related parts and components was 1073 percent from 2011 to 2021. Vietnam was the twelfth largest importer of phone parts and components in 2011, and after a decade, it became the third largest. Hence, to look into the production relocation of electronics manufacturing and the rapid global production system participation of Vietnam, mobile handset manufacturing will be our main focus sector of this book.

DATA COLLECTION

Two main data collection methods will be used. Our interest mainly lies in answering the "why" and "how" questions, that is, why and how different tiers of firms relocate their productions to Vietnam. Hence, firm-level case studies seem to be suitable (Yin, 2018). Compared to the studies of higher levels, the firm-level case study enables us to collect concrete, in-depth, and context-dependent knowledge related to the specific cases and firms of our interest (Flyvbjerg, 2006). To elaborate further, the firm-level case study enables us to have a detailed understanding of the situation by allowing us to gain deep and detailed insights into the inner workings of a particular organization. Besides, by examining a specific firm, we can contextualize our findings within the broader industry or market in which the firm operates. This can provide insights into industry trends and help in understanding the highly complex and dynamic electronics production networks. Through the firm-level case studies, we also discover some unique or rare phenomena that may not be easily observable through other research methods (see chapters 6, 7, and 8). Furthermore, we have also benefited from the longitudinal analysis enabled by the firm-level case studies as the connections we built allow us to keep monitoring the changing situations amid the COVID-19 pandemic remotely. This surely provides valuable discernment into the evolution of organizations and industries. To do so, in-depth interviews have been designed as the primary method to collect firsthand firm-level data. Apart from the firm-level investigation, to better understand the big picture and, more importantly, to avoid the firm-level case study's subjectivity issue caused by the biases and perspectives of the researchers, secondhand data, such as statistical data and reports from different sources, have also been collected and analyzed to ensure the validity and reliability of our collected data collected and findings.

Primary Data from Field Investigations and In-Depth Interviews

Firsthand data in this study has been mainly collected from firm-level interviews, which were primarily conducted on-site from December 2017 to November 2019. Two main rounds of on-field investigations were conducted in late 2017 and in the latter half of 2018 in two relatively developed regions with the highest level of inward FDI in Vietnam, namely the RRD and the Southeast region, as well as some surrounding areas.

Extensive face-to-face interviews were done in Hai Phong, Bac Ninh, Vinh Phuc, Ha Noi, and Bac Giang in the Red River Delta, and Ho Chi Minh, Binh Duong, Tay Ninh, and Dong Nai in the South East region with different tiers and levels of the firm and nonfirm actors from various origins that were involved in the networks (see figures 3.4 and 3.6). In addition to the on-site ones, interviews and follow-up interviews have been done online due to the flexibility of the time arrangement and, later, the travel limitations because of the COVID-19 pandemic. Sixteen online interviews have been conducted. Dozens of follow-up questions were asked through instant messaging tools, such as WeChat and WhatsApp, to further explore related topics and to keep updating the situations. Overall, a total of about fifty interviews, excluding the follow-up interviews, have been completed since 2017.

After connecting with several potential interviewees at the Vietnam Investment Seminar held in Hong Kong on September 15, 2017, by the Consulate General of S.R. Vietnam, the snowball method was used to get in touch with more targeted interviewees. By recruiting interviewees through referrals from other participants, we not only saved time and cost but also reached the rather hard-to-reach populations, that is, the relocated firms in Vietnam. One of the biggest advantages we realized is that the method can enhance the trust between us and the interviewees. Referrals from trusted sources can increase the likelihood that potential interviewees will participate in the study and share some of their rather sensitive ideas in terms of business and/or geopolitics with us. Semi-structured interviews were carried out in different parts of Vietnam, not only to understand the main questions listed below but also to explore the contextual information of the interviewees to better interpret their ideas. Each interview lasted an average of forty to ninety minutes, and they were recorded with the consent of the interviewees and transcribed to be used as anonymized quotations in this monograph.

Although the interview questions may be different as they were customized for each interviewee, the questions generally cover the following aspects. For the firm actors from different origins that have relocated to Vietnam, we focused on: (1) the motives and challenges of relocating; (2) the relationships with the parent companies and with other inter-firm actors, such as their suppliers of different tiers from different origins, before and after the relocation; (3) the relationships with the domestic firms and the nonfirm actors in Vietnam, such as the local suppliers, industrial park developers, and different levels of the host governments; and (4) different firm-specific strategies used in the relocation process, the rationales behind them, and the outcomes of the production network reconfigurations. For the domestic firms in Vietnam, we explored: (1) their situations and challenges in engaging in international production systems; (2) their relationships with the relocated TNCs; (3) the impacts of the expansions of the TNCs, both on them and on the region; and (4) their relationships with different levels of local governments. For different levels of Vietnam's governments, including national, regional, and local-level institutions, we examined: (1) the situations of the TNCs from different origins in Vietnam; (2) how governments see the firms from different origins and different tiers in the networks; (3) their relationships with the relocated TNCs as well as the domestic firms in Vietnam, especially the domestic suppliers; (4) the impacts of the relocations on the domestic firms and regional developments; (5) how different levels of government help the relocated TNCs as well as the domestic firms; (6) the relationships among different levels of governments and institutions in dealing with the FDIs and TNCs; and (7) the future planning of the governments regarding the FDI and TNCs. Follow-up questions to interrogate how these actors have responded to the current uncertainties and risks, such as the Sino-US trade war and the COVID-19 pandemic, were also asked, mainly via online tools.

Secondary Data from Reliable Sources

As mentioned by Hoa and Lin (2016), the quality of the statistical data of Vietnam is relatively poor due to the inconsistency and unavailability of many statistical items, particularly the subnational-level data. Therefore, the earlier in-depth interviews are crucial for this study. Yet, secondary data is still important for a better grasp of the general situations of the FDIs, regional developments, and internationalization of Vietnam. The secondary data used in this book was collected extensively from different official statistical publications, mainly from the General Statistics Office of Vietnam, the Customs of Vietnam, the Ministry of Planning and Investment, and the Vietnam Chamber of Commerce and Industry. The data was derived from different publications, such as the Report of International Merchandise Trade Vietnam, the Report of Economic Census, the Report on Labor Force Survey, the Statistical Yearbook of Vietnam, the Statistical Handbook of Vietnam, the Result of the Vietnam Household Living Standards Survey, the Report on Effectiveness of Business of FDI Enterprises, and the Report on Business

Results of All Enterprises of Vietnam, and so on. Unlike the statistical yearbooks of many countries that include provincial-level data, Vietnam does not. Hence, some information and data were directly obtained from different provincial/city-level governments during the field visits. In addition, FDI and international trade data was collected from different online databases of international organizations, such as the UN Comtrade Database, the World Bank Open Data, the Organization for Economic Co-operation and Development (OECD) Data, International Monetary Fund (IMF) Data, and the WTO Statistics Database. All values were adjusted to the current price and in US dollar to facilitate the comparisons.

The secondhand data were also collected from various official/professional reports published online by different public and private institutions, such as the Hong Kong Trade Development Council (HKTDC), Asian Development Bank (ADB), McKinsey & Company, and so on. Apart from these reports, different online archives, such as news and interviews, were also retrieved from well-recognized websites, such as Reuters, The Economist, CNN Business, Bloomberg, Forbes, South China Morning Post (SCMP), The Asian Post, The Wall Street Journal, The New York Times, and so on, so as to enrich the study, especially to keep updating the situation during the COVID-19 pandemic.

CONCLUSION

Using the production relocation of the electronics industry, especially the mobile phone manufacturing sector from China to Vietnam as the case study, this book comprehensively studies the current restructuring of the global and regional production networks in three empirical chapters. In the first empirical chapter, that is, chapter 5, the internationalization and the articulation of Vietnam into the production networks will be analyzed to get a better grasp of the broader picture of the emergence of Vietnam and the changing Asian electronics production network. Using mainly secondary data related to FDIs and international trades, the spatial, temporal, and sectoral changing patterns of the electronics production landscape, as well as the articulation of Vietnam into the global production systems, can be reflected.

After mapping out the big picture, how different tiers of firms from different origins have expanded their productions in Vietnam will be studied in chapters 6 and 7. The firm-level investigation in chapter 6 will focus on how the lead firms, contract manufacturers, and lower-tier suppliers from different origins in the electronics industry have expanded to the Red River Delta and organized their production activities using different firm-specific strategies. After collecting the firm-level data through on-site investigations and face-to-face semi-structured interviews, firm-specific strategies adopted by different TNCs will be systematically explored to see how they organized their production networks with different firms and nonfirm actors in the network, particularly the multi-scalar institutions in the host region, as well as the consequential coupling outcomes. Unlike chapter 6, which focuses on the relatively established TNCs, which are mainly from the NIEs, chapter 7 pays attention to the ones that originated in China, with particular attention to the privately owned and relatively small- and medium-sized ones that are becoming more important both in terms of the FDI volume and the production network reconfigurations. Instead, chapter 7 focuses on the South East region, which is another region where most FDIs concentrate and has the longest history of FDI attraction. Again, through analyzing the data collected from on-site investigations and interviews, chapter 7 investigates why and how these ETNCs have relocated and coordinated their cross-border production networks spatially and organizationally and how the inherent intuitional legacies have impacted the process.

To keep our study up to date, we also conclude our observations from our continuous study from 2019 to early 2023 in chapter 8. Many debates have been recently stirred about the future of electronics production networks under the current heightened geopolitical conflicts as well as the COVID-19 pandemic. In chapter 8, based on the latest released statistical data as well as the online interviews conducted by us and other business analysts and reporters, we hope to offer some empirically based preliminary findings on the impacts of both the Sino-US trade war and the COVID-19 pandemic, particularly on how these two incidents have impacted the electronics production networks. This not only can help to compare and contrast with the imaginations or presumptions raised by other observers toward the post-pandemic global production system but also can hopefully offer some practical insights for the actors in need.

This short chapter summarizes the overarching research design of our research project. In short, to understand the current wave of production relocations of firms to Vietnam under the changing global economic landscape, the observation will be more precise and insightful if different countries in developing Southeast Asia besides Vietnam and different industries besides the electronics sector have been taken into the study. However, due to the limited time and resources, one of the most important sectors—the electronics industry, which is the "backbone" of the global production systems (Kawakami & Sturgeon, 2010)—and one of the fastest-growing countries, as well as the biggest winner in the Sino-US trade war in the region, Vietnam, have been selected. To better capture the current wave of production relocations, the time period of study starts from the mid-2000s, especially after Vietnam's WTO accession. And instead of the generalized observations based on secondhand statistical data, in-depth firm-level interviews have been extensively carried out to understand the mechanisms of this wave of production relocations, particularly the questions of why and how besides "what." Yet, as extensive as the field investigations we did to collect the first-hand data, owing to our limited capabilities, there are still limitations in our research, especially regarding the data collection. For example, a structured questionnaire survey was originally designed to gather information from the relocated firms in the industrial parks where these firms from different origins are concentrated, with the help of the industrial park managing team. However, probably due to the nonobligatory nature of the survey, the survey did not hit the expected response rate, that is, lower than a 40 percent response rate, and the plan had to be discarded to avoid biased observation. That said, we would like to stress that the findings we obtained in this project, although verified by different parties, including the interviewees, still may not stand for the entire picture. One more thing to be noticed is that the study area, design, and methodology introduced earlier only give a relatively general idea of how the empirical studies in the following chapters of this book will be conducted. More detailed descriptions of the research design will be presented in the following chapters.

Chapter 5

Transformation of the Asian Electronics Production Networks

Articulation of Vietnam in Global Production Networks

The global value chains (GVCs) (Gereffi, 1994) and global production networks (GPNs) (Coe et al., 2004; Dicken et al., 2001; Henderson et al., 2002), including the newly developed GPN 2.0 (Coe & Yeung, 2015) frameworks, have been widely used to understand the geographical and structural configuration of the increasingly organizationally fragmented and spatially dispersed production networks since the 1990s. Coordinated by the lead firms, the GVCs and the GPNs are formed via cross-border investments in productive assets and the trades of inputs and outputs with different suppliers and customers worldwide. To stay competitive, lead firms from advanced economies, such as the United States, European countries, and Japan, as well as later the newly industrialized economies (NIEs), namely South Korea, Taiwan, Singapore, and Hong Kong, have started to "offshore" and "outsource" their relatively low value-added production activities to developing countries with lower overall production costs. As a result, developing countries, such as China, have been able to join the global and regional production networks coordinated by these leading firms (Borrus et al., 2000). Notably, in the electronics industry, a so-called "triangular trade" pattern (Baldwin & Lopez-Gonzalez, 2015) has been witnessed among the countries in East Asia after they have participated in the production networks over the past decades. China has become the "World Factory" by assembling the components and parts imported from the Asian NIEs and Japan into final goods and exporting them to external markets, mainly in the United States and European countries.

"The centuries-old international trade geography, where the South served as hinterlands of resources and captive markets for finished goods of the North, is changing" (UNCTAD, 2004: 1). Although the "triangular trade-" based understanding of the Asian electronics production network is still valid, it has not fully captured the emergence of the changing dynamics in the global economy and the related effects on the reconfiguration of the production network, particularly since the late 2000s. On the one hand, the rise of Asia and China has been reflected not just in the productive capacity but also in the rising demand from the increasing expansion of its middle-income population (Horner & Murphy, 2018; Horner & Nadvi, 2018). On the other hand, the increasing participation of the countries in developing Southeast Asia in the production networks has been noticed (Yeung, 2017). Since the 2000s, apart from "going west" to relocate to inland China, relocating to the neighboring countries nearby in developing Asia with lower production costs has been increasingly witnessed (Yang, 2016; Zhu & Pickles, 2014), the effects of which on the patterns of the Asian production networks remain underresearched in the academic literature. In response to the changing dynamics at national, regional, and global levels, this chapter, as the starting empirical chapter of this monograph, aims to offer an updated investigation on the configuration of the Asian production network since the late 2000s through the case of the electronics manufacturing industry, not only hoping to understand the latest changing dynamics in the global economy and their implications, especially on Vietnam, so as to provide a big picture of what happened to the global and Asian production network in the past few decades but also to provide some insights to push forward the traditional conceptualization of the global production systems to better grasp the potential research agenda in the coming future.

As illustrated by Sturgeon and Kawakami (2010), the electronics industry accounts for a growing and the highest share of the total manufactured intermediate goods trade compared to other industries common in the studies of global production systems, such as the automotive and apparel industries. Unlike other technology-intensive sectors that need the colocation of engineers and other capital-intensive sectors that the intermediaries are cost-inefficient to transport, it is relatively common for electronics firms to engage in the twin strategies of "offshoring" and "outsourcing" given the advanced technologies and cheaper transportation costs nowadays. Hence, under the fierce global competition, electronics firms are sensitive and would respond to the changing global economy in no time. Moreover, apart from the importance of the electronics manufacturing industry forming the production network at the global level, the industry is particularly important for the formation of the Asian regional production network as illustrated by Thorbecke (2016): not only was the intraregional trade volume in Asia in electronics parts and components three times more than the trade in the next leading category in 2014, but there has also been a tight relationship between the trade within the region and the exports of the final electronics products from the region to the world, forming a spatially wider network. Although the above article has pointed out that the Asian electronics production networks have started to transform, that is, with the increasing participation of Southeast Asian countries such as Vietnam, it warrants more attention as many questions are yet to be answered, for example: How have these developing economies joined the networks? What are their roles and the changing roles of the members already in the networks? And how have the networks reconfigured?

While studying the reconfigurations of the Asian electronics production networks, Vietnam in developing Southeast Asia deserves more attention due to its rapid participation in the electronics production networks (Sturgeon & Zylberberg, 2016; Thorbecke, 2016). Yet, despite the increasing research attention recently, the main focus has been placed on the national level to analyze the advantages and disadvantages of Vietnam in the global engagement for policy recommendations (see, e.g., Sturgeon & Zylberberg, 2016). Little effort has been made to understand the changing dynamics at a transnational level. Hence, this chapter offers an updated investigation of the transformation of the Asian electronics production networks, based on the participation of some developing economies, that is, Vietnam, to fill the aforementioned gaps. Particular attention will be paid to the changing trades and investments by established and emerging transnational corporations from relatively developed economies such as South Korea and emerging economies like China to Vietnam since the late 2000s.

The remainder of the chapter is organized into three sections. Following this introduction, a very brief overview of the literature on the reorganization of the global production networks of the electronics industry will be conducted to highlight the transformation of the regional production networks in Asia. It will then investigate the changing patterns of the Asian production networks, especially the integration of Vietnam into the network. This will be followed by an interpretation of the regional production networks by delineating the changing dynamics at global, regional, and national levels. Last but not least, we will also evaluate Vietnam's present role in the network. This chapter concludes with a summary of the main findings and, more importantly, a discussion and some suggestions for future research directions on global production systems.

REORGANIZATION OF THE ELECTRONICS PRODUCTION NETWORKS IN ASIA

The spatial reorganization of electronics production started in the 1960s when the electronics manufacturers in the United States, Western Europe, and later Japan began offshoring their production activities to Asian NIEs for lower production costs. While keeping the higher value-added activities at home, these TNCs managed to relocate their lower value-added production activities to the relatively developing NIEs at that time and export the final products back to the advanced economies. Starting from the 1980s, as the global electronics industry started to grow and become more competitive, given that the production process of electronics has become more standardized and modularized, the leading manufacturers began to outsource parts of their productions, mainly the manufacturing activities. The organizational shift of the electronics value chain from vertical integration (keeping all value activities in-house) to specialization (outsourcing some of the value activities, usually the lower value-added ones) not only increased the cost-efficiency of the production process but also provided an important chance for electronics firms in the NIEs to participate in the global production networks of electronics. The changing organizational structure of the electronics value chain gave rise to several higher-tier suppliers, such as the manufacturing service providers, modular manufacturers, specialized suppliers, and later the contract manufacturers, according to their divergent development paths, especially in the 1990s (Gereffi et al., 2005). Based on their corporate strategies and their "home-based advantages," and through participating in the global production networks as well as the nurturing by the national state, the firms in the NIEs became not only the suppliers of different tiers as aforementioned but also the lead firms themselves, such as Samsung and LG (Lee et al., 2016; Yeung, 2007).

The production relocation of the electronics industry has further extended beyond the NIEs since the 1980s. The export-oriented development model of NIEs was followed by China, particularly starting from the 1980s when firms in the TNCs started to move to the PRD in China mainly due to price pressure and growing competition from firms in other Asian countries (Yeung, 2001). Besides the FDI inflow to the PRD, the Yangtze River Delta (YRD) has become another FDI hotspot since the late 1990s. Taiwanese electronics and IT manufacturers, in particular, began establishing a new industrial cluster by expanding from Taiwan and the PRD region to the YRD region. A lion's share of investment from Taiwanese firms has been recorded in cities in the YRD region, such as Suzhou, Wujiang, and Kunshan (Yang, 2009). Since the 1960s–1970s, "Factory Asia" has been seen as a manufacturing power. China, carrying out the implementation of opening and reform at that time, replaced Japan and later the Asian NIEs to become the "World Factory" and contributed about one-quarter of the total manufacturing output of "Factory Asia." Nowadays, it has contributed more than half of the value. Notably, as pointed out by Baldwin and Lopez-Gonzalez (2015), a so-called "triangular trade" pattern has emerged and dominated the countries in East Asia over the past decades. It was found out that while components and parts have been imported from Asian NIEs and Japan, China has acted as the assembly hub by manufacturing and exporting the final products for external markets in the United States and European countries.

While the preceding paragraph has narrated the general situation of the relocations of electronics production activities over the past few decades, there are some variations between the paths of different sectors of the electronics industry. Tables 5.1 and 5.2 illustrate the changes in the top exporters of the automatic data processing machines and units thereof as well as of the radio-broadcast receivers, respectively. What is similar between these two tables is clear. One can see that before the year 2000, the top exporters of both electronics products were mainly the rather developed economies, such as the United States, Germany, Japan, and other European countries; while entering the twenty-first century, the top exporters have been replaced by the emerging and developing economies, such as China, Mexico, and other Southeast Asian countries like Malaysia. The differences between these two tables are also clear. Compared to a 100 percent global export value growth of the radio-broadcast receivers, which reached 12 billion USD in 2020, the export value of the automatic data processing machines and units has increased from just 12.6 to 305.4 billion USD from 1980 to 2020. Apart from the increasing market demand for the latter, the rapidly increasing value-added of the exported machines and units caused by the advancing technology could be another reason leading to a 2324 percent growth in its export value. In addition, by zooming in closely, one can also see the temporal differences of the changing top exporters in tables 5.1 and 5.2. Using the data from these two tables, figures 5.1 and 5.2 have been compiled by the authors to better showcase the changing landscape of the top exporters of the automatic data processing machines and units as well as the radio-broadcast receivers with time. Two observations could be spotted from these two figures, which illustrate the temporal and spatial changing production activities of these two electronics sectors. First, compared to the relocations of automatic data processing machines and units, the offshoring/production relocations of the radio-broadcast receivers to the Global South happened earlier. For example, China has become one of the top exporters since the 1990s. Second, compared to the production of automatic data processing machines and units, the landscape of the top exporters of radio-broadcast receivers was more spatially extended overall, especially in the Global South. This implies that one cannot see the electronics manufacturing industry as one in studying their temporal and spatial reconfigurations since different products are likely to have various production structures due to different levels of standardization of the productions and the codification of the transactions (Gereffi et al., 2005).

Although the "triangular trade" pattern among East Asian countries has still dominated, the transformation of the "World Factory" has been underway since the 2000s, especially in the aftermath of the 2008 global financial crisis.

Table 5.1 Top Ten Exporters of Automatic Data Processing Machines and Units Thereof (1980–2020)

1980			*1990*			*2000*			*2010*			*2020*		
Country	*Billion USD*	*World Share*	*Country*	*Billion USD*	*World Share*	*Country*	*Billion USD*	*World Share*	*Country*	*Billion USD*	*World Share*	*Country*	*Billion USD*	*World Share*
World Total	12.6	100.0%	World Total	69.9	100.0%	World Total	199.4	100.0%	World Total	295.8	100.0%	World Total	305.4	100.0%
United States and Puerto Rico	4.62	36.7%	United States	15.68	22.4%	United States	30.86	15.5%	China	139.06	47.0%	China	170.18	44.5%
Fed. Rep. of Germany	1.51	12.0%	Japan	12.17	17.4%	Singapore	19.42	9.7%	United States	23.93	8.1%	Mexico	32.00	8.4%
United Kingdom	1.42	11.2%	United Kingdom	6.84	9.8%	Taiwan	16.16	8.1%	Netherlands	16.55	5.6%	United States	24.78	6.5%
Italy	1.16	9.2%	Singapore	6.83	9.8%	Netherlands	15.18	7.6%	Mexico	13.33	4.5%	Hong Kong	24.23	6.3%
France	0.92	7.3%	Fed. Rep. of Germany	5.32	7.6%	Japan	14.85	7.4%	Thailand	12.85	4.3%	Germany	15.74	4.1%
Canada	0.66	5.3%	Taiwan	4.01	5.7%	United Kingdom	14.49	7.3%	Hong Kong	12.73	4.3%	Czechia	14.38	3.8%
Japan	0.54	4.3%	France	2.79	4.0%	China	10.99	5.5%	Germany	12.34	4.2%	Netherlands	12.52	3.3%
Sweden	0.42	3.3%	Ireland	2.51	3.6%	Ireland	9.87	4.9%	Malaysia	11.02	3.7%	Thailand	11.79	3.1%
Ireland	0.35	2.8%	Netherlands	2.26	3.2%	Germany	9.58	4.8%	Singapore	9.01	3.0%	Taiwan	10.62	2.8%
Poland	0.19	1.5%	Italy	2.20	3.1%	Rep. of Korea	9.29	4.7%	Czechia	8.33	2.8%	Singapore	7.32	1.9%

Source: Compiled by the authors according to data from the UN Comtrade database.
Note: Automatic data processing machines and units thereof were represented by SITC LTS 752.

Table 5.2 Top Ten Exporters of Radio-broadcast Receivers (1980–2020)

1980			1990			2000			2010			2020		
Country	*Billion USD*	*World Share*	*Country*	*Billion USD*	*World Share*	*Country*	*Billion USD*	*World Share*	*Country*	*Billion USD*	*World Share*	*Country*	*Billion USD*	*World Share*
World Total	6.0	100.0%	World Total	13.3	100.0%	World Total	19.4	100.0%	World Total	15.7	100.0%	World Total	12.0	100.0%
Japan	3.01	50.2%	Japan	2.48	18.6%	Hong Kong	3.4	17.5%	China	3.81	24.3%	China	3.95	33.0%
Hong Kong	0.84	14.1%	Hong Kong	2.12	15.9%	China	2.97	15.3%	Malaysia	1.74	11.1%	Mexico	1.53	12.8%
Singapore	0.64	10.8%	Singapore	1.58	11.8%	1	2.58	13.3%	Hong Kong	1.13	7.2%	Hungary	1.25	10.4%
Rep. of Korea	0.29	4.8%	China	1.43	10.7%	Mexico	1.45	7.5%	Portugal	1.1	7.0%	United States	0.92	7.7%
Fed. Rep. of Germany	0.28	4.7%	Rep. of Korea	1.38	10.4%	Japan	1.13	5.8%	Thailand	1.09	7.0%	Portugal	0.66	5.5%
Belgium-Luxembourg	0.17	2.9%	Malaysia	1.1	8.3%	United States	1.08	5.6%	USA	1.05	6.7%	Malaysia	0.53	4.4%
United States and Puerto Rico	0.13	2.2%	Fed. Rep. of Germany	0.5	3.7%	Singapore	1.03	5.3%	Mexico	0.98	6.3%	Thailand	0.49	4.1%
Netherlands	0.09	1.5%	Taiwan	0.45	3.4%	Portugal	0.64	3.3%	Germany	0.74	4.7%	Germany	0.34	2.8%
France	0.08	1.4%	United States	0.38	2.9%	Belgium	0.63	3.2%	Czechia	0.58	3.7%	Rep. of Korea	0.3	2.5%
United Kingdom	0.07	1.1%	Brazil	0.31	2.4%	Indonesia	0.61	3.2%	Israel	0.4	2.5%	Czechia	0.28	2.4%

Source: Compiled by the authors according to data from the UN Comtrade database. *Note*: Automatic data processing machines and units thereof were represented by SITC LTS 762.

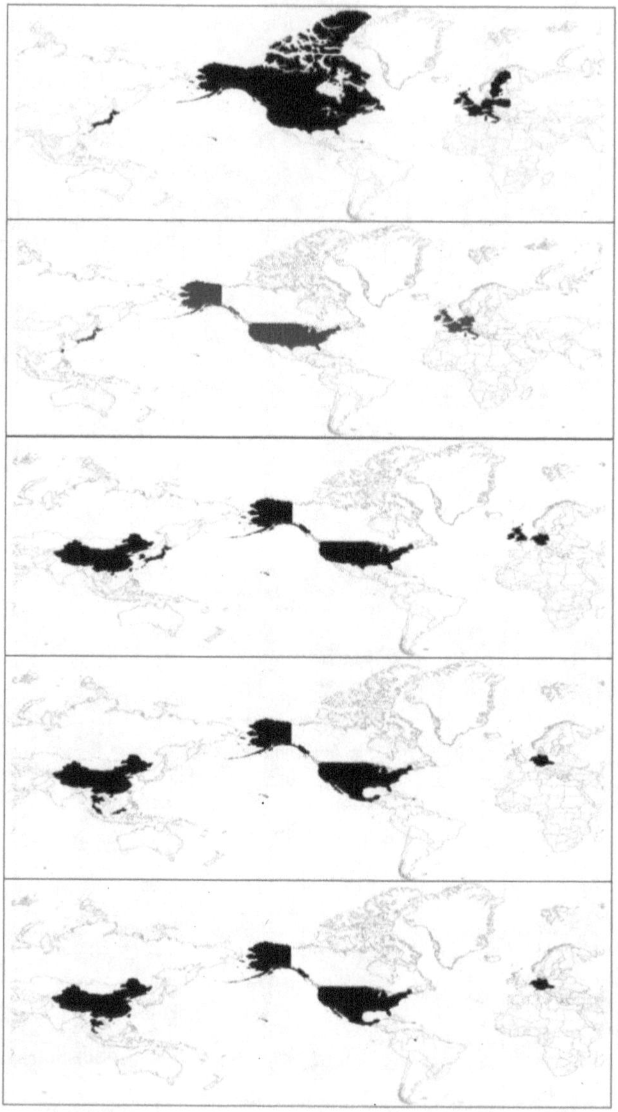

Figure 5.1 Top Ten Exporters of Automatic Data Processing Machines and Units Thereof (SITC LTS 752, 1980–2020). Note: From top to bottom, it is 1980, 1990, 2000, 2010, and 2020. In 1980, the regions of the United States and Puerto Rico were shaded only on the US region. In 1980 and 1990, the regions of the Fed. Rep. of Germany were shaded only on the Germany region. *Source*: Compiled by the authors according to data from the UN Comtrade database.

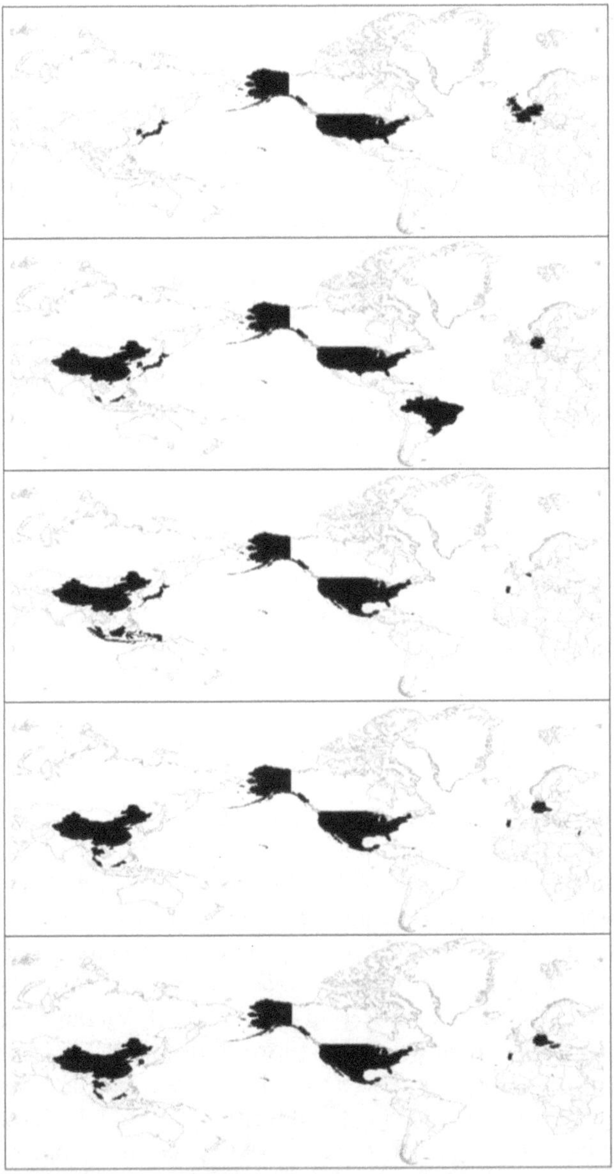

Figure 5.2 Top Ten Exporters of Radio-broadcast Receivers (SITC LTS 762, 1980–2020). Note: From top to bottom, it is 1980, 1990, 2000, 2010, and 2020. In 1980, the regions of the United States and Puerto Rico were shaded only on the US region. In 1980 and 1990, the regions of the Fed. Rep. of Germany were shaded only on the Germany region. *Source*: Compiled by the authors according to data from the UN Comtrade database.

The export-led regions in coastal China have faced unprecedented challenges, such as the rising cost of labor and land, policy changes, and shrinking market demand from Western advanced economies. These challenges have engendered spatial relocation of labor-intensive manufacturing firms from China to lower-cost locations, for example, inland China and neighboring Southeast Asia (Yang, 2016). While achieving a lower cost-capability ratio is not the only reason for the recent spatial relocations, increasing studies have pointed out that these relocations could also serve as a way for TNCs as well as domestic firms in China to "recouple" with the emerging market imperative in the vast domestic market in China and other developing economies (see, e.g., Fu et al., 2020; Horner & Nadvi, 2018; Yang, 2017). As pointed out by Yang (2016), the existing literature has primarily focused on the internal production relocation within China, while little academic attention has been paid to the restructuring of Asian production networks with the increasing participation of Southeast Asian countries, particularly the cross-border production expansion of established and emerging TNCs from China to these countries, such as Vietnam. This chapter will thus endeavor to advance the literature by understanding the restructuring of regional production networks in Asia and provide an up-to-date discussion toward the upcoming research trends.

VIETNAM'S PARTICIPATION IN THE GLOBAL AND ASIAN ELECTRONICS PRODUCTION NETWORKS

Before the start of the *doi moi* reform in the 1980s, Vietnam was a backward agricultural country. Since the late 1980s, Vietnam started to reform its economy and followed the path of China to open the door and leverage trade, inflows of FDI, and TNCs to achieve economic growth and reduce poverty. By integrating into global production systems via international trade, Vietnam has grown its competitive advantage in industrial performance. According to the UN Industrial Development Report (2018, 2022), Vietnam's competitive industrial performance ranking increased from fifty-ninth to forty-first within a short span of five years from 2010 to 2015 and ranked thirty-sixth in 2019. It has been proved that the export-led development model adopted by Vietnam over the past decades has had a positive impact on its ability to maintain economic growth in the long run (Hai et al., 2018). Notably, the inflows of FDIs and TNCs have been critical in this process. According to figure 4.1, one can see that, since the 1990s, the FDI inflow to Vietnam has been increasing significantly. After participating in the World Trade Organization (WTO) in 2007, the net inflow of the FDI balance of payment tripled from 2006 to 2008. Despite the global financial crisis in 2008–2009, the FDI inflow rebounded after 2011. This indicates that the rapid participation of Vietnam in the global and regional economies has been undeniably attributed to the inflows of foreign investors overseas since the mid-2000s.

From 2010 to 2016, the export values of phone sets and accessories, as well as computers and electronic products, have increased from USD 2.3 million and USD 3.6 million to USD 34.3 million and USD 19 million, respectively (table 5.3). The electronic products' contribution to Vietnam's total export value increased from less than 10 percent in 2010 to nearly 30 percent in 2016 (table 5.3). Consequently, Vietnam ranked twelfth in terms of electronics export values in the world in 2018 (VietNamNet Bridge, 2018) with phone and accessories (49.5 million USD) as well as computer and other electronic products (29.6 million USD) accounting for 20.3 percent and 12.1 percent of the total export value, respectively (table 5.3). And in 2020, the share of the total export value of phone and accessories together with computers and other electronic products reached a new height at 33.9 percent. After 2010, although the export value of primary products, such as wood and seafood, has kept increasing, their shares of the national total export value have been decreasing. This implies that the FDI-induced development model adopted by Vietnam after the *doi moi* reform has brought about the structural transformation of exports in Vietnam. In association with the transformation of the "World Factory" and the consequential production relocations away from coastal China, there has been increasing participation of Southeast Asian countries, such as Vietnam, in the Asian electronics production network.

According to data from the General Statistics Office of Vietnam, 57 percent of the accumulated registered capital of the FDI inflow to Vietnam having effect at the end of 2018 was invested in the manufacturing sector, rising from 53 percent in 2006. Vietnam has gradually emerged as an attraction for manufacturing investments by TNCs since the early 2010s. More in-depth analysis regarding the production relocations and shifting investment destinations between China and Vietnam could be demonstrated in table 5.4. China's share of Japan's outward FDI dropped from 5.4 percent in 2009 to 2 percent in 2017, while Vietnam's share increased from 1 percent to 3.7 percent during the same period. Among the destinations of South Korea's outward FDI, China's share fell from 15.7 percent to 7.8 percent during the period between 2009 and 2017, while Vietnam's share increased from 9.7 percent to 25.6 percent. Vietnam's share of Singapore's outward FDI also surged from 2 percent in 2007 to 21.9 percent in 2017 (table 5.4). Besides, the ratios of FDI invested by Japan, Korea, and Singapore to Vietnam compared to China have increased from 0.18, 0.62, and 0.1 in 2009 to 1.81, 3.26, and 1.93 in 2017, respectively. Particularly, the value of the investment from Korea to Vietnam was 3.26 times more than that to China. This implies that Vietnam has been replacing China as one of the major destinations for the FDI outflows by the

Table 5.3 Major Export Goods and Shares of the Total Exports in Vietnam (2010–2020, in million USD)

Item	*2010*	*Share (%)*	*2012*	*Share (%)*	*2014*	*Share (%)*	*2016*	*Share (%)*	*2018*	*Share (%)*	*2020*	*Share (%)*
Phone and accessories	2.3	3.2	12.8	11.2	24.0	16.0	34.3	19.4	49.5	20.3	51.2	18.1
Textiles	11.2	15.5	14.4	12.6	20.7	13.8	23.8	13.5	30.5	12.5	29.8	10.5
Computer and other electronic product	3.6	5.0	7.8	6.8	11.6	7.7	19.0	10.7	29.6	12.1	44.6	15.8
Footwear	5.1	7.1	7.3	6.4	10.2	6.8	13.0	7.4	16.2	6.6	16.8	5.9
Seafood	5.0	6.9	6.1	5.3	7.9	5.2	7.1	4.0	8.8	3.6	8.4	3.0
Wood and wood products	3.4	4.7	4.7	4.1	6.1	4.1	7.0	4.0	8.9	3.7	12.1	4.3
Crude oil	5.0	6.9	8.2	7.2	7.2	4.8	2.4	1.4	2.2	0.9	1.6	0.6

Source: Compiled by the authors according to data from the General Statistics Office of Vietnam.

Table 5.4 Comparison of FDI Inflows from Japan, South Korea, and Singapore to China and Vietnam (2009–2017)

		2009	*2011*	*2013*	*2015*	*2017*
Sources	*Destinations*	*FDI Amount (Million USD)*				
Japan	China	4,015	6,330	7,058	3,195	3,261
Korea	China	2,700	2,551	3,054	4,034	2,673
Singapore	China	3,605	6,097	7,229	6,905	4,763
Japan	Vietnam	719	2,306	4,769	2,083	5,895
Korea	Vietnam	1,661	1,540	4,466	6,983	8,720
Singapore	Vietnam	373	2,622	5,876	1,803	9,205
		Share of Respective Total Outflows of FDI (%)				
Japan	China	5.4	5.9	5.2	2.5	2.0
Korea	China	15.7	8.6	10.8	17.0	7.8
Singapore	China	19.5	19.4	16.6	22.0	10.9
Japan	Vietnam	1.0	2.1	3.5	1.6	3.7
Korea	Vietnam	9.7	5.2	15.7	29.4	25.6
Singapore	Vietnam	2.0	8.4	13.5	5.7	21.1
Ratios						
Japan to Vietnam/ Japan to China		0.18	0.36	0.68	0.65	1.81
Korea to Vietnam/ Korea to China		0.62	0.60	1.46	1.73	3.26
Singapore to Vietnam/ Singapore to China		0.10	0.43	0.81	0.26	1.93

Source: Compiled by the authors according to data from the World Investment Report 2018 from the UNCTAD (2018).

TNCs from Japan, South Korea, and Singapore. There emerged an increasingly shifting pattern of cross-border investments and expansion of manufacturing activities from China to Vietnam.

CHANGING DYNAMICS AND TRANSFORMATION OF THE ASIAN ELECTRONICS PRODUCTION NETWORKS

The production relocation and the reconfiguration of the production networks have not been solely led by the TNCs from Japan and the NIEs. According to table 5.5, Japan and Asian NIEs have contributed the most to Vietnam's FDI inflow since the 2010s. Yet, one can also see that Chinese firms have had an increasing contribution to Vietnam's FDI inflow, from only 2 percent in 2010 to 7 percent in 2018 (5 percent in 2020). It became the fifth-largest investor in Vietnam, just behind Japan, Korea, Singapore, and Hong Kong. As it is common for Chinese investors to venture abroad through Hong Kong, if the investments from Hong Kong are also included, China would become the third-largest investor in Vietnam, sharing 16 percent of the FDI inflow to

Table 5.5 Share of the Sources of FDI Inflows to Vietnam (2010–2020)

	2010	*2011*	*2012*	*2013*	*2014*	*2015*	*2016*	*2017*	*2018*	*2019*	*2020*
Hong Kong	1%	22%	4%	3%	14%	5%	6%	4%	9%	7%	7%
China	2%	5%	2%	10%	2%	3%	8%	65%	7%	4%	5%
Singapore	24%	15%	12%	21%	13%	9%	9%	16%	14%	14%	15%
South Korea	13%	10%	8%	20%	35%	29%	30%	24%	20%	19%	18%
Japan	12%	17%	34%	26%	10%	7%	11%	25%	25%	16%	16%
Taiwan	5%	4%	16%	3%	6%	6%	8%	4%	3%	9%	9%
ROW	43%	27%	24%	17%	20%	41%	28%	21%	22%	31%	30%

Source: Compiled by the authors according to data from the General Statistics Office of Vietnam.
Note: ROW = Rest of the World.

Vietnam in 2018. Although the share fluctuated in the late 2010s, Hong Kong and China together still shared 12 percent of Vietnam's FDI inflow in 2020. Notably, apart from the relatively large state-owned enterprises (SOEs), since the early 2000s, an increasing number of Chinese privately owned firms, most of which most of them are small and medium enterprises (SMEs), started to internationalize (Huang & Chi, 2014). According to China's Ministry of Commerce, the Outward Foreign Direct Investment (OFDI) stock shared by these private firms increased from 19 percent in 2006 to 51 percent in 2017. Unlike the previous literature, which postulates that the Asian production networks have been primarily driven by the established TNCs originating solely from Japan and the NIEs, this chapter argues that the emerging TNCs from emerging economies, such as China, have contributed to the current transformation of the Asian electronics production networks.

With the increasing participation of Southeast Asian countries, the "triangular trade" pattern and the roles of different economies in the Asian production network warrant an updated understanding. Besides the "World Factory," developing Southeast Asian countries, such as Vietnam, have emerged to become a manufacturing base for electronics products in the region. In particular, phone sets, computers, and other electronic products have been the main export items in recent years (table 5.3). According to table 4.1, even though China has still been the largest mobile phone exporter in the region, Vietnam has emerged rapidly from eighth place in 2011 to second place in the mid-2010s. Notably, the final electronics goods are mostly exported to advanced economies, particularly the United States. According to data from the UN Comtrade, the United States was the biggest destination for electronics products exported by Vietnam. For example, 27.1 percent of telephones for cellular networks exported by Vietnam in 2021 went to the United States. Besides the United States, most of the top electronics export destinations of Vietnam were relatively developed economies overseas, including the United Kingdom and European countries, like Germany and France, as well as East Asian countries, like Japan and Korea.

Apart from the East Asian countries becoming consumers, the ongoing transformation of the Asian electronics production networks has been characterized by the changing role of China as the main exporter of parts and components. Unlike what has been described as the "triangular trade" pattern in which China has been solely an intermediary importer, importing the parts and components largely from Japan and the NIEs, China has now become a major intermediary exporter, and Vietnam has imported a majority of its electronics parts and components from China. For example, according to figure 5.3, although Japan and the NIEs together contributed more than 50 percent of the parts and components for the automatic data processing machines and other electronics products, such as office machines imported by

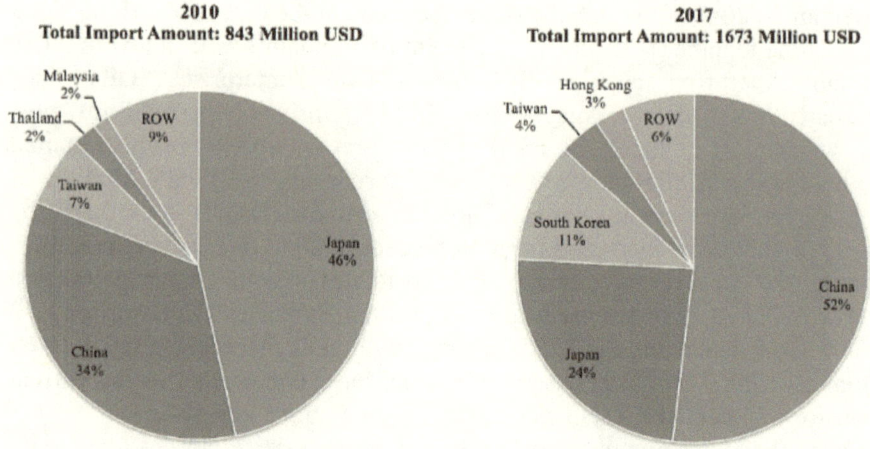

Figure 5.3 Top Importers of Vietnam's Electronics Parts, Accessories for Automatic Data Processing Machines and Office Machines (2010 and 2017). *Source*: Compiled by the authors according to data from the UN Comtrade database of the United Nations (https://comtrade.un.org/data/).

Vietnam in 2010, their shares were reduced in 2017 (to around 40 percent). Whereas China alone accounted for more than 50 percent of Vietnam's total import value of electronics parts and accessories for automatic data processing machines and office machines in 2017, rising from 34 percent in 2010. Apart from emerging as Vietnam's main investor, as aforementioned, China has also become Vietnam's dominant electronics intermediary importer, replacing Japan and the NIEs since the 2010s. This, indeed, shows that, apart from the relatively developed economies in the region, such as Japan and the NIEs, China has become more influential in the organization of the electronics regional production network in Asia nowadays, instead of the relatively passive role of simply acting as the "World Factory" in the past by importing the parts and components for manufacturing. In addition, the emergence of market imperatives in the vast domestic market in China has further increased China's role in restructuring of production networks at both regional and global levels (Fu et al., 2020).

This section interprets the aforementioned participation of Vietnam in the global and regional production networks based on the changing dynamics at global, regional, and national levels. On one hand, the push factors in relation to the current wave of production relocation of the labor-intensive industry away from China are mostly due to the more expensive production factors in China. According to a report from the Economist Intelligence Unit (2014), the manufacturing labor cost per hour in China was 177 percent of those in Vietnam in 2019, rising from 147 percent in 2012. Apart from the rising production cost, which has been the main research focus to date, the changing institutional environment that has not been as friendly to lower value-added manufacturing as it used to be could be another driver (Yang & He, 2017). On the other hand, the pull factors in Vietnam could be reflected by its efforts in regional and global economic integration. Since the *doi moi* reform and after joining the WTO in 2007, the FDI inflow to Vietnam started to boom (refer to figure 4.1). To promote integration with the global economy, Vietnam has also become a member of different trade associations at different spatial levels. For instance, Vietnam joined the Association of Southeast Asian Nations (ASEAN) as well as the ASEAN Free Trade Area (AFTA) in 1995, and in 2016, Vietnam signed the Trans-Pacific Partnership (TPP) and the updated Comprehensive and Progressive Agreement for Trans-Pacific Partnership (CPTPP) in 2018.

The transformation of the Asian production network has been driven by the changing dynamics at the national, regional, and global levels. Hence, besides the endogenous factors at the national level, as mentioned earlier, the exogenous factors at a broader spatial scale have also led to the reconfiguration of the regional and global production networks, particularly the changing international political economy. One of the factors is China's "Belt and Road Initiative" (OBOR), launched in 2015 with the main objective of promoting economic cooperation among countries in Asia, Europe, and Africa by different means, such as increasing trade and investment as well as strengthening the transportation infrastructure among the countries involved. Although it is not written as the official objective, different updated studies have found that the OBOR has indeed encouraged the production relocations of labor-intensive industries out of China (see, e.g., Chan et al., 2020; Lian, 2018), particularly to the nearby countries within the "Belt" and "Road," such as Vietnam and India, which have benefited from the trade agreements and initiatives (Lee & Zhou, 2019). Besides, it is worth noting that the outbreak of the US.-China trade war in 2018 also accelerated the production relocation from China to nearby countries to avoid the extra tariff imposed. According to the "winners" list of the trade war calculated by Economist Intelligence Unit (2018), Vietnam and other developing Southeast Asian countries have been big winners in the information and communications technology sector, while Malaysia and Vietnam are nominated as the winners with strong benefits. Of course, along with the explosion of the COVID-19 pandemic, it is certain that the global economic landscape and production systems will be restructured entering the 2020s. We will further stretch out these new yet remarkable dynamics in chapter 8.

UPGRADING OR DOWNGRADING? THE DECREASING DOMESTIC VALUE-ADDED OF VIETNAM'S EXPORTS

> The heavy concentration of final assembly global supply chain activities in the electronics industry in Viet Nam (Vietnam) is the result of the types of enterprises located in the country, what they produce, for whom and for which export markets, the type of skills required for their production activities, and in which activities or stages of the global supply chains they are located. (International Labour Organization, 2022: 22–23)

As pointed out in the earlier report and proved in the following chapters, the outsourcing of electronics production to Vietnam has been mainly led by leading brand names and manufacturers such as Apple, Microsoft, Google, Intel, Xiaomi, and so on, primarily to seek lower production costs. Of course, the proximity to regional suppliers and a relatively stable investment climate are also attractions (Sturgeon & Zylberberg, 2017). As a result, contract manufacturers such as Foxconn and Jabil, and other suppliers have started to expand to Vietnam. According to the 2021 Apple Supplier List, twenty-one first-tier suppliers to the brand company were operating in Vietnam. Apart from outsourcing, some also have their own factories set up in Vietnam. For instance, LG and Canon have their largest laser printer and inkjet printer factories worldwide near Hanoi (Organization for Economic Co-operation and Development, 2021). The rapid influx of electronics manufacturing firms and investments has helped transform the country's industrial landscape in a very short period.

Vietnam has participated in the GVC rapidly since the past decade. According to data from the OECD TiVA database, with an exceptionally high double-digit annual growth rate of 16.5 percent from 2010 to 2018, the 2018 GVC participation index of Vietnam was 62.1 (with the backward participation at 51.1 and the forward participation at 11.0), which was much higher than the Asian regional average level of 44.4. This implies that Vietnam has become a regional final assembly hub by importing GVC-intermediate goods from foreign countries. In 2018, China, Korea, and Japan contributed 28.2 percent, 10.9 percent, and 7.2 percent of shares in the total foreign content of Vietnam's exports. In spite of the fact that Vietnam has been one of the top electronics product exporters in the region and has seemed to "upgrade" its export structure (table 5.3), the trade in value-added reflects another side of the story. According to the OECD TiVA database, the foreign value-added of Vietnam's gross export increased from 5.1 billion USD in 2000 to 124 billion USD after two decades. According to table 5.6, the share of foreign value-added of Vietnam's gross exports surged from around 30 percent in 2000 to 48 percent in 2020, which was the highest among the countries in the

Table 5.6 Value-Added Share of Gross Exports of Vietnam and Other East Asian Countries (2000–2020, in %)

	Domestic Value-Added Share of Gross Exports								
	Japan	*Korea*	*China*	*Indonesia*	*Malaysia*	*Philippines*	*Singapore*	*Thailand*	*Vietnam*
2000	92.51	70.75	82.5	81.94	51.29	76.28	56.47	63.85	70.10
2005	88.81	68.23	76.33	82.07	56.39	65.84	51.65	59.07	63.81
2010	86.75	63.17	80.83	85.67	61.76	74.33	52.54	61.12	57.17
2015	84.44	68.46	84.08	85.81	65.47	79.66	52.3	64.89	52.82
2020	86.66	70.30	84.25	88.81	66.17	77.72	56.20	68.57	51.96
	Foreign Value-Added Share of Gross Exports								
	Japan	*Korea*	*China*	*Indonesia*	*Malaysia*	*Philippines*	*Singapore*	*Thailand*	*Vietnam*
2000	7.49	29.25	17.5	18.06	48.71	23.72	43.53	36.15	29.90
2005	11.19	31.77	23.67	17.93	43.61	34.16	48.35	40.93	36.19
2010	13.25	36.83	19.17	14.33	38.24	25.67	47.46	38.88	42.83
2015	15.56	31.54	15.92	14.19	34.53	20.34	47.7	35.11	47.18
2020	13.34	29.70	15.75	11.19	33.83	22.28	43.80	31.43	48.04

Source: Compiled by the authors according to data from the OECD-WTO TIVA database.

table. Notably, while the share of the foreign value-added in the exports of Vietnam increased by 60 percent within two decades, except for Japan, the shares of other Asian countries nearby either held the same or decreased. For example, the shares of foreign value-added in the gross exports of Indonesia and Malaysia dropped more than 30 percent from 2000 to 2020. On the other hand, compared to Vietnam's 52 percent, except Singapore, the domestic value-added shares of gross exports generally exceeded 60 percent in 2020 and the shares of some countries, such as Japan, China, and Indonesia, were even above 80 percent. Hence, table 5.6 showcases that not only has Vietnam had a relatively weak domestic industry compared to the peers nearby overall but also has Vietnam increasingly depended on the imports of intermediate goods from foreign countries over the past two decades.

Table 5.7 further illustrates the picture by sector. Accordingly, despite the growth of the value-added of Vietnam's gross export within the past two decades, the shares of the value-added by Vietnam's domestic industries of the main export sectors have declined more than double digits in general, with the mining and quarrying sector decreasing by more than 35 percent. While the shares of domestic value-added in agriculture, forestry and fishing, mining and quarrying, and total services of the business economy were higher than 50 percent (i.e., more than the foreign value-added), in 2020, the only sector which had foreign value-added exceeding domestic value-added was the manufacturing sector, with an overall 48 percent domestic value-added in 2020 (decreased from 60 percent in 2000). This means that the development of Vietnam's manufacturing sector has relied more and more heavily on the imports of foreign technologies as well as parts and components. Table 5.8 further displays the situations of the major subsectors within the manufacturing sector. Generally speaking, the foreign value-added ratios of all major manufacturing activities have increased since 2000. One rather apparent observation from table 5.8 is that compared to the relatively low-tech activities, such as the manufacturing of food products and basic metals, shares of

Table 5.7 Value-Added Share of Gross Exports of Vietnam by Sectors (2000–2020, in %)

	Agriculture, Forestry, and Fishing		*Mining and Quarrying*		*Manufacturing*		*Total Services of the Business Economy*	
	DVA	FVA	DVA	FVA	DVA	FVA	DVA	FVA
2000	79.2	20.8	90.5	9.5	60.4	39.6	79.2	20.8
2005	73.0	27.0	85.9	14.1	54.6	45.4	76.6	23.4
2010	70.9	29.1	67.5	32.5	50.9	49.1	72.1	28.0
2015	68.0	32.0	59.8	40.2	47.6	52.4	68.8	31.2
2020	64.9	35.1	55.1	44.9	48.2	51.8	70.8	29.2

Source: Compiled according to data from OECD-WTO TIVA database.
Note: DVA = Domestic Value-Added; FVA = Foreign Value-Added

Table 5.8 Foreign Value-Added Share of Gross Exports of Vietnam's Manufacturing Subsectors (2000–2020, in %)

	Food products, beverages, and tobacco products	*Textiles, wearing apparel, leather, and related products*	*wood and of products of wood and cork, except furniture; manufacture of articles of straw and plaiting materials; manufacture of paper and paper products; printing and reproduction of recorded media*	*wood and of products of wood and cork, except furniture; manufacture of articles of straw and plaiting materials*	*chemicals and non-metallic mineral products*	*basic metals and fabricated metal products, except machinery and equipment*	*fabricated metal products, except machinery and equipment*	*computer, electronic and optical products; manufacture of electrical equipment*	*computer, electronic and optical products*	*machinery and equipment n.e.c.*	*furniture; jewelry, musical instruments, toys, etc.; repair and installation of machinery and equipment*
2000	25.6	44.7	33.3	31.9	46.8	47.8	48.0	45.3	45.9	53.4	40.7
2005	28.8	40.2	41.1	41.8	41.5	55.5	53.6	53.7	53.1	57.3	40.1
2010	33.0	49.3	46.0	46.9	48.6	58.0	58.4	61.0	61.3	61.7	45.5
2015	36.6	53.0	46.3	46.4	49.0	53.3	49.0	51.3	50.0	66.4	47.9
2020	39.7	55.4	51.6	52.2	52.0	35.2	55.9	49.9	48.0	70.4	52.7

Source: Compiled according to data from OECD-WTO TIVA database.
Note: DVA = Domestic Value-Added; FVA = Foreign Value-Added

the foreign value-added have been higher in the relatively high-tech manufacturing activities such as textiles and apparel, fabricated metal products, computers, and machinery. This observation holds even within the same sector. According to Nakamura and Marukawa (2024), by decomposing Vietnam's major export items, that is, smartphones and printers, they pointed out that parts of the latter are more technologically accessible for domestic manufacturers to supply, while most of the former's parts are beyond the technical capabilities of local manufacturers and need to rely on imports. This clearly indicates that the rapid growth of Vietnam's manufacturing sector as well as exports in recent years has been driven by foreign counterparts rather than by the growth of domestic manufacturing capacity, as the share of value-added contributed by the domestic sector has been decreasing.

In short, aligning with other scholars' observations (e.g., Sturgeon & Zylberberg, 2017; Truong, 2022; Nakamura & Marukawa, 2024), in spite of the fact that Vietnam has rapidly integrated into the global production systems, changed its export structure, and become one of the biggest exporters in Asia, especially for the electronics sector, attributed to its latent comparative advantage of low production costs, a large percentage of these exports can be linked to foreign investors and manufacturing activities, particularly the relatively technology-intensive products, which predominantly consist of the assembly of imported intermediate inputs. Thus, unlike the case of China, which has been gradually moving up the chain to become not only the "World Factory" but increasingly an intermediate goods exporter, as shown in the last section, Vietnam has so far acted as a low value-added assembly hub in the region. The linkages of local Vietnamese firms with foreign investors and manufacturers remain very weak (Sturgeon & Zylberberg, 2017; Nakamura & Marukawa, 2024). Given the earlier situation, it would be interesting not only to see what the Vietnamese government officials have done and/or will do to upgrade the domestic industry, apart from attracting the FDIs, and how they have/will overcome the challenges, such as the big knowledge gap that hinders the spillover effect, to increase the value captured in the chains/networks, but also the countermeasures of the firms to exploit Vietnam's advantages. And these questions will be further explored in the coming chapters.

CONCLUSION AND DISCUSSION

Through the updated investigation of the configuration of Asian electronics production networks after the late 2000s, with increasing participation of Southeast Asian developing countries, this chapter not only intends to showcase the changing organizational and spatial configurations of the electronics production networks to lay a foundation for further studies and discussions in the coming chapters of this book but, more importantly, we also aim to shed light on the potential areas for further research development on the GPN literature.

Based on the case study of Vietnam, this chapter argues that the Asian electronics production networks have been transforming, led not only the TNCs from Japan and the NIEs but also by the emerging TNCs from China. The changing and rising roles of the emerging and developing economies, that is, China and Vietnam, have been reflected in the current reconfiguration of the production networks. Apart from China, Vietnam has gradually become the electronics assembly hub, particularly entering the 2010s, not only driven by the established TNCs from Korea, Japan, and other NIE countries like previous rounds of production relocations but also driven by the emerging TNCs, including the SMEs, from the rising economies in the region, that is, China. By importing the electronics intermediaries mainly from China, as well as Japan and the NIEs in the region, and exporting the final goods mainly to the advanced economies, such as the United States and the European countries, Vietnam has now actively participated in the global and regional electronics production networks. On the other hand, apart from being the "World Factory," China has emerged as a dominant investor driving the current production relocations to Southeast Asia and the biggest electronics intermediaries exporter in the region, outpacing Japan and the NIEs. In addition, the vast consumption market of China, as well as Southeast Asia, has been surging as well, which might further challenge the "triangular trade" pattern ends in the "Global North." Moreover, apart from the endogenous push and pull drivers at the national level, the exogenous factors at a broader spatial scale, in particular the situation of the international political economy, have also driven the current reconfiguration of the global and Asian regional production networks. Although the overview of the changing Asian electronics production networks has been shown earlier, more in-depth and empirical questions ought to be asked to better understand the ongoing reconfiguration. For example, how do the firms respond to the changing capitalist dynamics? How do the firms govern their production networks, upgrade, or participate in other networks? How do the firms decouple with the "old" regions/markets and recouple with the new ones?

Apart from offering an updated investigation on the restructuring of the global and regional production networks of the manufacturing industries in general and the electronics industry in particular, through the earlier case study, some inroads for further enriching the GPN literature have been discovered. The conventional conceptualization of the global production system has to be readjusted so that the research framework could be more attuned to pay attention to the increasingly influential actors and objects in the current changing global economy. Both GPN, including the GPN 2.0, and GVC frameworks have primarily conceptualized globalization as a set of geographically dispersed production activities coordinated by the lead firms, mostly from the developed countries, to maintain the control of the core nodes of value creation and retention in their home countries and to offshore and outsource the peripheral and lower value-added activities to the developing countries (Neilson et al., 2014). Compared to these lead firms, insufficient attention has been paid to the ETNCs from developing economies. Yet, since the changing power dynamics of global production systems have been seen as the firms originated from the developing economies nowadays have played a significant role in the spatial and organizational configuration of the value chains/production networks (see, e.g., Azmeh & Nadvi, 2014; Lee & Gereffi, 2015; Yeung, 2017), more research should be done to explore these ETNCs. For instance, how did they expand and govern their production networks given their limited resources, experience, and even market power? More fundamentally, why and how did they internationalize? Notably, unlike the four competitive dynamics mentioned in the GPN 2.0 framework, that is, cost-capability ratio, market imperative, financial discipline, and risk environment, some Chinese firms ventured abroad as part of the state's economic diplomacy (Yeung & Liu, 2008). That said, unlike the previous strategic coupling studies where the focus has been largely paid to the firms in the networks and the host institutions, there is a need to also concern the active role of the home governments of these ETNCs. Besides paying more attention to the home institutions, to better understand these ETNCs, their cultural legacies should also be taken into concern as these imprints are highly relevant to the strategies they used in orchestrating their production networks, both spatial and organizationally.

Apart from the firms per se, in the "Northern lead-firm centric" (Horner & Nadvi, 2018) definition of global production systems, the final market of the chain and the network is presumed to be the developed economies in the "North." Despite not being reflected by the earlier case study of Vietnam, different studies have clearly shown that the tails of the networks/chains have shifted gradually to the developing economies (e.g., Athukorala & Nasir, 2012). Although the domestic market-/emerging market-oriented reconfiguration of production networks is not uncommon, not much effort has been made to understand these restructurings and the related mechanisms hitherto. Notably, in looking into the question of how the lead firms and the domestic firms (re)couple with these emerging markets, ample research opportunities remain to be unpacked regarding the governance dynamics in the networks. Not only due to the "new" governance structure of the emerging leading firms, but the requirements of the new standards in these markets from the consumers and the institutions also deserve more attention as they affect the power and relationships among the actors involved as well as the upgrading opportunities available in the networks (see, e.g., Kaplinsky & Farooki, 2011).

Nowadays, different production networks have seemingly started to gradually narrow down spatially from "global" to "regional" and even "national," together with the emerging markets in the "Global South," for example, the vast domestic market of China, as well as the rise in trade protectionism and reindustrialization, for example, the Trump's "Made in America" campaign. Echoing Horner and Nadvi (2018), we have to scale down and focus more on the regional and domestic aspects of the production networks. Be that as it may, another lesson learned from our case study of Vietnam is that exogenous shocks could impact the operations of and interactions between multiple production networks/chains at different scales. For example, the trade friction between China and the United States has accelerated production relocations from China to the nearby Southeast Asian countries and the reconfiguration of the electronics production network in the region. In addition to the situations of international political economy, it would also be interesting to explore how the pandemic, for example, COVID-19, has influenced the production systems at multiple levels. Updated research has pointed out that, because of the coronavirus pandemic, the decline in production and trade due to the factory closures in China caused by the restrictions on labor's mobility could have a strong effect on countries further up and down the supply chain (Serić et al., 2020). Yet, whether this disruption, compared to the Sino-US trade war, will leave a long-term impact and lead to further pushback against the cross-border organization of production deserves continuous study. Hence, we urge for more awareness of the scalar dimension of the global production systems, and a truly "multi-scalar" understanding is earnestly needed for studying the constantly changing configurations and operations of the production networks nowadays when uncertainties and risks have emerged at different levels. And even though we will try to shed some light on parts of the aforementioned puzzle in chapters 6, 7, and particularly chapter 8, it will still be far from enough to obtain a full picture of the ongoing changes in global production systems, even under the same topic of electronics production relocation to Vietnam and in the post-pandemic future.

Chapter 6

Multi-scalar Strategic Coupling

The Bargaining between TNCs and Vietnam's Government

The core of the "new geography of trade" that emerged in twenty-first-century globalization has been the dramatic increase in South-South interactions, in which the "Global South" has been defined as the countries undergoing a process of economic development and structural transformation, such as developing Asia, including China and Vietnam. As pointed out by Horner and Nadvi (2018), global trade flows are no longer dominated by the South-North direction but increasingly South-South now. Not only can we see that Northern lead firms' global value chains (GVCs) and global production networks (GPNs) have been redirected toward the more rapidly growing "Global South," particularly after the global economic crisis in 2008 (Gereffi, 2014), but, nowadays, firms from newly industrialized economies (NIEs) and China have also expanded their production, particularly the labor-intensive manufacturing industries, into the developing economies in the "Global South," such as Vietnam, due to the increasing competitive pressures, to lower production costs and to feed the growing end markets (Yang, 2016; Yeung, 2019). Existing literature on the restructuring of production networks in the "Global South" has been focused on the notion of "de/recoupling" of the original regions, that is, coastal regions of China, yet, not much has been done to study the emerging strategic coupling of the destination regions in the GPNs (Yang, 2017), particularly in the "Global South" such as Vietnam, in this study. To understand the ways that different tiers of firms have expanded their production networks into the "Global South," with the nonfirm actors included, the recently developing GPN 2.0 framework, which defines different types of firm-specific strategies for organizing production arrangements (Coe & Yeung, 2015), and especially the notion of extra-firm bargaining focusing on the relations and interactions between the firm and nonfirm actors of different tiers and levels (figure 2.2), is an insightful analytical framework.

Taking the rapidly emerging electronics cluster in the RRD in Vietnam as a case, this chapter examines how different tiers of firms expanded their production networks and engaged with the host region. To be more explicit, after a broad picture sketched by the previous chapter, the current chapter focuses mainly on the extra-firm strategies, particularly the firm-state bargaining adopted by three different tiers of firms in the electronics production network and the related outcomes. By developing an analytical framework with reference to notions in international business (IB) literature as well as the GPN framework, this chapter aims to analyze the extra-firm bargaining outcomes by looking at the multi-scalar firm-state relationships and interactions. Although GPN 2.0 has emphasized the extra-firm bargaining strategy, as it is more focused on the question of "who gets what," the deliberation, as well as the actual tactics used by the firms, has been somewhat overlooked. By focusing solely on lead firms/tier 1 suppliers as most empirical case studies do, one may also overlook the firm-state relationship between lower-tier firms and different levels of host governments in a production network. Besides understanding the relocation of lower-tier suppliers as following the "order" from the lead firm, their extra-firm interactions with the host governments should also be understood, as the latter plays an important role in restructuring the production networks as well. Additionally, as the power of the tier 1 firms/suppliers in organizing production activities independently has surged recently (Azmeh & Nadvi, 2014; Yang, 2017), without a "must" to follow the lead firms, their roles and the extra-firm bargaining with the host governments are even more important in understanding the production relocation process. In other words, in some rather extreme cases, the extra-firm bargaining between these suppliers and the host government could determine the final production configurations without much to do with the lead firm.

In this chapter, we found that studies in the IB literature do provide an insightful view on understanding the detailed deliberation process between the firms and host institutions and on unpacking the actual tactics used by these actors. Besides further conceptualizing the firm-state relations and interactions in extra-firm bargaining, this chapter has also noted the multi-scalar bargaining process between different tiers of firms and various levels of host governments. The studies on the strategic coupling of a region so far have mainly focused on how firms have engaged with regional/provincial institutions, with the agency of national-level institutions being suppressed. Apart from looking at how local-level institutions have tried to make their localities nodes in the production networks, more studies should now see the strategic coupling as an assemblage of firms and state institutions at various scales. Not only can this chapter update the empirical literature regarding the current wave of production expansion to Southeast Asia, but it also sheds light on understanding the dynamic firm-state relationships and interactions as well as the multilevel intergovernment structures, which have received consistent academic attention since GPN 1.0, such as MacKinnon (2012), Murphy (2012), Smith et al. (2014), Fuller and Phelps (2018), and Gao et al. (2019), by analyzing the extra-firm bargaining between different levels of host institutions and different tiers of firms, that is, LG as the lead firm, Foxconn as the tier 1 partner, as well as lower-tier suppliers from China, from a fresh lens to explain the production relocation outcomes. Furthermore, at the same time, this chapter also contributes to IB literature by applying the studies to this multi-scalar geographical qualitative research.

The rest of the chapter is organized as follows. After this introduction, the next two sections review the theoretical development of the GPN framework to illustrate two specific research gaps. The effort is then spurred to develop an analytical framework by forging links between the notions of firm-state relations under extra-firm bargaining in GPN 2.0 and the building blocks of cooperative relations between transnational corporation (TNC) and host governments in the IB studies to understand the deliberation process and tactics used by firms more systematically. The fourth section introduces the detailed research context and methods. The fifth section explains the relocation processes of different tiers of firms by examining the firm-state relations and interactions. And the sixth section elaborates on the main findings, contributions, and policy implications of the current chapter.

EXTRA-FIRM BARGAINING, FIRM-STATE RELATIONSHIP, AND MULTI-SCALAR INSTITUTIONAL GOVERNANCE

To explore the expansions of production networks and the subsequent impacts, "strategic coupling" is an important concept as it represents the articulation of the "territorialized" regional assets and actors into GPNs. Coupling is characterized by different levels of congruence between the corporate production networks and the regional institutions, including the latter seeking to create the regional assets needed by the former for "value capture" purposes and leading to the territorial embedding of GPNs within particular places (Yang et al., 2009). In this vein, one can see that the nonfirm actors, especially the regional institutions, are crucial for realizing the strategic coupling as their willingness and capacity for creating the required regional assets are critical for the corporate relocation decision. Therefore, the GPN framework, compared to the GVC, is better for looking at this issue as these influential nonfirm actors are involved.

Yet, GPN studies have been accused of understating the power relations between territories and GPN firms and insufficiently conceptualizing the local states and institutions, as it is more concerned with their roles and activities rather than the deliberations and politics behind the relationships (MacKinnon, 2012; Murphy, 2012; Smith et al., 2014). Therefore, GPN 2.0 places prominence on "extra-firm bargaining" between GPN firms and the state, as well as nonstate and nonfirm actors, such as nongovernmental organizations (NGOs), that have impacts on GPNs, and this bargaining is defined as a contested two-way process of negotiation and accommodation to reach a mutually satisfactory outcome (Coe & Yeung, 2015). Yet, as Fuller and Phelps (2018) pointed out, the "extra-firm bargaining" strategy in GPN 2.0 focuses more on explicating the overarching outcomes, such as market power, proprietary rights, and social and political legitimacy, rather than actual practices per se. The processes of deliberation and governance in production networks advanced in GPN 1.0 may be overlooked by taking such an actor-centered approach.

Based on the foundation that TNCs look for legitimacy and distinctiveness (refer to Kostova et al., 2008), Fuller and Phelps (2018), by taking three types of micropolitical behaviors of TNCs identified by Dunning and Lundan (2010) as a reference, suggested a framework to conceptualize the causal mechanism underlying the coupling tendencies in which TNCs and their subsidiaries are implicated. Although it is said that the micropolitical approaches, that is, the notion of institutional "adaptation," "avoidance," and "experimentation," provide GPN 2.0 a way to look at the motives and practices constituting extra-firm strategies by way of its engagements with the issues of institutional legitimacy, the actual tactics used by the firms, especially when TNCs try to bargain with local institutions for better value capture, that is, the idea of "institutional experimentation," are still somewhat vague. It is still unclear how exactly firms utilize what power and method in the bargaining process and how they affect the outcomes. In addition, the ambition to include different and highly diverse extra-firm actors, for example, the state, worker groups, and consumers that may be articulated into the networks, further complicates the situation. For instance, the institutions could be further divided into formal and informal ones that come with different attributes and powers. Yet, among these actors, the state is arguably the most important one in the bargaining process as it can directly set up favorable industrial policies that sharpen the regional assets and thus influence the coupling process as well as the network reconfiguration and governance structure. Hence, we try to dig further into the firm-state relationship in this chapter as the deliberation process between the states and the firms should be understood further than simply defining the bargaining game as it is "dependent on firm-specific interests and pressures as well as the institutional capacity and priorities of these state actors" (Coe & Yeung, 2015: 155). Therefore, "a fuller appreciation of corporate agency has important implications for future research in the GPN approach, and its connections to perspectives deriving from the IB literature" (Fuller & Phelps, 2018: 157).

In the IB literature, institutional theory has been widely utilized to study the concepts of organizational field, legitimacy, isomorphism, mechanisms of institutional pressures, and so on. The degree of calibrating with the institutional environment directly affects the survival of an organization. As defined by Suchman (1995), "legitimacy" is a consciousness that the actions of an entity are desirable, proper, or appropriate within some socially constructed system of norms, values, beliefs, and definitions. While conforming to institutional pressures leads to isomorphism, which could be seen as a way to achieve legitimacy, it is important for firms to stay in the host region. Yet, recently, the conventional logic of institutionalism, that is, the ideas of organizational fields and legitimacy through isomorphism, has been challenged. For instance, Kostova et al. (2008) argued that it is difficult to identify the organizational fields and corresponding institutional pressures clearly, and whether "isomorphism" is the most important "medicament" to institutional challenges has been questioned. Pache and Santos (2010) highlighted that firms do not unthinkingly comply with institutional pressures nowadays. In emerging markets, such as China and Vietnam, where the institutional environments are still developing (Peng et al., 2008) and thus the institutional environments are much more dynamic and volatile than the developed or mature markets, the complexity of institutional pressures has been witnessed (Puck et al., 2013). As a result, recent literature calls for different responses to handle institutional pressures besides isomorphism, and these approaches in general call for more "agency" (Nell et al., 2015). That said, organizations now with more latitude to select their responses to institutional pressures. TNCs are relying more on other legitimacy-creating processes as they now have more ability, in general, to negotiate and influence the social construction of their status with certain stakeholders (Kostova et al., 2008). This has become a more popular and important way for them to gain legitimacy.

The institutional perspective aforementioned does provide insights into the dynamic nature of relationships in GPN, "encompassing the dynamics of contestation and stability as actors employ economic, discursive, and organizational strategies" (Levy, 2008: 33). It points out the importance of "legitimacy" for the firms to stay in the host region, not to mention their attempts to alter the institutional environment conducive to their operations. In other words, unlike inter-firm relations, a firm's power to influence its counterparts, that is, the host institutions, is not only determined by its power/position inside the firm network. While GPN 2.0 advances our understanding of the relationships within the network, as mentioned, it is conceptualized in terms of the end-state realm of bargaining, leaving the deliberation politics and actual tactics adopted by the firms understudied. Rather than being isomorphic, firms now would try to create a better institutional environment for themselves while maintaining "legitimacy" at the same time. It is insightful to investigate how and what actual tactics were adopted by firms in bargaining with multi-scalar host institutions.

Before conceptualizing the actual tactics used in the bargaining process, the recent rising attention to the multi-scalar institutional governance structure should also be highlighted. Although the GPN framework embraces a multi-scalar definition of institutions (Coe & Yeung, 2015), it has overlooked the analysis of the relational and scalar interactions between different levels of institutions, particularly in version 2.0 (Dawley et al., 2019). Empirical research so far has predominantly focused on regional-level strategies for the promotion of strategic coupling (Coe & Yeung, 2015), and the understanding of regional institutions has seemed to inhibit the agency of national states (Dawley et al., 2019). However, national states could also act as an important mediator in the process (Gao et al., 2019; Lee et al., 2014; Su, 2014). It is out of the scope of this chapter to discuss the agency of the national state (see, e.g., Jessop, 2001), nor does it investigate various roles that could have been played by the state in the GPN (see, e.g., Horner, 2017); it is our intention to draw attention to the institutional role beyond merely the local and regional levels to understand the extra-firm bargaining process at a multi-scalar level.

> The roles assigned to governments and their effectiveness in performing them differ. These differences derive in part from political choices. These choices determine the functional roles and powers of government . . . which responsibilities are assigned to different tiers of government and how different tiers relate to one another. (Gao et al., 2019: 5)

In the context of firm-state bargaining, this implies that local-level institutions, due to their limited capabilities, may not be able to fulfill the strategic needs raised by GPN firms, such as creating certain kinds of embedding environments, and may have to be handled by higher-level governments. On the other hand, as diagnosed by Yang (2012) through the case study of export-oriented industrialization in the PRD, due to the conflicting interests of the provincial and local governments with the state, the state-designated regional restructuring and relocation could be heightened by resistance from lower authorities. Hence, the multi-scalar relationships and interactions between firms and multi-scalar institutions as well as among different levels of institutions in the host region in the coupling process deserve more attention.

EXTRA-FIRM BARGAINING: CONCEPTUALIZING THE FIRM-STATE INTERACTIONS

The IB literature regarding the relationships between TNCs and host governments provides us with creative insights into the issues mentioned earlier. Conflict-based views of IB studies, supported by bargaining and transaction cost theories, provide us with a clear look into the interactions within the bargaining game between the firm and the state. For instance, the bargaining power of a TNC comes from its "contributed resources" or "ownership-specific advantages"; while a government's bargaining power comes from its "control of market access" or "location-specific advantages" (Boddewyn, 2016). Yet, scholars have started to realize that the relationship between TNCs and host governments is not a zero-sum game, in which one of them must lose, but rather a cooperative view that is based on strategic and sociological theories (e.g., Dunning, 1999). In turn, TNCs and governments are interdependent on each other for critical resources, and sharing these resources cooperatively creates more payoff for both parties. According to Luo (2001, 2004), unlike the earlier studies with the conflictual view that discuss the determinants of the relationship from the bargaining perspective, the cooperative view articulates these relational determinants from the angle of legitimacy and adaptation, which in turn escalates the cooperation with governments. As mentioned earlier, "legitimacy" is an important element for firms to stay in the host region while not being subject to sanctions as well as being able to attempt to change the institutions. Therefore, the cooperative view that sees the firm-state relationship as the strength or structure of a TNC's cooperative relationship with governmental authorities to benefit from various institutional supports would be a more updated way of thought. The closer the firm-state relationship, the better the chance the firms can benefit from the governments. This gives us new insights into the relationship and interaction between firms and governments by seeing the bargaining process as cooperation rather than a power conflict based on the powers, for example, contributed resources and ownership-specific advantages vis-à-vis the market control.

Based on the above understandings and the interaction between TNCs and the host governments being an intricate, dynamic, and interdependent process, and the development of the TNC-host government relations being both economically constructed and socially embedded, Luo (2001) categorized four building components of the relations, which are defined by the conditioning factors that reflect a TNC's organizational or managerial endeavors. These four components have been proven robust in the developing and emerging economy and at both national and regional levels. Most importantly, they unpack the actual tactics used by the firms in firm-state bargaining. In other words, these four building components systematically categorize the actual tactics adopted by the firms for having a closer tie with the host governments to enhance their likelihood of achieving their interests through the bargaining interactions. This framework not only allows us to study firm-specific strategies used in firm-state bargaining more systematically but also provides a way to predict (to a certain extent) the firm-state bargaining outcomes instead of the often-seen ex-post explanations.

In a nutshell, TNCs build closer relations with host governments, trying to maximize the economic returns from international expansion. Under this incentive, they will adjust their "political behavior" and "organizational commitment" in their interactions with host governments. This political behavior is showcased in political accommodation, and the organizational commitment is illustrated by resource complementarity and organizational credibility. Together, they represent a firm's deliberate effort to increase returns through improved ties with host governments. Political accommodation represents the extent to which a TNC can respond and contribute to governmental concerns or social needs. Resource complementarity refers to the extent to which a TNC's resources fit the government's will for development, while organizational credibility concerns the degree of a TNC's trustworthiness as recognized by officials and the public. Last but not least, in emerging markets, the institutional environment is much more dynamic and volatile; therefore, informal or social approaches, such as network-based, personalized exchanges with political institutions, are important to safeguard operations (Oliver, 1996). Personal relations are therefore also perceived widely as a key driver and mechanism for institutional attachment (Burt, 2009), and these relations could be seen as a way to build the tie as well. Table 6.1 summarizes four kinds of building components suggested by Luo (2001).

Although these four building components could be used to study a firm's deliberate attempt to increase the benefits through improved ties with host governments, to explain the firm-state relationships as well as the production expansions and results of different firms, the multi-scalarity of the interactions in the network cannot be ignored. That said, to understand the firm-state bargaining outcomes, apart from looking into the firm's deliberate attempts using the four building components aforementioned, which solely focus on a specific firm-level organization, the power and position of the firms in the production network also matter, especially in a multi-scalar setting. For example, governments prefer to attract lead firms rather than suppliers as the former, at a higher position in the network, is believed to better coordinate and control the lower-tier firms to follow them and bring more investments to the host region. Besides, rather than placing the analytical lens primarily on the national level as much IB and GVC literature does and on the regional level in GPN literature, the multi-scalarity of extra-firm actors, that is, governments and institutions, has to be addressed. Hence, by drawing upon the notion of extra-firm bargaining in the GPN 2.0 framework and the ideas of TNC-host government studies in IB literature, this chapter develops figure 6.1 as an analytical framework for understanding the firm-state relationships and interactions in the bargaining processes between different tiers of GPN firms

Table 6.1 Four Building Blocks of TNC-Government Relations

Firm-State Relation-Building Components	*Rationales and Characteristics*
Resource complementarity	• Resource invisibility between two parties is important for generating synergies from cooperation. • The greater the complementarity, the stronger the relationship between a firm and the host government
Political accommodation	• The bargaining position of firms can be best safeguarded if their business interests accommodate rather than neglect or dominate public interests in host regions. • Firms more politically responsive to a host country's social and political needs are more likely to maintain productive relationships with the host government.
Organizational credibility	• The credibility, reflected by the degree of a party's trustworthiness, is critical to establishing a desired relationship with a host government as it limits the likelihood of opportunistic behavior that is hot legit. • A firm's high credibility as perceived by the public or officials in a host region boosts its relationship with host authorities.
Personal relations	• Personal ties between firm managers and boundary spanners, who have considerable power, especially in emerging economies, can transform into interorganizational relational capital. • The stronger the personal tie, the stronger the relationship between a firm and the host government.

Source: Compiled by the authors, adapted from Luo (2001).

as well as various levels of host governments (with a focus on the dashed line) and the strategic coupling results.

By drawing upon the analytical framework we developed (figure 6.1) as well as the case study of the expansion of electronics production to the RRD in Vietnam, this chapter not only enriches the GPN literature by systematically conceptualizing the firm-state bargaining process and analyzing it at a multi-scalar level, but it also pushes forward the IB literature by validating and applying the studies of TNC-host government relationships to a quantitative case study with different firms and nonfirm actors at multiple levels. Additionally, this chapter updates the empirical studies on the restructuring of electronics production networks within Asia under the rise of the "Global South."

DETAILED STUDY AREA AND RESEARCH DESIGN

As pointed out in chapter 3, following the *doi moi* reform, in 1995, Vietnam started to sign different cooperation agreements and joined various

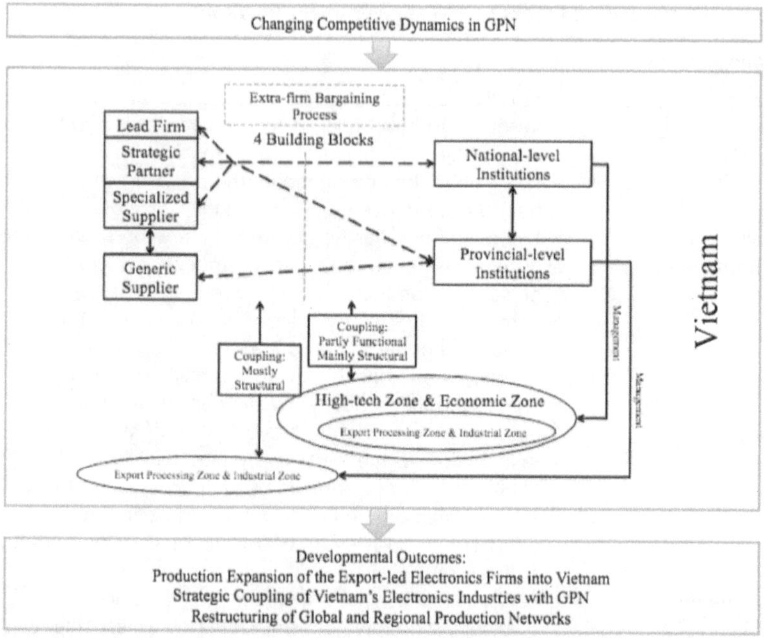

Figure 6.1 Analytical Framework of Strategic Coupling with a Focus on the Multi-scalar Extra-Firm Bargaining. *Source*: Compiled by the authors.

trade associations. As shown in figure 4.1, since joining the WTO, the FDI inflow to Vietnam tripled in volume. And as shown in table 6.2, according to the updated data released by the General Statistics Office of Vietnam, accumulated until 2021, nearly 60 percent of FDI stock in terms of the total registered capital flowed into the manufacturing sector. According to table 5.3, the electronics hardware manufacturing sector in Vietnam has grown explosively in the past few years. Notebook computers, mobile phones, and other electronics hardware are now among Vietnam's most important exports with large investments from global lead firms (e.g., Samsung and LG), contract manufacturers (e.g., Foxconn), and different component suppliers, including platform leaders (e.g., Microsoft and Intel), forming a relatively complete supply chain (Sturgeon & Zylberberg, 2016). Although Vietnam has participated in the global electronics production system, echoed by Sturgeon and Zylberberg (2016), chapter 5 has revealed its primary role as an assembly hub. Despite the fact that according to the UN Comtrade Database, Vietnam's trade balance of telephone sets (including the mobile and landline phone sets) and parts (refer to the category of SITC Rev.4 76411, 76412, and 76418) grew from negative to positive, the import value of the parts increased seventy-seven times from 2008 to 2016. This implies that the growth of

Table 6.2 FDI Projects Licensed by kinds of Economic Activity (Accumulation of Projects Having Effect as of December 31, 2021)

Kinds of Economic Activity	*Total Registered Capital (Mil. USD)*	*Share*
Agriculture, forestry, and fishing	3,730	0.9%
Mining and quarrying	4,898	1.2%
Manufacturing	248,653	59.2%
Electricity, gas, steam, and air conditioning supply	36,300	8.6%
Water supply, sewerage, waste management, and remediation activities	2,908	0.7%
Construction	10,847	2.6%
Wholesale and retail trade; repair of motor vehicles and motorcycles	9,079	2.2%
Transportation and storage	5,777	1.4%
Accommodation and food service activities	12,727	3.0%
Information and communication	4,261	1.0%
Financial, banking, and insurance activities	891	0.2%
Real estate activities	64,363	15.3%
Professional, scientific, and technical activities	4,147	1.0%
Administrative and support service activities	992	0.2%
Education and training	4,436	1.1%
Human health and social work activities	1,743	0.4%
Arts, entertainment, and recreation	3,392	0.8%
Other service activities	740	0.2%

Source: Compiled by the authors according to data from the statistical yearbooks of the General Statistics Office of Vietnam (2021).

exports in Vietnam has been somehow supported by the increased import of parts and components. The data from the official report—Vietnam's Exports and Imports of Goods—International Integration and Development 2005–2015—further proves Vietnam's role by revealing its triangular trade pattern with main trading partners in which Vietnam exports to the EU and North America and imports from China, South Korea, Japan, and other Asia-Pacific Economic Cooperation (APEC) countries, with China ranking the top.

In this current wave of production relocation within the region, according to the UN Industrial Development Report 2018, among Southeast Asian countries, Vietnam had the highest growth rate (159.1 percent) in manufacturing exports per capita from 2010 to 2015, and its impact on the world manufacturing trade exceeded Indonesia and ranked second in 2015. Hence, to understand the rise of emerging economies and the rapid production expansion of labor-intensive manufacturing industries within the "Global South," Vietnam is an ideal study area. Instead of the entire Vietnam, the RRD in the northern part is selected (refer to figure 3.5). Despite the South East region being opened first since the early 1990s (Jandl, 2013), the economic development of the northern part, that is, the RRD, has been catching up quickly as shown in figure 3.4. In terms of export value, according to the Vietnam Customs Portal, the RRD has also been catching up, and compared to the 38 percent growth rate of the South East region, the RRD grew 43 percent from 48.8 billion USD to 69.8 billion USD in 2013–2017. The fast development of the RRD is partly owing to its strategic physical location and low production costs. On one hand, the northern part of Vietnam connects to China, Vietnam's biggest importer, physically and therefore, it is relatively cost-efficient for firms to expand their production networks from China to the RRD in terms of transporting intermediate goods. On the other hand, the labor cost in the northern part of Vietnam is generally lower than in the South East region (see table 3.2). As the RRD has emerged as an electronics cluster within a short time with the influx of different tiers of electronics firms, it is ideal for studying how these different-tier firms interact with the multilevel host governments and the consequent results. Moreover, due to the multi-scalarity of its institutional governance structure on industrial development and FDI policies, studying Vietnam also enables us to investigate the multi-scalar extra-firm bargaining process, not only limited to the regional- and local-level governments but also the national one.

The present chapter is primarily based on the authors' two-year extensive field investigation in the RRD from late 2017. A total of twenty-eight in-depth interviews were conducted with different levels of governments and official institutions for attracting and managing FDI, TNCs and domestic firms involved, and industrial park (IP) developers (see table 6.3). Semi-structured interviews with open-ended questions were conducted with the interviewees, who were all at the senior management level. Questions mainly included their strategies toward firms/nonfirm actors at different scales, the rationales behind them, the regional/extra-regional assets they sharpened and/or embedded in, and their interactions with one another in the cross-border production relocation. All interviews lasted between 45 and 100 minutes and were transcribed to be used as anonymized quotations to protect the interviewees and their companies/institutions. Notably, the parties interviewed may not represent the overall population. Follow-up interviews via instant message tools were done to keep updating the issue. In addition, considerable secondary data from various resources, such as firm reports, statistical yearbooks, and publications by governments and research institutions, were also used.

Table 6.3 Summary of Interviews Conducted in the RRD (Excluding the Follow-Up Interviews)

Interview No.	*Name of the Firm/Institution*	*Tier of the Firm/Level of the Institution*	*Location*	*Source of Origin*
1	Deep C (Deep C Hai Phong IP developer)	N/A	Hai Phong	Belgium
2	Red Star Group (Nam Dinh Vu IP developer)	N/A	Hai Phong	Vietnam
3	VSIP (VSIP Hai Phong IP developer)	N/A	Hai Phong	Singapore
4	KinhBac City (Que Vo IP developer)	N/A	Bac Ninh	Vietnam
5	Vina CPK (Ba Thien 2 IP developer)	N/A	Vinh Phuc	Vietnam
6	Capella Land (Thanh Liem Industrial Park IP developer)	N/A	Ha Man	Vietnam
7	Fugiang (Van Trung IP developer)	N/A	Bac Giang	Taiwan
8	SHP (Trang Due IP developer)	N/A	Hai Phong	Vietnam
9	Youtech	Specialized supplier	Hai Phong	Korea
10	GoerTek	Specialized supplier	Bac Ninh	China
11	Xinxin Electronics	Generic supplier	Bac Ninh	China
12	SWACOO	Generic supplier	Bac Giang	Japan
13	Yuanxing Electronics	Generic supplier	Bac Giang	China
14	Haiphong Trade, Investment, Tourism Promotion Center	Provincial-level government	Hai Phong	N/A
15	Haiphong People Committee	Provincial-level Government	Hai Phong	N/A
16	Bac Ninh Industrial Zone Authority	Provincial-level government	Bac Ninh	N/A
17	Vinh Phuc Investment Promotion Agency	Provincial-level government	Vinh Phuc	N/A
18	Vietnam Academy of Social Sciences	N/A	Hanoi	N/A
19	Investment Promotion Center—North, Ministry of Planning and Investment Vietnam	National-level government	Hanoi	N/A
20	Diptronics Manufacturing	Generic supplier	Hanoi	Taiwan, China
21	RPS Vina	Generic supplier	Bac Ninh	Korea
22	Temas Technical	Generic supplier	Hanoi	Vietnam
23	WNC Vietnam	Generic supplier	Bac Ninh	Taiwan, China
24	IDC Vietnam	Generic supplier	Hanoi	Vietnam
25	Vision Battery	Generic supplier	Hanoi	China
26	Hank Electronics	Generic supplier	Hanoi	China
27	Samsung	Lead firm	Bac Ninh	South Korea

Source: Compiled by the authors.

Before starting the analysis section, as mentioned earlier, one ought to pay attention to the multi-scalarity of Vietnam's institutional governance structure on industrial development and FDI policies since functional roles and powers are assigned to various tiers of government differently. To fully analyze the firm-state relationships and interactions, it is important to understand different levels of institutional governance of the industrial zone policies in Vietnam as the majority of the TNCs would invest and locate in these zones. Table 6.4 summarizes four major types of development zones in Vietnam. One highlight point is that, in general, the financial incentives offered in economic zones (EZs) and high-tech zones (HTZs) are much higher compared to industrial zones (IZs) and export-processing zones (EPZs). For example, firms can have four years of tax holiday and 50 percent of income tax reduction for the subsequent nine years in the EZs and HTZs, compared to only two years of tax holiday and 50 percent of income tax reduction for the subsequent four years offered in EPZs and IZs. The administrative levels of EZs and HTZs are higher as well in general, as reflected also in figure 6.1. The establishment and expansion of the former two require approval from the national-level institutions. Although firms can enjoy more preferential treatments overall, unlike the EPZs and IZs, which are specialized for manufacturing and exporting, EZs and HTZs are indeed multifunctional zones, which Vietnamese governments aim to utilize to achieve a functional strategic coupling with the production networks instead of solely the structural one (refer to figure 6.1). Therefore, the thresholds of these two zones are comparatively higher; for example, only certain sectoral investments and/or certain minimum amounts of investments would be accepted.

MULTI-SCALAR EXTRA-FIRM BARGAINING BETWEEN THE HOST INSTITUTIONS AND TNCS

The Case of LG as a Lead Firm

LG Electronics announced the opening of the first phase of its Hai Phong campus in March 2015. After the first round, a total of 1.5 billion USD worth of investment from LG Electronics, LG Display, LG Innotek, and LG Chem also expanded into the Hai Phong campus with another 2.5 billion USD investment. Partly due to its strategic transportation location (refer to figure 3.5), rich supply of land and labor, and low production costs, all four LG firms are located in Hai Phong Trang Due Industrial Park, where around 80 percent of the investment inflow was from the LG Group (Interview with SHP, the developer of Trang Due Industrial Park, in Hai Phong, December 2017). The lower-tier generic suppliers of LG from different origins, mostly China, have been found to appear in the surrounding IPs nearby during our field investigation.

Table 6.4 Four Different Types of Development Zones in Vietnam

Development Zone	*Related Regulation*	*Main Roles and Characteristics*	*Incentives*
Export-processing zone	Decree No. 29/2008/ND-CP and 164/2013/ND-CP	• Zones specialize in the production of export goods and the provision of services for the production of export goods and export activities. • Export processing enterprises may sell their liquidated assets and goods in the inland market but relations of exchanging the produced goods between export processing zones and enterprises and other areas in the Vietnamese territory, except for nontariff areas, are regarded as import and export relations. • Establishment and expansion are normally under the approval of the provincial People's Committee.	Lower (e.g., Corporate Income Holiday: two years of exemption; 50 percent for the subsequent four years)
Industrial zone	Decree No. 29/2008/ND-CP and 164/2013/ND-CP	• Zones specialize in the production of industrial goods and the provision of services for industrial production. • Establishment and expansion are normally under the approval of the provincial People's Committee.	
Economic zone	Decree No. 29/2008/ND-CP and 164/2013/ND-CP	• Zones, including coastal and border-gate economic zones, with an investment and business environment, which is especially favorable for investors. • Establishment and expansion are normally under the approval of the prime minister and the Ministry of Planning and Investment.	Higher (e.g., Corporate Income Holiday: four years of exemption; 50 percent for the subsequent nine years)
High-tech zone	Decree No. 99/2003/ND-CP	• Multifunctioned economic-technical parks aim to research, develop, and apply high technologies, nurse high-tech enterprises, train high-tech manpower, and produce and trade in high-tech products. • Establishment and expansion are normally under the approval of the prime minister and the Ministry of Science and Technology.	

Source: Compiled by the authors according to interviews with the Ministry of Planning and Investment of Vietnam.

As aforementioned, it is important to understand the firm-state relationships and interactions when analyzing the coupling of the lead firms with the RRD. One crucial compromise that the Vietnamese government took to keep LG investing in Hai Phong and Vietnam, after a long negotiation, was expanding the boundary of Dinh Vu-Cat Hai EZ to include the entire Trang Due IP in August 2013 (refer to figure 6.2). This allowed LG and their suppliers located in the same IP to enjoy higher financial incentives; otherwise, LG would have invested elsewhere outside Vietnam. The case is exceptional in the sense that it does not follow the normal laws and procedures regarding the establishment and expansion of EZs in Vietnam. Not only because it was applied bottom-up instead of the top-down arrangement, but the expansion of EZ also did not strictly fulfill the locational conditions for setting up an EZ, such as a connection to the sea or a national border gate (Interview with Foreign Investment Agency under the Ministry of Planning and Investment in Hanoi, December 2017). Indeed, this case illustrates a multi-scalar extra-firm bargaining process between LG and both levels of host institutions. As what LG asked, that is, the expansion of EZ, could not be fulfilled by the provincial government or the regional one, LG's extra-firm bargaining strategies then had to involve the national-level government. To systematically look deeper into the firm-state relationships and interactions that led to the expansion of EZs and the coupling between Hai Phong and LG, four components in the

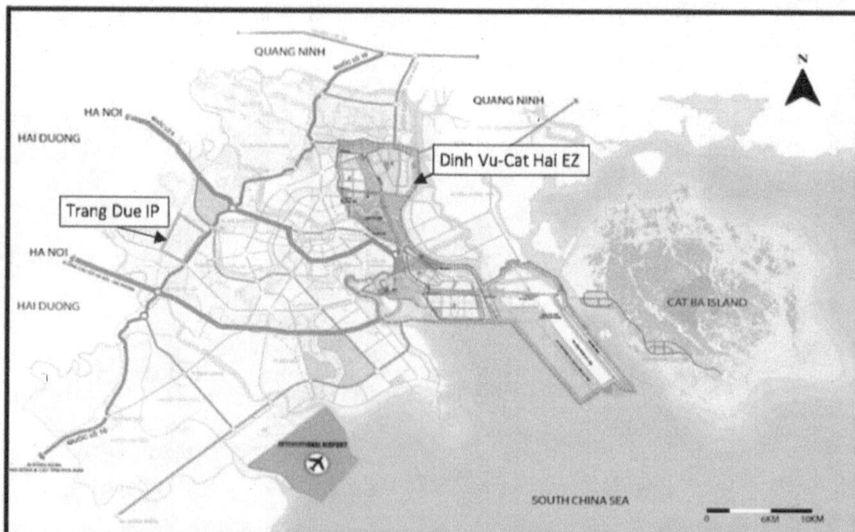

Figure 6.2 The Location of Trang Due Industrial Park and Dinh Vu-Cat Hai Economic Zone. *Source*: Compiled by the authors.

aforementioned analytical framework used to categorize the firm's tactics are analyzed below.

The greater the resource complementarity between two parties, the better interplay relationships are likely to accrue. According to Coe and Yeung (2015), the extra-firm actors in host locations, particularly territorially based organizations, are often keen to attract higher-value activities from foreign firms as they may induce local technological innovation, industrial upgrading, and so on. In our case, not only home appliances but products having higher technology levels and value-added, such as smartphones and LED display panels, are also produced by LG in Vietnam. According to Tibken (2015), R&D operations, for areas such as software and automobile infotainment have also been taking place inside Vietnam. Different levels of Vietnamese government officials believe that apart from turning Hai Phong into a simple electronics manufacturing hub, LG's technologies would also spill over to local sectors by various means, such as the local procurement process and the movement of labor. A case in point is the cooperation signed in 2018 between LG Chem and VinFast, a domestic vehicle manufacturer, to produce eco-friendly batteries that meet international standards.

As a firm's corporate citizenship is increasingly considered by the host government nowadays, the firm has to be more accommodating to the social needs of the host region to build good relationships with host governments by mitigating the liability of foreignness as perceived by the officials. Apart from providing employment opportunities, LG responds to the different social needs of Vietnam. For example, highly appreciated by the prime minister and the trade and labor union, LG Display provides canteens and dormitories for the workers. Another case in point is that according to an interview with the plant director of LG's factory in Hai Phong (Tibken, 2015), LG provides on-the-job training not only to blue- and white-collar staff for one to four months but also to R&D-centric employees for up to three years with scholarships and internships, and this had rarely been rarely seen in other firms.

Thirdly, a positive organization's credibility and trustworthiness, which includes social responsibility image, adherence to social norms, institutional harmony, previous trustworthiness, and so on, are important to boost its relationship with the host authorities. In our case, for example, the development of the LG-funded IT Library and the trade and labor union both reflects the social responsibility image and corporate reputation of LG in the RRD. As mentioned by the general director of LG Electronics in Vietnam in an interview, LG wished to support the development of Vietnam and firstly the city of Hai Phong. In 2017, LG donated an IT library to Hai Phong Industrial Vocational College under the "Vocational Development for Disadvantaged Youth in Hai Phong City" project with an estimated budget of 225,000 USD (World Vision, 2017). Also, until 2018, 91.2 percent of the total labor in LG Display joined the trade and labor union of the company with the support from LG Display itself, and according to the managing director of the company, LG Display would abide by Vietnamese law and work with trade unions at all levels to better protect the legitimate rights of its workers (Vietnamplus, 2018). Furthermore, from our interviews, various levels of host governments disclosed a positive view toward the investments from LG and their contributions. Therefore, by realizing the promises to support the development of Hai Phong and Vietnam as a whole, LG has earned relatively positive credibility and trustworthiness.

Personal relation is another building component of the relationship, particularly in developing and emerging economies where formal institutional constraints are relatively weak. In our case study, the personal relationship between the lead firm, that is, LG, and the local governments is of two scales. At the provincial level, personal relations between the managers of LG and the chairman of the Hai Phong People's Committee were close since they would regularly meet with each other (Interview with Hai Phong's Department of Planning and Investment in Hai Phong, December 2017). As aforementioned, different tiers of government are assigned different roles and responsibilities, and the provincial-level government's capacity in Vietnam is limited to the planning of IPs, provision of infrastructures and consultancies, approval of investment and business licenses, and so on. Yet, what LG asked for, indeed, could not simply be handled by the provincial government. So, besides the provincial government, the first director of LG Electronics had a very close relationship with the prime minister (Interview with SHP in Hai Phong, December 2017). Apart from the direct personal relation between LG and Vietnamese governments, in our case, the close personal tie between the industrial park developer and the governments was also found to be a crucial addition in strengthening the firm-government relationship. SHP, the developer of Trang Due IP, wanted not only the investment from LG but also the inclusion of the IP into the EZ since having the EZ status could attract more investors. Sharing the same goal as LG did, the chairman of KinhBac City, the parent company holding 90 percent charter capital of SHP, who has had a very close personal relationship with the prime minister as being a member of the 13th National Assembly, a full member of the APEC Business Advisory Council, and a senior advisory board member of Vietnam's Post-WTO Action Plan appointed by the prime minister, supported LG by becoming the mediator in the lobbying between LG and the prime minister (Interview with SHP in Hai Phong, December 2017). As a result, apart from the personal relationships built between regional-level institutions, the one between LG and the national-level government was relatively tight due to the mediation by the IP developer.

Last but not least, the position of LG in the production network was also crucial in explaining the extra-firm bargaining result, apart from what LG has done to build up a close relationship with the host governments. As it is able to coordinate the organizations of production activities as well as other firm actors in the network due to its lead firm's power, it has been widely believed by different tiers of Vietnamese governments that after attracting LG, a large group of its vendors from different origins will follow and/or be forced to relocate nearby where LG is located (Interview with Hai Phong's Department of Planning and Investment in Hai Phong, December 2017). Therefore, they welcomed LG before the belief had even turned out to be true. And after LG's expansion, a huge number of firms from mostly Korea and China relocated to Hai Phong. The majority of the investors located in Trang Due Industrial Park were, in fact LG's suppliers from Korea (Interview with SHP in Hai Phong, December 2017).

To wrap up, from the case study of the production expansion of the lead firm, LG, we see that, with its top position in the production network, LG also developed a very close firm-state relationship with different levels of host governments to achieve and maximize its benefits through bargaining. As a result, in August 2013, Trang Due IP was successfully included in the EZ. Not only could LG enjoy more preferential treatments and capture more value, but the host region could hopefully benefit from LG's partial functional coupling, besides solely the structural one, and upgrade.

The Case of Foxconn as a Tier 1 Supplier

At the end of 2006, Foxconn announced its production expansion plan to Vietnam. A cooperation framework was signed with the Ministry of Planning and Investment, pledging to invest in a series of projects in Vietnam. The opening of two plants mainly to produce camera modules, mainboards, and connectors, worth 160 million USD in total, in Que Vo IP in Bac Ninh province in the RRD in 2007 marked the beginning of Foxconn's expansion plan. In the ceremony, Foxconn's CEO Terry Gou revealed that Foxconn could bring up to 300,000 job opportunities to Vietnam over the coming three to five years according to the plan to invest up to 5 billion USD and to become the largest foreign investor in Vietnam, posting the highest export turnover. Besides Bac Ninh, Foxconn also planned to set up facilities in Bac Giang and Vinh Phuc, two northern provinces close to the capital Hanoi (refer to figure 3.5), and in central and southern provinces and cities like Binh Dinh and Ho Chi Minh.

However, the production relocation led by Foxconn has not been smooth; it has not yet realized its 5 billion USD promise as well as different investment projects in Vietnam. Foxconn has not yet successfully expanded its production network in the RRD and Vietnam as planned. For example, Foxconn was granted the investment license to build a 200 million USD base in Vinh

Phuc for manufacturing mobile phones and other electronic devices in 2009. The factories in Vinh Phuc were expected to operate in 2010 with an annual output of 89 million mobile phones. Yet, Foxconn's investment license was canceled by Vinh Phuc's government in 2015 since the project failed to make any progress. Another example is the Van Trung IP in Bac Giang. Foxconn initially planned to set up large-scale production facilities inside; however, the project eventually turned into a real estate project managed by Fugiang Company under Foxconn and Rowi Investment from Singapore. Focusing on the extra-firm bargaining between this tier 1 firm and host institutions, a manager working at Foxconn mentioned that an important reason why Foxconn could not set up the production facilities as promised is that its relationship with the Vietnamese government has been broken and the latter did not fulfill the strategic needs of Foxconn, such as providing a huge number of cheap labor (Follow-up interview, May 2018). In other words, one main reason why the Vietnamese government was reluctant to offer the preferential incentives asked by Foxconn is the relatively weak firm-state relationship between Foxconn and the host institutions. In fact, the weak relationship between Foxconn and the host institutions was at both provincial and national levels. The relatively weak firm-state relationship leading to the lagged production expansion progress of Foxconn could be better explained by the framework above.

The relatively weak resource complementarity was one of the reasons why the relationship between the two parties was feeble. Apart from being the biggest FDI exporter in Vietnam and making Vietnam its second biggest production base after China, the chief financial officer (CFO) of Foxconn Vietnam revealed that the company has treated expansion to Vietnam as a way to lower production costs and diversify the risk (Economic Daily News, 2007). However, instead of labor-intensive and low value-added manufacturing, various tiers of governments in the host region emphasized in our interviews that they prefer to attract higher-tech, value-added, and value-added as well as more environmentally friendly industries. In other words, what Foxconn provides is not complementary to what host governments, especially the national-level ones, want.

The second building component of the relationship is political accommodation, which represents the extent to which a TNC can respond and contribute to governmental concerns or social needs. Unlike what LG did to promise to help the development of Hai Phong and Vietnam, such as donating an IT library to Hai Phong, Foxconn has not made clear commitments or actions so far in response to the social and political needs of the RRD and Vietnam, probably as it only sees Vietnam as an assembly base besides China. Therefore, from the host government's viewpoint, Foxconn was not as contributive to the local society as LG would be and hence, this is also a reason for weakening the power of Foxconn in the firm-state bargaining process.

Thirdly, compared to LG, Foxconn did not have high credibility as it could not realize its promises. Not only has not yet fulfilled its promise to Vietnam's national government made in 2007 that it would invest 5 billion USD in total within two to three years, but it also failed its promise made to the provincial government as its 200 million USD smartphone project in Vinh Phuc had made no progress since 2008, and in 2015, the investment license was revoked (VietnamNet, 2016). Besides, in the same province, Foxconn also committed to investing in the infrastructure of Binh Xuyen II Industrial Park; however, due to slow implementation, the project has been adjusted from 485 to only 45.6 hectares (Dautu, 2015). Foxconn's CEO Terry Gou not only failed his investment promises to Vietnam but also to Indonesia, India, as well as the United States (see MarketWatch, 2017). With the history of making and breaking promises in different regions across Vietnam, various levels of government officials in Vietnam have doubted whether Foxconn could realize its investment commitments eventually (Dautu, 2015). As for the personal relationships between the managers of this tier 1 supplier and the government officials, there is no clear evidence to indicate whether their personal ties have been tight or not.

Some recent studies point out that the power of the contract manufacturers, for example, Foxconn, has been increasing as they can somehow coordinate the restructuring of production networks nowadays. They can relocate the production and even attract their suppliers to follow. Yet, in this case study, Foxconn's impact on Vietnam was less than LG's due to its own firm strategies. Unlike LG, which would bring along its suppliers, according to an interview with the CFO of Foxconn Vietnam, Foxconn did not have specific plans to do so (at least at the beginning of expansion) (Economic Daily News, 2007). This also weakened the bargaining power of Foxconn when facing the host institutions. To sum up, our case study shows that the expansion to the RRD of the power-rising tier 1 supplier, that is, Foxconn, has lagged behind its schedule. The unwillingness of the host governments to fulfill Foxconn's needs in the bargaining process was due to the broken bargaining firm-state relationships resulting from Foxconn's low degrees of resource complementarity, political accommodation, and organizational legitimacy, as well as its strategies in organizing its production network in Vietnam.

The Case of Tier 3 and Tier 4 Suppliers

Unlike the two earlier cases that their relocations were somehow decided and initiated by themselves, the majority of the relocated lower-tier Chinese suppliers we interviewed in the RRD were "asked" by their clients, that is, the lead firms and/or the tier 1 suppliers, on one hand, and pushed by the home institutional environment, on the other hand, which will be explained in detail in chapter 7. They were mostly located within a two-hour driving distance from their clients. Although the relocation was risky for them due to their limited resources, they had to do so to keep the business with their clients, who account for large portions of their incomes. As they, being generic suppliers, are relatively easy to be substituted, it is crucial for these suppliers to stay near to their clients. A manager of a tier 3 supplier from China revealed that "in order to stay in here (Bac Ninh) without disturbances, we strictly follow the laws and rules here . . . And we have never asked for anything extra from the governments" (Interview in Bac Ninh, December 2017).

A director of another tier 3 Chinese supplier revealed that his firm, like many other tier 3 firms, is not particularly important for the local economy (Follow-up interview, July 2018). Therefore, they did not ask and dared not ask for more from the host governments as they realized that they could not contribute as much as firms like LG and Foxconn both in terms of investment amount and the technological spillover (Interview in Bac Giang, December 2017). These suppliers produce low value-added intermediates like plastic shells, wires, and anti-shock rubber pads. As their positions and power are generally low in the network, unlike the lead/tier 1 firms that have some lower-tier "followers," these tier 3 and tier 4 suppliers could not affect, to a great extent, the configuration of the networks or bring in more investors for Vietnam. Staying away from disturbances was all they wanted to achieve through maintaining firm-state relationships. As this goal does not need to be fulfilled by the national-level institutions, in this sense, these firms had to bargain with the local governments. It is clear that the resource complementarity, as well as the organizational commitment of these lower-tier suppliers, were weak as their products are relatively low value-added and they do not have as many resources, financially and technologically, as their clients do to contribute to the host region.

As for organizational credibility, there was no solid evidence to determine the degree of these suppliers' trustworthiness as perceived by the public and officials. Yet, we did find that, even though the two earlier building components, that is, resource complementarity and organizational commitment, were weak, the strong personal relationship between the managers of these lower-tier Chinese suppliers and the local and regional government officials could be the reason why the former could achieve its goal, that is, staying away from the disturbances in relocating to the RRD. According to a director of one tier 3 supplier, he, along with other managers of similar kinds of firms from China located nearby and the provincial government officials, were good friends and would gather at least once a month (Follow-up interview, July 2018).

Apart from their limited efforts to build the four components of firm-state relationships, their positions in the production networks must be considered as well. As they are in a low position in the network, and can hardly coordinate and control any production activities, they could hardly bring in any extra investments in Vietnam. In turn, they would easily move out from the host regions when their clients, for example, lead firms and CMs, relocate and decouple. To sum up, due to these constraints, that is, lacking financial and technological capital—the lower-tier suppliers did not have strong resource complementarity and organizational commitment. Be that as it may, unlike LG and Foxconn which tried to bargain to maximize their value captures, these suppliers did not ask for anything but just tried to stay close to their clients while staying away from the disturbances in their cross-border expansions. In this vein, firm-state bargaining here is mainly at the local level, as the local officials could already handle their needs. Despite an overall weak firm-state relationship as well as the low position inside the production network, thanks to the relatively strong personal ties built between the officials and the managers of these suppliers, according to our observations, the requests of the latter could be fulfilled, and their production expansions to Vietnam by structural coupling could still be realized.

CONCLUSION AND DISCUSSION

Insufficient attention has been paid to investigating the current wave of production expansions into Southeast Asia. This chapter studies the production relocation of electronics industries within the "Global South" to understand the expansions of various tiers of GPN firms using different firm-specific strategies in multi-scalar firm-state bargaining. Although GPN 2.0 has placed special attention on extra-firm bargaining, the focus has mainly been on explicating the overarching outcomes while leaving the dynamic deliberations, actual tactics, and causal mechanisms largely unexplored. Unlike many empirical studies that focus primarily on the regional level, this study puts back the "multi-scalarity" of the GPN studies by examining the bargaining between different tiers and levels of firms and host governments. Since the interactions between TNCs and the institutional environment are critical to understanding of the coupling process, this study contributes to the GPN and strategic coupling literature by interpreting the firm-state relationships from the institutionalist perspective inspired by the IB literature. Apart from the position in the network, legitimacy is a must for the firms to survive in a host region, not to mention alter the institutions there to maximize their profits. We developed an analytical framework that systematically categorizes the actual tactics used by the firms in the firm-state interactions into four building components. Rather than viewing the process as a simple power contestation, the current study takes a cooperative view of the firm-state relationships, and these four components manifest a firm's deliberate attempt, through building up a strong tie with the host governments, to better achieve its needs via bargaining interactions. By considering the attempts of firms to build closer firm-state relationships together with their positions in the production networks, one can better study, compare, explain, and perhaps even predict the bargaining outcomes, as well as the strategic coupling results.

Hence, this chapter enriches the developing GPN 2.0 framework by further conceptualizing the firm-state bargaining process and unpacking the actual tactics used by the firms in a systematic fashion. Moreover, this chapter reinforms the multi-scalar nature of the regional institutional governance structure in the context of the extra-firm bargaining process. At the same time, this chapter also contributes to IB literature by applying the studies to a multi-scalar qualitative study and by showing the importance of investigating firm-state relationships from a broader network perspective. Apart from the theoretical contribution, this chapter provides an updated empirical study regarding the current relocation of labor-intensive industries, that is, the electronics manufacturing sector, to Southeast Asia in the context of emerging strategic coupling between the RRD in Vietnam and the global electronics manufacturing networks.

In short, this chapter argues that by having higher degrees of these four building components, the firm-state relationship will be closer, and together with a higher position in the production network, the likelihood of the firm achieving its needs via bargaining will be higher. Hence, the relocation and coupling process shall be smoother. Due to its higher degrees of "resource complementarity," "political accommodation," "organizational credibility," and "personal relations," LG had a stronger firm-state relationship both at national and provincial levels; together with its top position in the production network, it could achieve its goals, including incorporating Trang Due IP into the EZ, through extra-firm bargaining and expanding its production to the RRD. Comparatively speaking, due to the weaker firm-state relationship between Foxconn and the host governments and a relatively lower position in the production network, the expansion of Foxconn into Vietnam has lagged as the host governments were not willing to fulfill its strategic needs. As for the lower-tier suppliers from China, the firm-state relationships between these suppliers and the local states were weak due to the lower degrees of resource complementarity and political accommodation. Yet, unlike the previous two firms that sought to maximize their value captures through bargaining, these lower-tier suppliers just hoped to minimize disturbances, as they had to physically stay close to their clients. Thanks to the higher degree of personal relations developed with the local-level governments, their needs could be handled by local officials and thus, their production expansions into the RRD were also smooth on average. In return, through the expansion of the EZs, instead of strategic structural coupling, the coupling of the RRD with LG's production network has been, at least, partly functional. Furthermore, we point out that in coupling with a region, different tiers of firms with different extra-firm bargaining goals would bargain with the host institutions of different/multiple scales rather than a single, overarching layer of "regional institutions" since different levels of host institutions do have their own governance capabilities.

It is important to interrogate the multi-scalar firm-state bargaining deeper and more systemically, as it is critical for understanding the anchoring of production networks to a certain place. The findings of this chapter provide fundamental policy implications for the governments in Asia, especially for the emerging and developing economies in Southeast Asia, by understanding the importance of their roles as host governments and of the firm-state relationships in restructuring and coupling with the production networks. One highlight is that the power relationships between TNCs and host institutions are not a zero-sum game since the cooperation could bring more payoff for both parties. Learning from the RRD's lesson, one should also notice the potential of setting up a multilevel industrial governance institution in the host region for different kinds of investors and coupling goals. As the "Global South" continues to rise in the global economy, production expansions within Asia are expected to increase in the coming decades. More studies should be carried out to examine the restructuring of production networks in various industries, with particular attention to the firm-state relationships and interactions, as well as the consequent implications for regional development in Southeast Asia and the "Global South." What's more, with the rise of the "Global South," as we slightly discussed earlier and will further dig into in the next chapter, one should also shed light on the emerging TNCs originating from these developing economies apart from the established ones from the Western economies and/or the NIEs, as these ETNCs have accounted for an increasing portion of outward FDI recently.

Chapter 7

Institutional Escape and Embeddedness in the Cross-border Production Networks

Relocation of Chinese Electronics Small and Medium-sized Enterprises to Vietnam

In the previous chapter, we have paid attention to the multi-scalar strategic coupling and the extra-firm bargaining behind the scenes between different tiers and levels of transnational corporations (TNCs) and host institutions. As pointed out at the end of the previous chapter, one cannot ignore the emerging TNCs from the emerging and developing economies in studying the current wave of production relocation in the "Global South." Therefore, as the title of this chapter suggests, we will focus our efforts on these emerging TNCs (ETNCs). As pointed out in previous studies (Fu et al., 2020; Yang & He, 2017), the regional assets in coastal China have started to unfit the strategic needs of the TNCs due to unprecedented challenges, especially the rising production costs together with the shrinking market demand of the developed economies. Labor-intensive manufacturing firms have started to upgrade and/or relocate away from the coastal regions of China. However, in comparison with numerous studies focusing on the internal "transformation" of the "World Factory" (e.g., Yang & He, 2017; Zhu & Pickles, 2014), for example, upgrading to survive or moving to the inland regions, less attention has been paid to the cross-border production relocation to neighboring Southeast Asian countries, such as Vietnam (Yang, 2016). Moreover, as aforementioned, the majority of existing studies on production relocation, especially those in relation to the electronics industry (e.g., Yeung, 2007, 2019), have focused on the established TNCs, for example, the ones that originated from Japan and newly industrialized economies (NIEs). A growing body of literature has recently been devoted to examining the participation of ETNCs from emerging economies, for example, China, in the reorganization of global and regional electronics production networks, which has mainly focused on the large-scale firms with relatively abundant resources and experiences going abroad, as well as the state-owned enterprises (SOEs) with support from the national state. Little attention has been paid to the privately owned small and medium enterprises (SMEs), which have increasingly engaged in relocation away from China to nearby countries, for example, Vietnam, and participated in the current restructuring of global and regional production networks (Yeung, 2017; Yeung & Liu, 2008).

In the recently developed GPN 2.0 framework (Coe & Yeung, 2015), the causal drivers of the GPN actors, including nonfirm actors such as different levels of government, have been further emphasized to better understand the underlying determinants for the actors when interacting with various firms and nonfirm actors in organizing their production networks. Although increasing efforts have been made to incorporate political-economic forces into the GPN framework, room for improvement still exists in the institutional analysis in the literature (Coe & Yeung, 2019). In particular, the authors reckon that the static analysis of institutional embeddedness in the host region has endangered the understanding of the dynamic interplay between the institutions at home and in the host regions involved in the cross-border production networks. On the other hand, apart from cost-based studies, an institutional perspective has been increasingly adopted to explain production relocation in the international business (IB) literature. However, the emerging notion, that is, institutional escapism, has overlooked firm-level strategies in the post-escape situation.

This chapter enriches the literature in both conceptual and empirical domains. First, we will offer a critical review of previous empirical studies regarding production relocations to showcase that the overemphasis on capitalist dynamics runs the danger of ignoring the role of institutions. Then, we will also critically look into the institutional analysis in the GPN and the IB studies to identify the loopholes in theories. By cross-fertilizing the notions of institutional escapism and institutional embeddedness, the authors forge a new dynamic connection between the home and host institutions to build an analytical framework for a better understanding of the mechanism of how both institutions drive production relocation simultaneously. After the introduction of the study area and research design, in the fourth section, we will update the empirical literature by looking into the relocation and production network reorganization of privately owned SMEs originating from emerging economies, that is, China, which have been understudied yet play an increasingly important role in the changing regional and global economy based on the extensive field investigations in the Southeast region of Vietnam, especially the in-depth interviews carried out in both home and host regions since 2017. Particular emphasis will be placed on the interplays between institutional environments in these two regions. In the concluding section of this chapter, a summary of the research findings and contributions will be presented.

CONCEPTUALIZING THE CROSS-BORDER PRODUCTION NETWORK RECONFIGURATION: TOWARDS THE INSTITUTIONAL PERSPECTIVE

Cross-border Production Relocation of ETNCs, Especially the Ones from China

In the aftermath of the global financial crisis in 2008, despite more studies focusing on the transformation of the "World Factory," existing studies have mainly paid attention to the internal dynamics, while the dynamics and patterns of production relocations away from China have received insufficient attention (Yang, 2017; Yang & He, 2017). Take the electronic industry as an example; existing literature has mainly concentrated on the production relocation of established TNCs originating from relatively developed economies, for example, Japan and the NIEs, which are primarily lead firms and power-rising strategic partners such as Samsung and Foxconn in the global production networks (e.g., Lee & Gereffi, 2015; Yeung, 2019). In contrast, the cross-border production relocations of ETNCs from emerging economies, especially SMEs from China, have been overlooked (Yang, 2016). Although it has been receiving increasing attention to date, the focus has been put on the relatively "celebrated" cases, that is, the emerging giants like Huawei, Haier, and Lenovo, and the SOEs that usually receive support from the Chinese state (e.g., Xu, 2014; Yeung & Liu, 2008). Rather, a large number of SMEs that have increasingly engaged in cross-border relocations have been relatively underresearched (Yeung, 2017). It is essential to explore why and how these SMEs, which have increasingly participated in the reconfiguration of global and Asian regional production networks, have relocated and reorganized their production networks to better understand the whole picture.

Existing studies on the going out of Chinese firms have overemphasized the capitalist dynamics, particularly those based on firm-level analysis (e.g., Alon et al., 2018; Deng, 2012), have tended to adopt a resource-based view (RBV) highlighting the firm-specific characteristics. In addition, theoretic underpinnings like Mathews's link-leverage-learn (LLL) framework (Mathews, 2017) and Dunning's OLI paradigm (Dunning, 2001) have been used frequently. These directions, nevertheless, may lead to an insufficient understanding of the story. First, since these frameworks were primarily developed upon the case studies of established Chinese TNCs, and as their firm-specific attributes are drastically different from SMEs, they are not readily applicable to SMEs.

Second, as these frameworks have prominently focused on the capitalist dynamics, the institutional drivers have been somewhat ignored (Wu & Deng, 2020). Thirdly, embedded in the expanding global and regional production networks and taking on important transnational characteristics, it is urged that the internationalization of Chinese business needs to be located and investigated within the global production networks (Pan, 2009).

Institutional Embeddedness Perspective in the GPN Framework

Unlike the GVC perspective, which sees the institutions as "the external architecture that chains inhabit" (Bair, 2008; Neilson & Pritchard, 2009), the GPN approach takes

> explicit consideration of extra-firm networks, it necessarily encompasses the broad range of non-firm organizations . . . that may shape firm activities in the particular places absorbed into GPNs. (Coe, 2012: 390)

A focal notion of the GPN literature involves the "strategic coupling" of global firms and their networks to the institutional and geographical contexts within which global production takes place (Yeung, 2016).

> "(M)ulti-scalar 'regional institutions' are important because they can provide the glue that ties down global production networks in particular localities" (Coe & Yeung, 2015: 20). "(A)n institutional lens will be crucial to understanding how the 'vertical' dimension of production networks intersects with their 'horizontal' embeddedness in particular places and localities." (Coe, 2012: 393)

The important notion—"embeddedness"—in the GPN perspective has been stressed (Hess, 2004). In particular, "territorial embeddedness" concerns the degree to which the actors are "embedded" in particular territories. To support the formation of new nodes within the global production networks, national and local government policies may be used to attract the economic actors to embed in certain places. And when they become embedded, these actors may absorb and sometimes become constrained by/locked into the economic activities and social dynamics of that territory. Many economic geographers have therefore focused on seeing how institutions in the host region have attracted and interacted with the economic actors, which originated overseas, for regional economic development. While the concept of strategic coupling, and later decoupling, as well as recoupling, has been widely adopted to understand empirically how different networks and industries have tied and untied with certain regions over time (e.g., Horner, 2014), the focus has been mainly on the roles of government agencies in the host regions. Hence, the home institutions and the interplays of institutional environments of home and host regions associated with production reorganization have been rather overlooked in the literature.

> (T)he intention of GPN research has been to incorporate the state as an active agent in global production networks rather than relegating it to being part of the background institutional context. (Coe & Yeung, 2019: 782)

In fact, the role of the home institutions has merely been seen as the institutionalized patterns of political, economic, and cultural processes that play a role in explaining the ways firms go abroad in the GPN studies (Yeung, 2007). In the recent review of the newly developed GPN 2.0 theory, the original authors admitted that the political-economic forces could be further looked into and stated explicitly that the role of the state should have been emphasized (Coe & Yeung, 2019). In particular, the three competitive dynamic forces in the GPN 2.0 seem to be delineated in a definitive and reductive way in that the "state activity is positioned as one of many factors in the risk environment" (Neilson et al., 2018: 417). The active role of the state in creating the institutional environment in the first place, which has provided the context for the competitive dynamics faced by firms, seems to be understated in the firm-centric GPN 2.0 theory.

> (T)he institutional settings, or territorial influences, are more than mere influences on value capture trajectories through strategic coupling but to be considered as independent variables driving the actor practices. (Neilson et al., 2018: 417)

That said, in relation to the studies of production reorganization, apart from the three competitive dynamic forces, that is, cost-capability ratio, market imperative, and financial discipline, the institutional environment, largely built by the home state, should not be ignored. it could directly alter the interplay between the competitive dynamics in the cross-border production networks.

The presumed "conductive" role of the state could be another issue in the institutional analysis of the GPN literature. So far, within the attention to the role of the state in the GPN literature, "a major emphasis has been on initiatives that will meet the 'strategic needs' of key firms in GPNs to produce a strategic coupling, and thus capture value, within the production networks of global lead firms" (Horner, 2017: 5). However, apart from being the facilitator in the strategic coupling, the state could also act as the regulator setting the rules of the game; the producer operating its SOEs in the networks; and the buyer through large-scale public procurement (Horner, 2017). The state may not always be "conducive." For instance, acting as the producer, the state could act as the competitor to privately owned firms; while acting as the regulator, the state could lead to the strategic decoupling of certain firms and industries.

Insights from the Institutional Escapism in the IB Literature

"(M)ainstream (IB) literature ignores the vital role of institutional contexts in shaping the nature of firm strategic choices in and out of emerging markets" (Wu & Deng, 2020: 338). Similar to the GPN literature, which has mainly focused on the host region where the GPN firms are tied while ignoring the role of the home institution, the direct and active role of the home institution in driving firm-specific responses has been overlooked in IB studies. Instead of the presumed "conducive" institutional environment, the formerly useful elements of the business system, that is, the institutional structure, may lose their utility or become an obstacle to the ability of firms over time. The needs of firms and the affected elements of the business system would then become misaligned (Michael & Lewin, 2007). Apart from acquiescence, abatement, and diminution, escape is one of the responses to avoid misalignment and associated costs. Recently, IB scholars started to contend that the cross-border activities engaged by firms in emerging markets, for example, China, may be either forced or pushed by their less munificent home country institutions (e.g., Yamakawa et al., 2008). The core viewpoint of institutional escape, an integral part of institutional theory, is that firms venture abroad as a strategic exit from domestic institutional constraints and/or biases that hinder them from fulfilling their goals. With an escape response, they establish a footprint overseas to circumvent home-based harsh institutional hurdles. Compared to the big, resource-rich firms, which could handle the institutional constraints in various ways, and the SOEs, which are generally with strong government support, institutional escape is more applicable to privately owned SMEs with limited resources to deal with the constraints (Boisot & Meyer, 2008).

Although institutional escapism has been increasingly applied to study the relocation of TNCs, four research gaps have been identified. First, the destination for the escaped firms is still under debate (Barnard & Luiz, 2018; Wu & Deng, 2020). Yet, it is commonly believed that the firms will "shift their operations to outside the borders of the local economy to a location with institutional and other conditions that they perceive as more amenable to their operations" (Barnard & Luiz, 2018: 607). Second, the notion of institutional escapism has been mainly derived from deductive analysis or aggregated country-level data, while empirical case studies have been insufficient. Third, and in relation, while focusing on the country level, the previous research has ignored subnational institutional differences. Fourth, and most importantly, the previous studies have been relatively partial as they have mainly focused on the rationale behind the escape of the firms while ignoring the post-escape activities that are critical for us to grasp the whole picture (Wu & Deng, 2020).

TOWARDS AN INSTITUTIONAL INTERPLAY FRAMEWORK FOR EXPLORING CROSS-BORDER PRODUCTION NETWORKS OF CHINESE ELECTRONICS SMES: CONNECTING INSTITUTIONAL ESCAPE AND EMBEDDEDNESS

The institutional embeddedness and institutional escape notions from the GPN and IB studies have been somewhat separated. On the one hand, although the important concept of embeddedness in strategic coupling has been pointed out in the former literature, previous studies have primarily focused on the institutional environment in the host region while ignoring various dynamic roles of the home institution in driving the firm's activities. On the other hand, although the latter literature does point out the direct and nonconductive impact of the home institution on firms, it has not paid enough attention to the activities after the "escape." To go beyond the static institutional analysis and to build up an analytical framework that captures production reorganization of firms, particularly the cross-border relocations, under the dynamic interplay between the home and host institutions, the authors realized the potential from the recent calls to cross-fertilize between the economic geography and IB theories (e.g., Barnes & Sheppard, 2010; Deng et al., 2020).

In addition to the capitalist/competitive dynamics, relocation of domestic firms, particularly SMEs, could be a way to escape from home institutional constraints/bias to seek living spaces. In general, these firms "are not quite ready for meaningful international operations after their escape overseas" (Wu & Deng, 2020: 340). Although we do agree that one should not cast Chinese businesses as distinctively Chinese in unitary and national terms by cultural coherence and homogeneity (Pan, 2009), these firms, that is, SMEs, are likely to retain their inherited legacies. Their ways of production relocations and reconfiguration of production networks could greatly reflect their practices in China. For instance, one of the dominant legacies inherited in Chinese firms is the *guanxi* utilization as a strategic mechanism to overcome competitive and resource disadvantages, particularly for SMEs, during cross-border relocations (e.g., Ko & Liu, 2017; Park & Luo, 2001). These SMEs, with relatively less experience and fewer resources going abroad, are likely to spatially "lock in" to their origins (Hess, 2004).

The "psychic distance" in the cross-border expansion of a firm "concerns the cultural, linguistic, institutional, developmental level and other dimensions of difference between a firm's country of origin and other countries to which it may internationalize" (Child & Rodrigues, 2005: 385). Facing a heterogeneous cultural, societal, and institutional environment, "firms have to bridge these differences, establish efficient communication between agents with various cultural backgrounds and adjust their organizational practices in the host country" (Bathelt, 2005: 209). The distance can give rise to costs associated with the need to adapt to local contexts. The larger the distance, the higher the associated cost (Denk et al., 2012). In particular, a recent study found that, in relation to Chinese firms, compared to the cultural and societal distance, which will not have a significant effect, the institutional distance will have a robust negative correlation with the investment volume of Chinese firms in certain countries (Ren & Yang, 2020). This implies that the higher the institutional distance, the less likely Chinese SMEs will relocate to that country due to the higher extra cost associated. And compared to large, resource-rich firms, this is especially true for SMEs. As such, these firms prefer to embed into a similar institutional context to their home ones, that is, the territorial embeddedness. In other words, the institutional legacies inherited in the firms, especially the SMEs, do affect their post-escape cross-border relocation and destination locations. Therefore, to better understand production relocations under the dynamic interplay between the institutions in the home and the host region, apart from the push from home institutions, the efforts of the host institutions to lower the sociocultural and institutional distance should not be ignored.

> the national and local government policies (training programs, tax advantages, etc.) may function to embed particular parts of larger actor-networks in particular cities or regions, in order to support the formation of new nodes in global networks. (Hess, 2004: 177–178)

Figure 7.1 illustrates the institutional interplay analytical framework we built for the current chapter. Under the changing dynamics in global and regional economies, to better grasp the emerging opportunities, institutional environments in both home and host regions will evolve/change accordingly. As the home institutional environment may no longer fit the strategic needs of certain firms in certain industries, these firms will then be forced to relocate as an escape response to the institutional constraints/bias. These firms, particularly the SMEs with limited resources and experience, are then likely to relocate and reorganize their productions with their home institutional legacies inherited. Meanwhile, under the pressure of the changing global and regional economic situations as well as the national-level dynamics, the institutional environment in the host region is also subject to change. For instance, to attract and anchor down these "escaped," firms which are considered to be

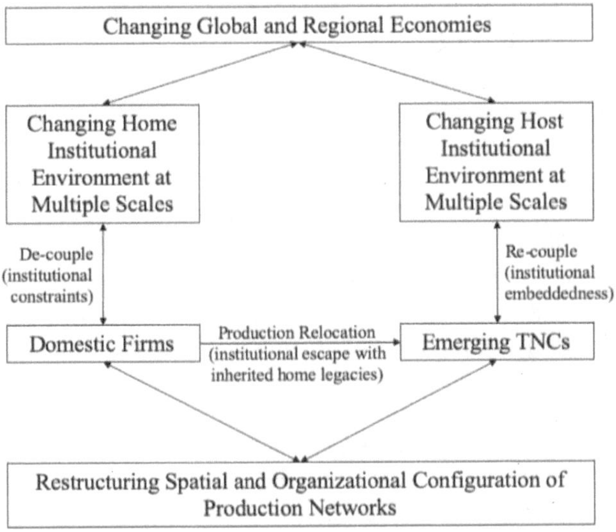

Figure 7.1 The Institutional Interplay Analytical Framework. *Source*: Compiled by the authors.

beneficial to the host region, the effort from the host institutions at multiple scales to fulfill the firm's inherited home legacies, that is, to minimize the institutional distance, could be seen and is crucial in driving the relocation process. By incorporating the notion of institutional escape and institutional embeddedness, instead of static analysis, we forge a new connection of the dynamic interplay between the home and host institutions to build an analytical framework for a better understanding of the mechanism of how both institutions have codriven the production reorganization as well as the pre- and post-escape activities of the relevant firms.

DETAILED STUDY AREA AND RESEARCH DESIGN

This chapter sheds light on the rise of Vietnam as an alternative location for electronics SMEs in the reorganization of their production out of China. Taking the communication device manufacturing sector as an example, although China has been the largest exporter, Vietnam's export share has been following and rising since the 2010s (table 4.1). Electronics products have become a main export category of Vietnam, and the export values have boomed entering the 2010s (table 5.3).

Vietnam has been selected in this study as it not only has participated in the electronics production networks in a short span but has also become one of the main attractions for Chinese investors recently (refer to chapter 5). The current wave of production relocation is not solely driven by firms that originated from relatively advanced economies in the region, such as the NIEs and Japan. It has also been driven by Chinese firms. The electronics industry has been an ideal sector to illustrate the changing global economic landscape since, as aforementioned, it shows the backbone of the global production systems accounting for the growing and highest share of the total manufactured intermediate goods trade compared to other industries common in the studies of GVC/GPN (Kawakami & Sturgeon, 2010). The electronics TNCs are geographically extensive and sensitive to the changing dynamics in the global economy, and that in turn helps us to better keep up with the current wave of production relocations from China to Vietnam.

The sectoral differences in institutional dynamics are also a main cause for us to focus on the electronics firms. Since the 2000s, labor-intensive, low value-added manufacturing sectors, such as textiles and garments, and electronics manufacturing, in coastal China have been forced to relocate (Yang, 2016). Among various industries, the rapid development of the electronics industry in Vietnam is not a coincidence. Rather, it is the institutional effort that comes into play. In comparison with other manufacturing industries, the electronics industry has been assigned particular importance in Vietnam since the mid-2000s. For example, in 2007, electronics, information, and telecommunication technologies were identified as key sectors among the top ten priority sectors, and incentive policies were introduced (Bích et al., 2019). Therefore, as the electronics industry has presented unique institutional dynamics across the border, it is advisable for us to look into its cross-border production relocation from an institutional perspective.

To study the production relocation in detail, instead of taking Vietnam as a whole, the current study focuses on the Southeast region in Vietnam (figure 3.6). According to figure 3.4, the Southeast region has attracted most of the FDI inflow since the 2010s. Not only has it attracted the majority of the FDI inflow, but it has also been the main destination of China's OFDI in Vietnam. Although no exact records of the spatial distribution of Chinese investors have been found, it is pointed out that Chinese investments have been present in sixty-three provinces in Vietnam and concentrated in the densely populated regions, especially the Southeast region where Tay Ninh province alone accounted for 14.8 percent of China's total registered investment capital in Vietnam in 2019 (Ha, 2019).

As the current chapter focuses on SMEs, all of the cases are privately owned SMEs with 50–3,000 employees. Only one firm has more than 2,000 employees, and the rest have fewer than 1,000. These firms generally have less experience and fewer resources going abroad, and they receive no support from the Chinese national state. Instead of the lower-tier suppliers, who have little autonomy in their relocations as they have to follow their customers, this study focuses on firms that have upgraded along the chains and become specialized suppliers, original equipment/design manufacturers, and even OBMs. Through relocation to Vietnam, these Chinese SMEs can develop their own production networks and markets. Although these SMEs have increasingly contributed to the changing regional and global production networks, they have been underresearched in the literature.

A chain-referral sampling method was applied to reach the target interviewees after connecting with the CEO of an investment consulting firm for Chinese investors in Vietnam. Through his referral, we started to reach and connect with different Chinese SMEs in Vietnam. Among the seventeen Chinese enterprises the authors interviewed in the Southeast region, nine are OBMs, and eight are suppliers at different tiers, mostly specialized suppliers, in the electronics production networks. While the majority of these enterprises (10/17) manufacture relatively low-tech electronics products, such as portable radios and home appliances, and their related accessories and components, others (7/17) are in relatively high-tech sectors, that is, mobile phones. The majority of the interviewed firms (13/17) relocated their production to Vietnam after 2008. To ensure representativeness, the interviewees are mostly at the management level, and some are the vice president and the CEO of the firms. All interviews generally lasted between 90 and 120 minutes and were recorded and transcribed to be used as anonymized quotations in this chapter. Besides face-to-face interviews, follow-up interviews were conducted via online messaging tools to keep updating the issue. It is to be noted that although the interviewed firms are representative, they may not stand for all Chinese SMEs relocated to Vietnam.

INSTITUTIONAL ESCAPE AND INSTITUTIONAL EMBEDDEDNESS IN THE CROSS-BORDER RELOCATION OF CHINESE ELECTRONICS SMES TO VIETNAM

Institutional Escape in Production Relocation Out of Coastal China

Unlike what has been described in the previous studies emphasizing market access, access to resources and production factors, and the state's diplomacy as the main driving forces for the "going out" of Chinese firms (Yeung & Liu, 2008), this study demonstrates different motivations for Chinese SMEs to move to Vietnam. As illustrated in table 7.1, only 20 percent (2/9) of the interviewed SMEs saw seeking lower costs and market potential as their primary motivation. In contrast, ten out of seventeen interviewed firms saw pressure from home institutions as the most important driver for them to relocate.

Table 7.1 Main Reasons for Relocation of Chinese Electronics SMEs to Vietnam

Reasons for Relocation	*The Most Important Driver for the OBM SMEs*	*The Second Most Important Driver for the OBM SMEs*	*The Most Important Driver for the Suppliers of Different Tiers*	*The Second Most Important Driver for the Suppliers of Different Tiers*
Seeking for lower production cost	One firm (11%)	One firm (11%)	0	One firm (12.5%)
Seeking for market potential	One firm (11%)	Three firms (33%)	One firm (12.5%)	Two firms (25%)
Seeking for financial resource	0	0	0	0
Pressure from the customer	0	0	Four firms (50%)	Two firms (25%)
Pressure from the home institution	Seven firms (77%)	One firm (11%)	Three firms (37.5%)	Two firms (25%)
The changing political economy, for example, the Sino-US trade war	0	Four firms (44%)	0	One firm (12.5%)

Source: Compiled by the authors according to interviews.

Among various policies, the anti-low value-added manufacturing programs carried out by different levels of government in home regions of China since the 2000s, such as the "empty the cage for new birds" of the Guangdong provincial government and the most recent campaign to eliminate backward and excessive production capacities by both national and subnational governments, have become the main push factor for these SMEs to escape from their home to survive.

Pointed out directly by the vice president of a low-tech portable electronic gadget manufacturer, "We were given three options at that time (the early 2010s). We could either shut down, upgrade, or relocate . . . It was not an easy decision for us to come here (Vietnam) from both perspectives of business operation and personal life" (Interview with the vice president of a low-tech portable electronic gadget manufacturer, September 2018). Although it was said that the relocation was not easy with limited resources and experience, it was the only option for them. Compared to the cost of relocation, the cost of upgrading was hardly affordable. "Unlike production relocation in which we basically need to pay to change our location of production and maybe sales, we may have to upgrade all of our machines, staff, and production procedures to produce products with higher tech levels . . . It is too costly and risky for a tiny enterprise like us" (Interview with the CEO of an electric home appliance manufacturer, March 2019). To be more specific, instead of paying hundreds of thousands of USD to upgrade their production, the firm spent only around

50–60 percent to move to Binh Duong in Vietnam from Guangdong in China (Interview with the CFO of an electroplating factory, October 2018).

Unlike the long-established "World Factory" in coastal China where the supply chain has been well-developed, more time and/or transportation costs have to be incurred by the relocated firms to look for and/or to ship the intermediate goods. This could be even more difficult for the SMEs given that their market power is generally lower. "It is not realistic to ship all the parts and components from China in terms of the shipping cost and time . . . Switching suppliers has been one of the most challenging problems" (Interview with the vice president of an electric home appliance manufacturer, September 2018). Apart from the difficulties faced when looking for suppliers, poor-quality labor was another issue, even though the labor cost in Vietnam was only half of that in China (Shortell, 2019). The productivity of Chinese workers in the interviewees' eyes was more than double that of Vietnamese workers in general. On the other hand, the emerging consumption market in Vietnam was not that attractive, to be honest. According to the data from the World Bank, although the household final consumption expenditure in Vietnam increased from 493 USD to 1,329 USD per capita from 2000 to 2018, the expenditure per capita in China reached 3,148 USD in 2018, more than two times in Vietnam. "Despite it has become more competitive, China's domestic market is much larger than Vietnam's . . . Besides shipping our products to developed economies, we also export a part of our products back to China" (Interview with the manager of a high-tech electronic gadget manufacturer, September 2018).

While the traditional capitalist drivers, that is, access to markets, resources, and production factors, clearly were not strong enough for these firms to relocate, the challenging institutional environment at home against them did. As expressed by the majority of the interviewed firms, if the institutional environment at home remained the same, they would rather stay in China even with increasing production costs. Unlike the related studies at the beginning of the 2010s (Yang, 2012), in which, despite the pressure from the national government, with the resistance from the governments at the lower levels, these firms in the labor-intensive manufacturing industry still managed to struggle to stay in the coastal region. "Starting from the mid-2010s, the bias of the governments (in China) towards the small-sized private firms in the traditional manufacturing sectors has been strong" (Interview with the CEO of an investment consulting firm for Chinese investors, November 2019). Compared to the Notice of the State Council on Further Strengthening the Elimination of Backward Production Capacities issued during the National 12th Five-Year Plan (2011–2015), which targets mostly the extraction and heavy industries, the Guiding Opinions of the State Council on Resolving Serious Production Overcapacity Conflicts issued in 2013 and the Guiding Opinions of Elimination of Backward Production Using Comprehensive Legal Standards co-issued by sixteen national institutions in 2017 have extended the range of the backward production capacities further to the environment-polluting and labor-intensive low value-added light manufacturing industries. The provincial and local government officials in the coastal region, such as Guangdong and Dongguan governments, have actively responded to these guiding opinions this time. "Unlike the SOEs or the state-related firms who could receive a helping hand from the governments, we received no help but pressure to leave where the company was 'born.' As we were not able to upgrade in a short period, they labeled us as 'low-end' enterprises . . . Although not spoken out directly, their (the officials') purpose is clear. By a more frequent checking schedule, such as environmental monitoring and labor inspection, they just wanted to kick us out to free the land" (Interview with the CEO of a component supplier for electric home appliances, October 2019). "Their (the local officials') hidden agenda was to get rid of the labor-intensive and low value-added small firms like us and they were very determined" (Interview with the senior manager of an electronic component manufacturer, January 2020). Hence, as the pro-"labor-intensive manufacturing" institutional environment in the "World Factory" in which many domestic firms have been deeply embedded has started to change and turn to become the "institutional constraints" for these SMEs, particularly since the 2010s, these Chinese SMEs had no choice but to escape abroad.

Institutional Building in Host Regions in Vietnam

Vietnam's central government decided to launch the *doi moi* economic reform in 1986. Different legal frameworks and policies for attracting businesses were then set up. Apart from the Foreign Investment Law, following the successful lesson from China setting up special economic zones (SEZs) in the 1980s, the central government in Vietnam started to establish different industrial zones in 1994. Reflected in various studies, despite the differences in ownership structures, incentive policies, and development speeds, the general business and institutional environments of the SEZs in China and Vietnam have been, in fact, highly similar, particularly in how these SEZs are operated and managed (Akinci & James, 2008; Freeman, 1994).

Besides national-level governments, the subnational ones have also actively participated in the institutional building process. Since the accelerated fiscal decentralization in 1996, and particularly since 1997 when the issuance of investment licenses and the administration of land use have been delegated to the People's Committees, there has been intense internal competition for the FDI inflow among provinces in Vietnam (Meyer & Nguyen,

2005; Vo et al., 2007). Apart from some of the industrial zones, such as high-tech zones with the most favorable incentives, which are directly governed by the national government (refer to chapter 6), provincial governments have actively attracted different investors by building up industrial zones and export-processing zones and creating an investor-friendly business climate (Freeman, 1994; Meyer & Nguyen, 2005). The decentralization process has thus enabled the provincial authorities to use their newly gained "freedom" to deal with foreign investors innovatively (Nguyen et al., 2004).

> The ambiguity of many laws and regulations issued at the central level gives local authorities an important role . . . Discrepancies between official policy and local implementation . . . are a natural outcome of the interaction between informal and formal institutions. (Meyer & Nguyen, 2005: 70)

This enables the local authorities to better facilitate the administrative processes and create investment incentives for the investors. According to the interviews, although the subnational government officials were banned from offering extra fiscal incentives to investors in recent years to prevent the "race to the bottom," the provincial and local government officials in Vietnam are still proactively helping investors to relocate to and embed into the institutional environment they built.

Interplay between Institutional Escape and Institutional Embeddedness in the Cross-border Relocation: Inherited Home Legacies

As the interviewed Chinese SMEs were forced to escape from the institutional constraints/bias at home, instead of expansionary relocation, the majority (twelve out of seventeen) of interviewed firms have adopted complete relocation as they simply could not survive under the "worsen" institutional environment, particularly since the mid-2010s. Since these firms have only limited cross-border relocation experience and fewer resources, their ways of going out greatly reflected their inherited home legacies, both in sociocultural and institutional aspects.

One of the commonly used inter-firm strategies by these SMEs is to rely on social capital to build their production networks. As pointed out and agreed upon by most interviewees, with less experience, fewer resources and particularly lower market power, reorganizing their production networks has been the most challenging task in the process. The majority have admitted that they have set up their supply chains by building up inter-firm relationships with the suppliers in Vietnam based on ethical and personal relationships to a certain extent, as they used to do at home. Except for some specialized intermediate products, which are not available in Vietnam, the interviewed firms tended to source locally for better cost-efficiency. Yet, as they have little market information, sourcing locally has been easier said than done. To do so, social capital in this unknown market has been crucial. "(T)o find our suppliers, we have asked for the opinions and contacts (of the suppliers) from our friends who have already been here (in Vietnam) . . . We have also joined different Chinese business associations in Vietnam . . . Instead of working with the unknown domestic suppliers by trial and error, we preferred a relatively low-risk solution" (Interview with the senior manager of a phone accessory manufacturer, December 2018). Added by an interviewee, "instead of speaking the same language, I think the main reason to do so (sourcing mostly from the Chinese suppliers in Vietnam) is the 'trust' among the Chinese community . . . It is the way how Chinese people do business" (Interview with the CEO of an electric home appliance manufacturer, September 2018). A similar socio-cultural atmosphere also helps to embed the interviewed Chinese SMEs. "We also think that the business cultures and the social norms here are somewhat similar to the ones in China, as compared to the Western world. Since this (Vietnam) is a place with a big Chinese community and society, it somehow makes us (the Chinese investors) fit in more easily" (Interview with the vice president of an electric home appliance manufacturer, March 2019).

The home institutional legacy has been another important factor driving the firms to escape to Vietnam. Deep territorial embeddedness was found between the industrial zone development model in Vietnam and the interviewed SMEs. As aforementioned, due to their limited resources and experience, these privately owned SMEs could hardly bridge the institutional distance between the home and the host regions. To anchor down these escaped SMEs, the efforts from the host institutions to provide a similar institutional environment with minimal "psychic distance" have been crucial in explaining this wave of production relocation. The institutional environment that caters to the SMEs with their home institutional legacies inherited has been created through the two-way deliberations between these firms and the host institutions in Vietnam. All interviewees agreed that the subnational officials have proactively assisted them in setting up their business, from planning to application, and even operation. "Similar to the local governments in China a few decades ago, the officials from the industrial zone management board and the People's Committee have been friendly and have been actively participating in our production relocation . . . They helped us to handle all the paperwork and they even provided a helping hand in our recruitment process" (Interview with the vice president of a high-tech electronic gadget manufacturer, May 2019). The decentralization mentioned earlier has offered a certain degree of "freedom" for the subnational institutions to build up competitive business and institutional environments.

Besides the "top-down" approach, the institutional environment was also designated "bottom-up." For example, to better attract these investors, "(w)e (the industrial zone management board) set up 24-hour hotlines and hold meetings with all the investors (in our zone) regularly to better understand and satisfy their needs" (Interview with the director of the industrial zone management board of Ho Chi Minh City, September 2018). Moreover, "according to the trend, we expect more Chinese firms will come to Vietnam . . . We have visited China many times to learn from the local governments there and we have also taken into serious consideration the ideas and opinions of the investors" (Interview with the deputy manager of the investment promotion division of southern Vietnam, October 2019).

The deep territorial embeddedness has not been solely accomplished through "formal" institutional building. "To be honest, we like to move to this place not simply due to the preferential (industrial) zone policies; the somewhat 'free' institutional environment is what makes Vietnam unique and similar to the 'old' Pearl River Delta" (Interview with the CEO of a component supplier for electric home appliances, October 2019). Pointed out bluntly by an interviewee, besides the ordinary firm-state interactions, "by keeping close relationships with local officials here (Vietnam), like the ways they (the Chinese firms) did at home, they can take advantage of the 'grey area' and this is not unfamiliar to these SMEs" (Interview with the CEO of an investment consulting firm for Chinese investors, September 2018). "We are good at dealing with the officials here . . . The game here is very similar to China" (Interview with the vice president of an electronics component supplier, September 2018).

Therefore, one can see that not only due to the similar sociocultural background but the institutional environment satisfying the institutional legacies inherited in these SMEs, which has been created intentionally by the host institutions at multiple levels, also acts as a pull factor to attract and anchor down these SMEs, which have escaped from the institutional constraints/bias at home. With no surprises, more than 75 percent (13/17) of interviewed firms were able to set up their production network again within the first four months, with nearly half (9/17) of them claiming that the relocation cost them less time and money than expected. Around 60 percent (10/17) of the interviewed firms reckoned that this cross-border production relocation has been easier than expected in general.

CONCLUSION AND DISCUSSION

This chapter goes beyond the static analysis of the institutional context in the studies of production reorganization to understand the dynamic interactions between the home and host institutions in driving cross-border production relocation of emerging TNCs from China to southern Vietnam. The institutional perspective in the GPN and IB studies is somewhat partial. By cross-fertilizing from the notions of institutional escapism and institutional embeddedness, an analytical framework for understanding the alternative mechanism of cross-border production relocations was established.

Although dramatic transformations of the "World Factory" in China have been witnessed in recent years, cross-border production relocations from China to neighboring Southeast Asian countries, for example, Vietnam, have received insufficient attention. In particular, cross-border relocations engaged by Chinese electronics SMEs as emerging TNCs have been understudied, despite their surging appearance in regional and global economies. Taking the production relocations of these Chinese firms as a case, in this chapter, we argue that: apart from the conventional capitalist competitive drivers, the cross-border relocation of these Chinese SMEs has been a response to escape from the recent anti-low value-added manufacturing campaigns in coastal regions in China, on the one hand, and, on the other hand, to embrace the pro-"manufacturing" institutional building in the host region advocated by different levels of the Vietnamese governments. In practice, cross-border production networks have been established in which the inherited Chinese institutional legacy has acted as an important factor in driving the Chinese SMEs to escape from the institutional constraints in home regions—while attempting to "embed" into various industrial zones in southern Vietnam. The results of this chapter show the important roles and interplay of both home and host institutions. Besides, unlike the supportive roles of the home governments in helping domestic firms to internationalize shown in previous studies, the current chapter does reflect the multiple roles of institutions in driving production relocation and reorganization.

In a nutshell, this chapter updates the developing literature on the changing dynamics in global and Asian regional production networks by the empirical evidence of production relocation engaged by emerging TNCs from China and enriches the institutional perspective highlighted in both the GPN and IB studies by connecting the interplays between the host and home institutions. The case studies showcase the dynamic interplay between the institutional escape of Chinese electronics firms from the home region and the institutional embeddedness in the host institutions in Vietnam, which had aligned with the inherited home institutional legacies.

Yet, given this initial attempt to forge the links between the host and home institutions and the cross-border production reorganizations, more case studies of emerging TNCs in other sectors, such as the garment industry, which have engaged in cross-border relocation, should be done to validate the analytical framework developed in this chapter. More empirical studies of production relocation involving other sectors and other countries in Southeast Asia would help for a fuller understanding of the presumed sectoral differences in institutional dynamics in the restructuring of production networks. A more comprehensive investigation warranting further research includes a comparative study of the emerging Chinese TNCs and the established TNCs to generate the so-called "China model" and "Western model" of cross-border production networks (Zhao, 2010). It will be interesting to explore the institutional changes and interplays between regions in China and Southeast Asian countries amidst the One Belt One Road (OBOR) initiatives and the resultant effects on the reconfiguration of the Asian regional production networks. Of course, facing the dual impacts of the rising geopolitical attention and the pandemic, updated investigations must also be carried out to better grasp the latest dynamics in the global production networks, which are crucial for the post–COVID-19 recovery.

Chapter 8

Geopolitical Risks of Strategic Decoupling and Recoupling

Insights from the Sino-US Trade War and COVID-19 Pandemic

Since the early 2010s, the global electronics industry, particularly the mobile phone sector, has undergone dramatic reconfiguration, characterized by the emergence and evolution of regional production networks in Asia (Thun et al., 2022; Yeung, 2022b). Numerous research has explored the production shift from China to Southeast Asian countries, among which Vietnam has turned into an increasingly attractive destination for labor-intensive manufacturing, mainly due to lower labor costs, favorable business environments, and its strategic geographical location. Another strand of literature has been devoted to reflecting the increasing participation and strategic coupling of Vietnam in the global production networks (Sturgeon & Zylberberg, 2016; Wrana & Nguyen, 2019). Vietnam has emerged as a key player in the reconfiguration of the Asian electronics production networks, which could be attributed to the interplay between the institutional "escape" from China's coastal regions and institutional embeddedness in southern Vietnam (refer to chapter 7). Existing research, including the previous chapters of this book, on the production shift and strategic coupling of regional development in Vietnam in the cross-border production networks has been mainly conducted before the outbreak of the Sino-US trade war and the COVID-19 pandemic, as the notable dynamics with profound impacts on global production.

The trade war and the pandemic have unexpectedly disrupted global and regional trade and supply chains, causing a shortage of components (export/import restriction, factory closure), surging transportation costs (transportation detours to avoid tariffs, disrupted transportation systems), and delay in production. TNCs in mobile phone production have turned to working closely with their suppliers to ensure that they have sufficient inventory of critical components and identify potential disruptions in their supply chains, to adjust their production schedules and manage their inventory levels more effectively. To this end, decoupling from China has been put forward as a vivid strategy induced by the trade war and pandemic. One of the measures has been the diversification of supply chains by reducing their reliance on China and seeking alternative suppliers and sourcing components from multiple regions. This chapter, however, argues that the fashionable discourse of decoupling has already been practiced by various TNCs, known as the "China Plus One" strategy, before the trade war and pandemic. What warrants exploration is the new practices of "decoupling" and "recoupling" and the resultant effects on local development in host regions/countries and the reconfiguration of global and regional production networks in the post-COVID-19 era.

The follow-up investigation on the mobile phone production relocation from China to Vietnam amid the trade war and pandemic illustrates that TNCs have continued engaging in the "China Plus One" strategy by decoupling from China's coastal regions and recoupling with multiple regions in neighboring Southeast Asian countries. Among these, Vietnam deserves more attention, particularly in the heightened Sino-US relations, as it has been well-recognized as the "biggest winner" (Jamrisko, 2019). It is worthwhile to explore the novel measures and mechanism of recoupling in the changing geopolitical dynamics and risk environment. Conceptually speaking, this chapter advances the literature on the focal notion of strategic coupling in the Global Production Networks (GPN) theory, by offering a vivid multi-scalar analysis of the changing decoupling and recoupling dynamics in the reconfiguration of regional production networks in Asia under the uncertainties and risks of global political economy. Empirically, the theory-grounded empirical research is conducted not only based on extensive field investigations and personal interviews with concerned actors in both home and host regions, namely the PRD in southern China and the Red River Delta (RRD) in northern Vietnam during the latter half of the 2010s, as the previous chapters in this monograph do, but also based on the follow-up observation and online interviews from early 2020 to early 2023 amid the trade war and the COVID-19 pandemic. There are twofold goals of this chapter. Firstly, it aims to explore the changing dynamics of decoupling and recoupling in the production relocation from China to Vietnam, with particular emphasis on the Sino-US trade war and the COVID-19 pandemic-induced geopolitical risks in the reconfiguration of the cross-border mobile phone production networks. Secondly, it investigates the changing mechanisms of recoupling with the RRD in northern Vietnam, engaged by various tiers of TNCs amid the uncertain geopolitical risks of the production shift.

The remainder of this chapter is organized as follows. After this introduction, the strategic coupling literature in the GPN theory, particularly the geopolitical dynamics and changing mechanisms of de/recoupling in the global production networks, will be critically reviewed under the reconfigurations of the global mobile phone production networks. A multi-scalar analytical framework will be developed for investigating changing decoupling and recoupling dynamics in the cross-border production relocation from China to Vietnam before and during the Sino-US trade war and the COVID-19 pandemic. The research context and methods will be briefly presented in the third section. The empirical analysis in the fourth section will first explore the changing dynamics of the cross-border relocation from China to Vietnam in the geopolitical tension and risk environment, by the cases of different tiers of TNCs, namely Apple, Samsung, Foxconn, and lower-tier supplier firms. It will then examine the changing mechanisms of recoupling of the RRD in the reconfigurations of mobile phone production networks, through which the RRD has developed into an emerging mobile phone production cluster. The chapter concludes with a summary of the main research findings, conceptual and practical implications, and suggests potential issues for future research on examining geopolitical risks in the evolving strategic coupling of regional development in the changing global economic landscape.

GEOPOLITICAL RISKS IN STRATEGIC COUPLING OF REGIONAL DEVELOPMENT AND CROSS-BORDER PRODUCTION NETWORK

Changing Geopolitical Dynamics in the Global Production Networks Reconfiguration: Insights from GPN 2.0 Theory

Since the publication of the seminal GPN 2.0 theory (Coe & Yeung, 2015), a growing body of empirical research to examine the changing dynamics and reconfiguration of global production networks in various industries has emerged. GPN studies have enabled exploring the "often contested and evolutionary relationships between lead firms and other actors in inter- and extra-firm settings" (Coe & Yeung, 2015: 58).

Existing research has usually focused on the analysis of the causal role of the three competitive dynamics, namely cost-capability ratios, market, and finance, within the broader risk environments in shaping firm strategies (Yeung, 2016, 2009b). There is an insufficient systematic investigation of the causal role of the cost-capability ratio in the unprecedented risk environments of global production networks in specific industries (Bryson & Vanchan, 2020). In the GPN 2.0 theory, the dynamic concept of the cost-capability ratio is conceptualized to describe the optimization process that allows different tiers of firms in the production networks to achieve greater firm-specific capabilities and value capture over time. Yeung and Coe (2015: 35) argued that "while cost reduction is an important capitalist dynamic compelling lead firms to engage in outsourcing and subcontracting to independent suppliers both at home and abroad, cost is a relative concept." The factor of cost must be conceptualized in combination with the actor-specific capabilities of these firms for a complete picture of its causal influence on the formation and evolution of global production networks. There are four scenarios of cost-capability ratios (low cost-low capability, low cost-high capability, high cost-low capability, and high cost-high capability) confronting both lead firms and their suppliers. As pinpointed by Yeung and Coe (2015: 37),

> (b)y optimizing their ratios through international production and outsourcing arrangements, lead firms may be able to maintain or regain their international leadership in end markets. By articulating into the global production networks . . ., independent suppliers can also optimize their ratios over time.

Cost reduction alone cannot be the fundamental driver of evolving global production networks. Rather, "both costs and firm-specific capabilities are relative and subject to change over time under global competition" (Yeung & Coe, 2015: 37). There is not enough in-depth analysis of the cost-capability ratio with empirical evidence concerning the risk environment in the reconfiguration of the production networks at global and regional levels.

Another innovative improvement of GPN 2.0 theory lies in its conceptualization of risk environments, particularly the "*GPN risk*" (Yeung & Coe, 2015: 42, original italic) in the emergence and evolution of global production networks. While the five forms of risk, including economic, product, regulatory, labor, and environmental risk, have existed in the Fordism era of vertically integrated mass production, their nature and effects have a broader geographic scope and faster temporal transmission in the contemporary interconnected world. The GPN risk defined as the "qualitative nature and causal effects of risk play out differently in the context of global production networks" (Yeung & Coe, 2015: 42) has been debated in the COVID-19 pandemic-induced disruption of supply chains (Bryson & Vanchan, 2020; Yeung, 2021b). The industry-specific GPN risk is particularly visible in the global electronics industry (Yeung, 2007; Sturgeon & Kawakami, 2011) due to its geographically dispersed nature. However, there is a lack of updated empirical exploration of new dynamics and patterns by the current two consecutive GPN risks, that is, the trade war and the pandemic, in reshaping the strategic coupling of regional development in the evolving production networks of the electronics industry in the late 2010s. Looking into these two GPN risks surely will let us better understand the firms' responses to organizational and spatial anchoring of the network and help us gain some insights into the post-pandemic era. As pointed out by Fuller (2021) and Völlers et al. (2023), the "risk" has been treated as an objective economic concern in which "once these unknown outcomes (caused by the uncertainties and risks) can be predictable . . . management strategies can be developed accordingly" (Coe & Yeung, 2015: 110). The risk-or-reward calculative thinking runs the danger of decontextualizing the organizational decision-making in the GPN studies by disconnecting the perception of and response to the risk from the simulative decision-making environment and spatial-relational context where the firms and their managers stay in. That said, apart from the rational balancing of cost and capability in risk-or-reward thinking, the logic of risk as a broader driver for GPN actors cannot exclude the firm-based sensemaking of reality and the strategy-making process that is beyond the rational calculation. Rather than a static and objective perception, the risk is indeed a fluid and subjective interpretation of the crisis and the tolerance by the firms and their managers. As summarized by Völlers et al. (2023), the risk perception and interpretation are processed by organizational decision-makers, including both firms and nonfirm actors, who are societal, territorial, and network embedded within a relational web of social relations, place-specific contexts, and decision-making environments. And the ambiguity of risk perceptions may trigger different risk expectations and narratives as well as the strategic responses to the same risk phenomenon within a global production network. In this vein, the hardly predictable COVID-19 pandemic and the Sino-US trade war offers an invaluable case for us to study how different actors of various tiers and levels have responded to the risks with the dynamic de/recoupling mechanisms in the global production networks.

Multi-scalar De/Recoupling of Regional Development in the Cross-border Production Networks

Since the 2000s, the focal notion of strategic coupling in the GPN literature has been increasingly adopted to explain how local regions in the "Global South" could develop through participating in the global production networks in various industries and sectors (Coe et al., 2004; Coe & Yeung, 2019; Hess, 2018). There is a growing body of literature on strategic coupling, particularly decoupling and recoupling in the regional development in the "Global South," in the GPN literature (Horner, 2014; MacKinnon, 2012; Yang, 2013). There has been the fashionable "decoupling from China" discourse in the media recently (e.g., Sweeney, 2022), which simply refers to the unwinding of the current level of technology, investment, finance integration, and interdependence between the United States and China. In contrast, the "decoupling" in the GPN theory is conceptualized as a break, or a reduction, in the prevailing form of linkage between a particular GPN(s) and territory, an outcome that may be the result of either a firm-based decision or the initiative of territorial, including state, institutions (Horner, 2014; MacKinnon, 2012). Similar to the notion of strategic coupling, how GPN actors decouple with a territory or vice versa also varies according to the regional assets, the status of TNC affiliates within the parent company, the power relations between global firms and regions, and so on.

Recent sympathetic reviews (as well as chapter 2 of this book) have argued that the GPN framework on the "multi-scalar" institutions of strategic coupling remains inadequately explored (Coe & Yeung, 2019; Dawley et al., 2019). As identified by Dawley et al. (2019: 856), the understanding of regional institutions as an overarching category has tended to suppress the agency of national states as empirical research has largely focused on regional-level strategies for the promotion of strategic coupling. As exemplified by Yang (2012) and Gao et al. (2019), the functional roles, powers, and responsibilities and thus the preferences of different levels of actors, for example, governments, in the strategic coupling with the global production network differ. As diagnosed by MacKinnon et al. (2019: 117), "from a GPN perspective, strategic coupling processes between regional assets and GPN actors foster path creation, resonating with the traditional regional development concern with FDI and transplantation." Recent efforts have been made to "theorize 'regional worlds' as territorial networks of interconnections that capitalize regional specific assets and yet tap into extra-regional markets, production capabilities and flows of people, capital and technology" (Yeung, 2021a: 990). However, existing research has mainly focused on the static analysis of endogenous dynamics of decoupling and recoupling mainly at the national and/or local levels, with few exceptions. Drawing on the formation of Sino-German production networks in environmental goods and services in China, Fu and Lim (2022) underscored the crucial role of the national-level government as well as the cross-scalar and dynamic aspects of strategic coupling. Hence, one should not ignore the multi-scalar institutions and their cross-scalar interactions, which may significantly sharpen the regional assets and thus the coupling outcomes.

Moreover, there has been little research conducted on the multi-scalar mechanism of strategic coupling within the changing dynamics and risk environment of global production reconfiguration. As argued by Yeung and Coe (2015), the different scales and effects of risks under changing circumstances explain why some risks are more causally efficacious in shaping firm-specific strategies, because more value can be captured, or losses minimized, through the mitigation of these risks. As added by Völlers et al. (2023), since a single or a collective of GPN organizational decision-makers are processing information according to their embedded relational context environment, not only the societal and territorial embeddedness but also the network embeddedness matters. The ways the collectives of organizational decision-makers are connected through interorganizational relationships in the network can also cause cognitive bias in the risk expectations among the actors in the same network and lead to their different responses. Hence, the omission of multi-scalarity ought to be filled in the study of risk-induced decoupling and recoupling dynamics in the cross-border reconfiguration of production networks.

A Multi-scalar Framework for Investigating Geopolitical Risks of Strategic Coupling of Regional Development in the Cross-border Production Networks

Among the four major explanatory variables of competitive dynamics including the cost-capability ratio, market imperatives, financial discipline, and the broader risk environment, this chapter highlights the changing dynamic of the cost-capability ratio in explaining the ongoing production relocation from China to Vietnam over the risks induced by the Sino-US trade war and the COVID-19 pandemic. To reiterate, instead of taking it solely as cost, one should not ignore the capability part as one competitive dynamic driving the actor strategies and reconfigurations of the network under geopolitical risks. Moreover, as aforementioned, the perception and interpretation of risk are produced within the nexus of the decision-making environment, the relational spatial-contextual factors, and the strategic agency bound to the organizational decision-maker cognition (Völlers et al., 2023). The risk in production networks should be seen as a specific driver of organizational behavior for each different actor, which is socially constructed. In the context of the Sino-US trade war and the COVID-19 pandemic, the multi-scalar GPN framework can help understand how the changing risk environments have affected the relocation of different firm actors from China to Vietnam. Although these two risks have created unprecedented challenges for global production networks and exposed their vulnerabilities, few studies so far have included these two most influential risks in the late 2010s into the analysis even though their impacts would likely add on each other and alter the firms' anticipated contemporary dynamics and strategies over time. And in connection, the mobile phone manufacturing sector is an ideal testbed due to its comparatively high-tech and value-added nature, highly geographical dispersion organization, and highly specialized production tasks and labor which make it relevant in both risks.

At the above conceptual and empirical backdrops, a multi-scalar analytical framework is developed to examine the regional development through de/recoupling in the production shift in the geopolitical risk dynamics (figure 8.1). This analytical framework elucidates the dynamic strategic coupling between various tiers of TNCs engaged in cross-border relocation, and variegated types of regional assets, that is, industrial zones developed by different levels of host governments drawing the development path transplanted

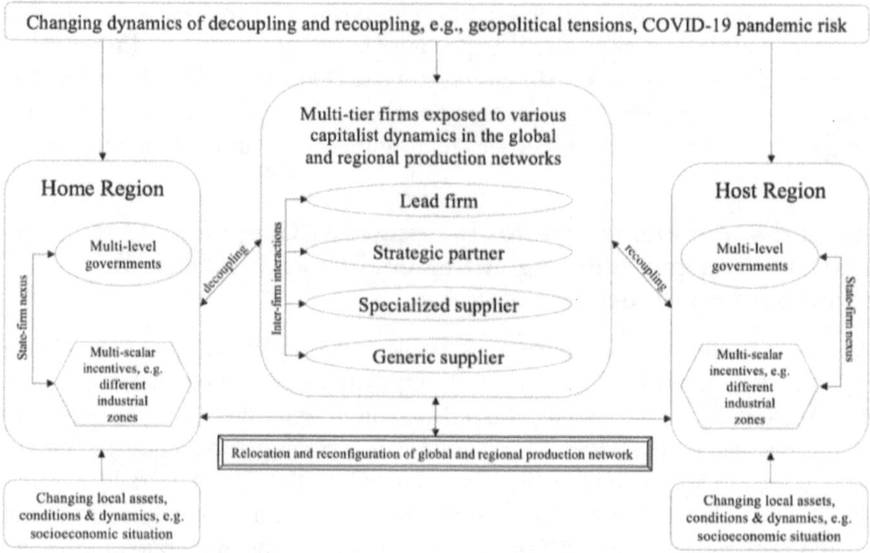

Figure 8.1 A Multi-scalar Analytical Framework for Investigating the Changing Dynamics of Strategic Coupling of Cross-border Production Networks. *Source*: Compiled by the authors.

across national borders under the changing GPN dynamics, with particular emphasis on the GPN risks at a broader scale. As indicated, the multi-scalar dynamics involve two parallel processes and concerned actors at multiple scales of dynamics associated with the cross-border production configuration. The first multi-scalar process refers to the cross-border relocation engaged by various tiers of firms in GPNs. The second multi-scalar process involves the development of regional assets, for example, industrial zones, by various levels of government in host regions. Apart from the formal institutions shaping the multi-scalar regional assets, the local dynamics of the region also contribute to molding the embedding soil for the GPN actors. In short, local/regional economic development could be understood through the strategic coupling engaged by various TNCs and host institutions, which aim to tide a node with the global production networks, in a way that maximizes the value created and captured for both sides. And as we also showed in chapter 6, the organizational mechanism for strategic coupling could be facilitated by the explicit multi-scalar matching among different tiers of GPN firms and divergent assets shaped by various levels of host institutions/governments. Last but not least, one should not see this as a static process but instead, as a temporal and spatial contingency of which the changing uncertainty and risk at different levels, for example, intra-firm/organization, inter-firm/organization, and extra-firm/organization, and the changing subjective perceptions and responses of actors of different social-spatial embeddedness levels meet. Hence, the resulting de/recoupling should be fully considered in a liquid and multi-scalar fashion. This analytical framework demonstrates the explicit scaling dynamics in the evolving processes of strategic coupling among different actors, which will be verified specifically by a vivid empirical analysis of the changing mechanism of strategic de/recoupling with the home region PRD and the host region RRD in the reconfiguration of the Asian regional networks of mobile phone production networks amid the Sino-US trade war and the COVID-19 pandemic in the following sections of this chapter.

DETAILED RESEARCH CONTEXT AND METHODS

The export-oriented development model was adopted by China, particularly starting in the 1980s when the TNCs started to move to the PRD mainly due to the price pressure and the growing competition from the firms in other Asian countries (Yeung, 2001). Besides the PRD, the Yangtze River Delta (YRD) has become another hotspot for the inflows of FDI, particularly for Taiwanese investors, since the late 1990s. Since the 2000s, the export-led regions in coastal China have faced unprecedented challenges. Apart from moving to inland China, such as Chongqing (Gao et al., 2017; Yang, 2013, 2017), there witnessed a growing number of TNCs moving out and establishing their manufacturing facilities beyond China, usually in the neighboring countries in Southeast Asia (Sturgeon & Zylberberg, 2016; Zhu & Pickles, 2014).

Since the late 1980s, Vietnam has started to reform and followed China's path to open the door. Massive inflows of FDI to Vietnam have been led by NIE TNCs, mainly from Japan, South Korea, and Singapore, which accounted for 11 percent, 20 percent, and 29 percent of the FDI inflow to Vietnam in 2021 (figure 8.2). The investment increase by these top investing countries was paralleled by the decrease in their investment in China during the same period (Chan & Yang, 2022b). Moreover, China has become an important investor in Vietnam reflected by the increase of China's FDI share from only 2 percent in 2012 to 7.7 percent in 2021 (figure 8.2). While the Sino-US trade war started in 2018 has not affected the growth of Vietnam's FDI overall (the FDI from Hong Kong and China to Vietnam even doubted in 2018–2019), the COVID-19 pandemic did as the value of the total registered projects in 2020 dropped 20 percent from 2019.

Vietnam, as an emerging electronics cluster, contributes a lion's share of electronics products in the world nowadays. As illustrated in table 8.1, Vietnam's phone exports have developed rapidly, accounting for 11.2 percent of the world total, in 2021, just following China. Surging from the eighth in 2011 to the second-largest phone exporter in 2021, the rapid development

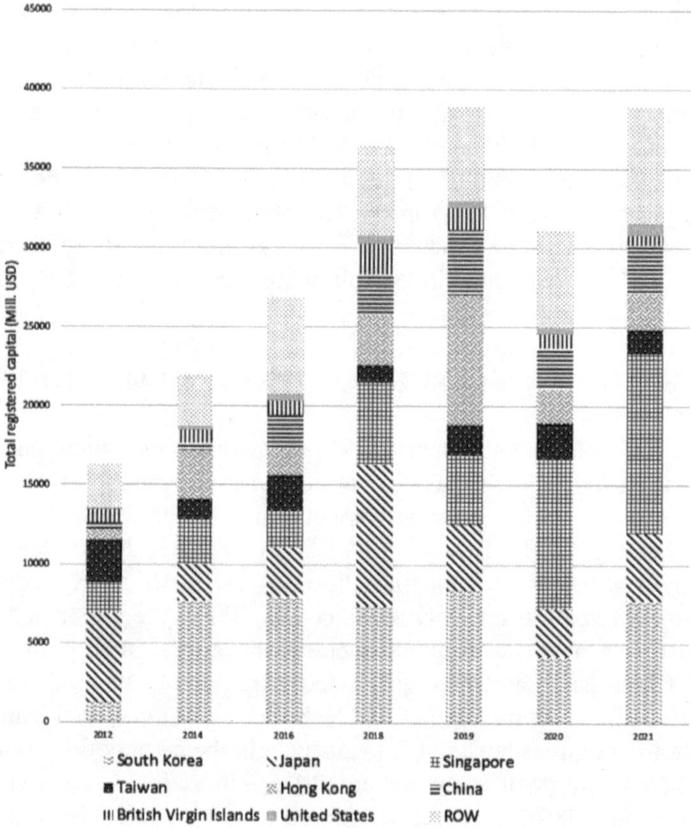

Figure 8.2 Foreign Direct Investment Projects Licensed by Main Counterparts by Year (2012–2021). *Source*: Compiled by the authors according to data from the General Statistics Office of Vietnam. Note: ROW = Rest of the World.

of Vietnam in a short span of ten years has been attributed to the inflow of notable lead firms in the global mobile phone industry, particularly Samsung. Samsung, having one of the largest production bases in Vietnam, focuses on manufacturing and distributing mobile phones and tablets in the RRD. Along with the relocation of TNCs out of China, various industrial zones as prevalent development paths in China's coastal regions have been followed and widely established by Vietnamese governments to attract and retain TNCs since the 2010s (Chan & Yang, 2022a; Kuchiki, 2007; UNIDO, 2015). While existing literature on this production relocation has mainly been conducted on the analysis of the push and pull factors at the national levels, there are inadequate updated investigations into the emerging risk dynamics in the changing geopolitical economy on driving the capitalist dynamics, such as the cost-capability ratio, and thus the cross-border relocation. The firm-specific

Table 8.1 Top Ten Phone Exporters and Their Respective Export Volume and Share in the World (2011–2021)

2011			*2013*			*2015*		
Top Ten Exporters	*Billion USD*	*Share*	*Top Ten Exporters*	*Billion USD*	*Share*	*Top Ten Exporters*	*Billion USD*	*Share*
China	64.80	38.2%	**China**	97.15	44.8%	**China**	125.51	51.9%
South Korea	15.09	8.9%	**Vietnam**	19.49	9.0%	**Vietnam**	25.22	10.4%
Hong Kong	10.98	6.5%	Hong Kong	17.14	7.9%	Hong Kong	22.48	9.3%
Taiwan	10.57	6.2%	South Korea	13.18	6.1%	United States	11.09	4.6%
Hungary	10.41	6.1%	United States	10.29	4.7%	South Korea	10.38	4.3%
Mexico	7.25	4.3%	Germany	6.08	2.8%	Singapore	6.19	2.6%
United States	7.05	4.2%	Taiwan	5.75	2.7%	Germany	5.53	2.3%
Vietnam	6.06	3.6%	Mexico	5.03	2.3%	United Arab Emirates	4.54	1.9%
Germany	4.89	2.9%	Singapore	4.80	2.2%	Slovakia	3.79	1.6%
Singapore	4.77	2.8%	Hungary	3.94	1.8%	Taiwan	2.81	1.2%
2017			*2019*			*2021*		
Top Ten Exporters	*Billion USD*	*Share*	*Top Ten Exporters*	*Billion USD*	*Share*	*Top Ten Exporters*	*Billion USD*	*Share*
China	127.53	49.5%	**China**	125.95	46.4%	**China**	147.66	49.2%
Vietnam	29.76	11.6%	**Vietnam**	34.26	12.6%	**Vietnam**	33.66	11.2%
Hong Kong	24.18	9.4%	Hong Kong	30.95	11.4%	Hong Kong	32.45	10.8%
United Arab Emirates	14.43	5.6%	United Arab Emirates	17.88	6.6%	United Arab Emirates	21.20	7.1%
United States	12.37	4.8%	United States	10.56	3.9%	United States	13.03	4.3%
South Korea	6.98	2.7%	Czechia	6.81	2.5%	Germany	5.98	2.0%
Germany	6.26	2.4%	Germany	5.57	2.1%	Czechia	5.55	1.9%
Slovakia	4.79	1.9%	South Korea	4.75	1.8%	Singapore	5.42	1.8%
Singapore	4.58	1.8%	Singapore	4.74	1.7%	South Korea	4.93	1.6%
Czechia	3.85	1.5%	Slovakia	3.85	1.4%	India	4.89	1.6%

Source: Compiled by the authors according to data from the UN Comtrade database.
Note: Telephone (including cell phone and smartphone) refers to category 76411 according to the SITC Rev. 4 commodity code.

strategies and causal effects on the multi-scalar strategic coupling of Vietnam's regional development in the reconfiguration of networks of mobile phone production lack conceptualization and empirical updates.

By catching up with the southern region in Vietnam, the share of FDI stock and the number of FDI projects in the RRD in northern Vietnam surged by 163 percent and 216 percent in a decade from 2011 to 2021 according to the General Statistics Office of Vietnam. In 2021, the RRD shared 34 percent and 30 percent of the total FDI project number and registered capital. According to our interviews, the physical connection to China, Vietnam's largest importer (figure 3.5), also serves as an attraction as it is more cost-efficient to import intermediates from China. After Vietnam joined the WTO, different electronics lead firms and their suppliers, such as Samsung, LG, Canon, Foxconn, and Flextronics, established their factories in the RRD, forming a relatively complete supply chain and making the RRD an electronics manufacturing hub (HKTDC, 2020; Sturgeon & Zylberberg, 2016). While the Government's Action Plan mapped out several new orientations and visions to make the RRD Vietnam's largest economic driver, the general secretary also asked party committees and organizations at all levels, sectors, and the entire political system in the localities to quickly devise exact plans to popularize and implement the resolution. Hence, various levels of Vietnam's government sharpening and implementing different policies ought to be interrogated.

This chapter is primarily built on the authors' study presented in chapter 6 of this book and is mainly based on our follow-up observation and online interviews from 2020 to early 2023. As stressed in figure 8.1, identifying how different tiers and levels of firms, host institutions, and regional assets interact under the GPN risks at multiple scales is important for understanding the changing de/recoupling dynamics. We intentionally kept contacting and updating various tiers of TNCs to analyze their strategies toward the multi-scalar dynamics and transition of strategic coupling with the RRD in the mobile phone production networks. Apart from the firsthand data, extensive secondary data from various sources, such as online interviews done by the media, firm reports, statistical yearbooks and publications by governments, research institutions, and business analysts, was also studied to validate our observations amid the pandemic when the travel ban was in place.

GEOPOLITICAL DYNAMICS OF DECOUPLING AND RECOUPLING IN THE MOBILE PHONE PRODUCTION SHIFT FROM CHINA TO VIETNAM

Previous analysis of production shift has mainly focused on either domestic conditions as push factors or external ones in host regions as pull factors.

Comprehensive and updated investigations into the interplay among multiple dynamics at various levels involving geopolitical and economic dynamics together are lacking. We argue that the shift in mobile phone production is due to a combination of factors, including not only the rising costs in China but as much as the tensions between China and the United States and the desire for companies to diversify their supply chains, particularly resulting from the disruption during the COVID-19 pandemic. The emerging decoupling and recoupling dynamics could be understood based on the established multi-scalar analytical framework in figure 8.1.

Changing decoupling and recoupling dynamics have emerged in relation to cost-capability optimization within the network through cross-border relocation. Companies' concerns when picking places to make their goods are not only about the manufacturing price and the time it takes to ship the finished products to market but also, increasingly, about the diversification of the locations. Local-level conditions highlighted in figure 8.1 contribute significantly to explaining the spatial reconfigurations of production relocation. Figure 8.3 illustrates that more provinces in northern Vietnam, particularly in the RRD, have been ranked as "excellent" and "high" for their provincial competitiveness index (PCI) composed of business costs, infrastructure, policy implantation, and so on. However, the reason for this shift away from China is not down to the environment and cost alone as labor and manufacturing account for less than 2 percent of the cost of a phone (Interview in Hai Phong, December 2019). One should also consider the capability. Compared with the RRD as an emerging cluster of mobile phone production, echoed by Chan and Yang (2022a), China indeed has advantages in skill sets in manufacturing operations and engineering talent and access to a network of suppliers that can act quickly and react to changing market conditions (Online interview, April 2020). Apart from the local conditions, global-level GPN dynamics should also be highlighted in altering TNCs' strategies (figure 8.1).

Second, the decoupling dynamics that have emerged since the Sino-US trade war initiated during the Trump administration reflected by increased tariffs on a wide range of goods have had a significant impact on the shift of production. The trade war has been driven by several factors, including the US protectionist stance to maintain dominance in global trade and China's aspiration to move up the technological ladder. The Sino-US tensions had tightened before the trade war, but the tariff increase has put more urgency on manufacturers to diversify production. The higher US tariffs on a wide range of Chinese exports have directly driven manufacturers to relocate from China toward alternative manufacturing hubs in Vietnam. While keeping China for advanced functions such as producing higher value-added components, the lower-end manufacturing tasks have been moving to Vietnam,

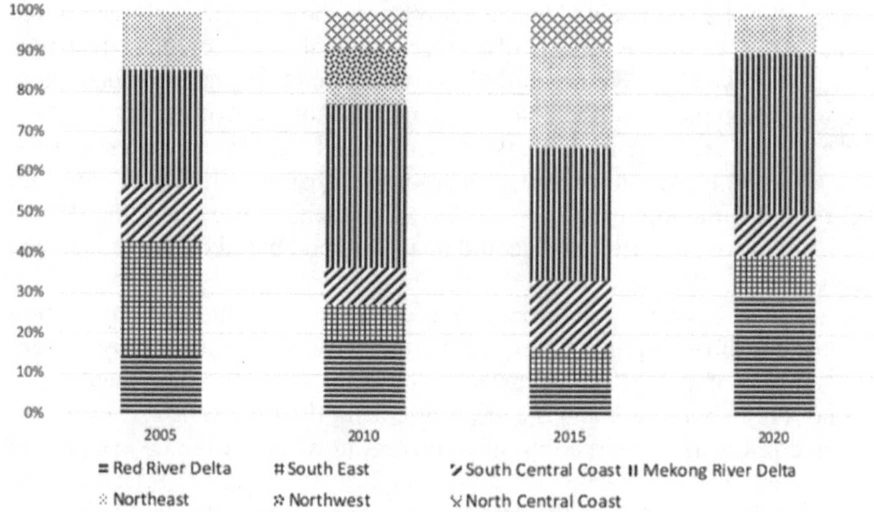

Figure 8.3 Regional Share of the Provinces Ranked as "Excellent" and "High" in the Provincial Competitiveness Index (2005–2020). *Source*: Compiled by the authors according to data from Vietnam Chamber of Commerce and Industry (VCCI).

which indicates a partial relocation, rather than a complete relocation, as the common discourse of "decoupling from China."

Interestingly, as commented by the interviewed firms, "China Plus One" is more easily said than done. As noted, even though manufacturing in China has been more expansive, China is still the "World Factory" not only because it has abundant labor but also because that labor force is increasingly higher skilled and includes more than 200 million people who can flexibly move across producers as demand fluctuates. As Jay Foreman, the CEO of Basic Fun, has put it: "China offers a suite of benefits . . . a highly trained labor force, a well-financed infrastructure, a great safety and quality control regime, excellent transportation and communication points" (Harvard Business Review, 2021). He acknowledges that moving operations is difficult. "For example, if we went to Vietnam . . . it's only 10% of the size of China. So, if you just moved 5% or 10% of Chinese production into Vietnam, you're going to max out the capacity . . . You can go to India . . . but India's infrastructure is really not set up for this." Companies that are heavily dependent on China for their upstream activities may also face difficulties independent of tariffs or labor but the supply of intermediaries. That said, the "China Plus One" strategy induced by the Sino-US trade war can only be partly explained by the cost-capability ratio as China still has its competitive edge but needed to concern about the risk dynamics beyond the region.

"The move was requested by Apple," said a person with knowledge of the plan inside Foxconn (Lee, 2020). Apart from the lower-tier manufacturers following the calls of the brand-name lead firms, lead firms and some domestic suppliers in China expanded to Vietnam actively trying to avoid the risk associated with the trade war. According to a senior executive with one of China's biggest original product manufacturing facilities in Shenzhen in the Pearl River Delta (Online interview, May 2019), they felt very lucky that their products had not been on the list of tariffs so far. Although they were very low-key and did not make any opinion on trade war-related topics in fear of getting the United States' attention, they together with other Chinese firms decided to expand to Vietnam and set up factories. "Our clients (brand-name firms) did not push us to expand at this moment. But what if our products were listed (on the tariff list) next time? We do not want to lose our business," said one senior executive (Online interview, May 2019), "to be honest, we cannot tell whether the relocation at the end is beneficial or not . . . but a lot of our friends moved to Vietnam already." It is not surprising to see a rocketing 112 percent increase in the FDI from China and Hong Kong to Vietnam in 2018–2019 (figure 8.2).

Third, our follow-up interviews indicate that the relocation of mobile phone production from China to Vietnam has kept on even during the COVID-19 pandemic. Of no doubt, this global-level risk affects both China and Vietnam as much as other countries with export-led economies. However, summarized explicitly by the chairman and president of the Vietnam Chamber of Commerce and Industry (VCCI) (2020), "despite the unavoidable negative effects from the pandemic, thanks to its impressive efforts to contain the virus and investors' shifting strategy, Vietnam remains in a position to take advantage of U.S.-China trade tensions to cement its role as one of the world's factories. It is imperative . . . in attracting foreign firms that are seeking to diversify away from and move out of China." Although there was a temporary drop in 2020, Vietnam's FDI inflow rebounded in 2021 to 2019's level (figure 8.2). Echoing the provincial competitiveness index (PCI) reports of 2020 and 2021, the majority of TNCs we interviewed were busy dealing with the setbacks brought by the pandemic, such as lockdowns and transportation restrictions that caused disruptions in production and distribution; nevertheless, their cross-border relocation activities have been only curtailed not stopped.

They, however, would not change, at least in the short term, their overall business strategies, including investing and expanding in Vietnam. "Although it (the pandemic) has made us more careful in making investment decisions, we still needed to invest here (Vietnam) . . . While the pandemic is inevitable, the trade war is not . . . We cannot predict how long will COVID-19 last . . . As going out of China is a must, it should be done sooner than later," explained a Chinese supplier that expanded to Vietnam in 2020 (Online interview, November 2020). Apart from the rebound of inward FDI, as further proven by the PCI report (VCCI, 2020), 41 percent of Chinese foreign-invested enterprises (FIEs) in Vietnam in the 2020 sample (of over 1,500 FIEs in total) are new entrants and among these new entrants, 40 percent of them are exporters, more than a double in share compared to previous years. Interestingly, one year later in 2021 when COVID-19 was still severe, improving from 41 percent in 2020, 48 percent of FIEs in Vietnam considered expanding in the next two years (VCCI, 2021). Nearly half of the FIEs, especially the export-oriented ones, believed that they could operate indefinitely in Vietnam given the current economic and COVID-19 conditions and were expecting a V-shaped recovery of the global market. "There is no other country stricter than the 'zero-COVID' policy here (in China). If we can survive here, there should not be more challenging staying in Vietnam," said a Chinese generic supplier's manager (Online interview, July 2021).

Based on the earlier in situ investigations and online interviews amid the pandemic and follow-up observations after the release of travel restrictions in late 2022 and early 2023, instead of the popular "decoupling" discourse of leaving China completely, we saw that the "China Plus One" as a reconfiguration strategy has been prominent for the electronics manufacturers of various tiers. After analyzing foreign investment survey reports by VCCI over multiple years, compared to other alternative destinations like China and Thailand, stable politics and fewer policy uncertainties were the top two attractions of investing in Vietnam in 2020, with the latter one's significance surging from 2015. As pointed out in 2020 by Foxconn chairman Liu Youngway, moving some production to Vietnam is to provide "two sets of supply chains" as the Sino-US trade war had split the world into two (Lee, 2020). Even though the global-level uncertainties as indicated in figure 8.1 have significant impacts on GPN firms' strategies to reorganize their activities thus leading to the dynamic de/recoupling in the region, the risks of the Sino-US trade war and the pandemic perceived by the actors and hence their responses were indeed different. Our interviews revealed that while the trade war was a fundamental shock stimulating the relocation, the pandemic was regarded as a rather short-term hardship that slowed down the process.

As aforementioned, apart from the rational thinking between cost and capability, the logic of GPN risk as a broader driver cannot exclude the firm-based sensemaking of reality and the strategy-making process that is beyond the calculation and embedded within a relational web of social relations, place-specific contexts, and decision-making environments. According to our observations, apart from those who were asked by their clients, since the Sino-US trade war has been perceived by the firms as a risk that could last for a long period, and together with the decoupling of other surrounding firms with social connections, the decision-makers decided to relocate to Vietnam even without a clear and detailed cost-capability calculation. On the other hand, owing to the perception of the firm decision-makers that the pandemic is a global-level risk that might not last long and, more importantly, that the anti-pandemic policies are the strictest in China, the relocations from China to Vietnam had been rebounded in a short span even amid the pandemic. As our follow-up investigations demonstrated, different GPN firms did have their attributes and ways to cope with these impacts in different stages of these risks. The institution of the firm's origin also matters. While Japanese firms, which are known to be relatively conservative in their FDI strategies according to our interviews, originally planned to postpone their relocation plan, after the announcement of a 2.2 billion USD fund by the Japanese government to pay its manufacturers to move out of China in April 2020, their investments to Vietnam have been increased in 2021 as shown in figure 8.2. Overall, Vietnam has become an increasingly popular destination for companies originally coupled with China looking to diversify their production facilities. Besides the societal and territorial embeddedness, which could affect the risk interpretations and subsequent strategies as shown earlier, the network embeddedness also does (Völlers et al., 2023). That said, how an actor is embedded in what network does affect how they perceive the GPN risks and how they respond. And as pointed out, this is seldom an objective decision. Thus, what remains underexplored is how and in what ways the different tiers of TNCs have engaged in relocation and the changing mechanism of strategic coupling of the RRD in the reconfigured cross-border production networks.

DECOUPLING AND RECOUPLING OF REGIONAL DEVELOPMENT IN THE RECONFIGURATION OF CROSS-BORDER PRODUCTION NETWORKS

Distinctive Decoupling from China: Samsung vs. Apple

Drawing upon the lead firm-centered reconfiguration framework conceptualized by GPN 2.0 theory (Coe & Yeung, 2015), we identified different practices of lead firm-led decoupling and recoupling in the reconfiguration of cross-border production relocation, reflected by the cases of Apple and Samsung in the pre-, amid, and post-pandemic geopolitical context when the Sino-US relationship remains tense.

In 2019, Samsung closed its last mobile phone plant in China, moving assembly to lower-cost locations like Vietnam (and India), in part because it was reportedly losing out China's market to Chinese competitors like Huawei and Xiaomi. In an attempt to couple with Vietnam, Samsung Electronics has established a plan to produce 46 percent of its total mobile devices in Vietnam's Thai Nguyen and Bac Ninh provinces, both located in the RRD, in 2023, which indicates the company's increasing reliance on Vietnam as a production base (Etnews, 2022). Since it granted its first Investment Registration Certificate in 2008, Samsung has multiplied its investment capital in Vietnam by thirty-two times. According to the latest data (Lăng, 2022), with a nearly 19 billion USD investment, Samsung has established six manufacturing factories (four in the RRD region) with an R&D center in Hanoi. Apart from smartphones, Samsung will further relocate its screen and semiconductor productions in Vietnam in the short future (Hoang, 2022; Reuters, 2020). As affirmed by the general director of Samsung Vietnam Mr Choi (Lăng, 2022; Giang, 2023), Samsung has had no plan to relocate to India and has not changed its pace of development in Vietnam despite the complications of the COVID-19 pandemic. It will also encourage its vendors to expand to Vietnam together. Hence, despite suffering a heavy blow from the fourth COVID-19 wave in 2021, Samsung announced in January 2022 that its total revenue in Vietnam reached 74.2 billion USD, up 14 percent compared to 2020.

Different from Samsung, which started the expansion in the late 2000s, Apple's plan to expand to Vietnam has recently started to come up the water surface. Being a dual player who has a high extent to which they are focused both on upstream activities and on downstream activities, as described by Black and Morrison (Harvard Business Review, 2021), Apple's best strategy to deal with the recent challenges, that is, the Chinese government favoring indigenous players and the import tariffs imposed by the United States, is to use an *in* China *for* China strategy (originally italic). While keeping the production network in China, it has effectively decoupled to try to establish other production networks for other markets besides China. Yet, it is easier said than done, although Apple got a more concrete plan to move its MacBooks production from China to Vietnam with the assistance of its top supplier, Foxconn, very recently (Forbes, 2023). Currently, Apple still assembles 100 percent of its more than 200 million iPhones in China each year. A CNN Business article titled "Why Can't Apple Quit China?" (Iyengar, 2022) recently pointed out that China is still its biggest market outside the United States accounting for nearly a quarter of Apple's global sales. On the other hand, Apple's CEO, Tim Cook, once noted: "China has moved into very advanced manufacturing, so you find in China the intersection of craftsman kind of skill and sophisticated robotics and . . . computer science . . . That intersection, which is very rare to find anywhere . . . is very important to our business because of the precision and quality level that we like" (Harvard Business Review, 2021). Despite the common saying that the turmoil caused by China's "zero-COVID" strategy, with strict lockdowns in major parts of the country halting production at several factories—including those of Apple's contract manufacturers Foxconn and Pegatron—and disrupting global supply chains, is the direct driver leading to

Apple's moving decision to Vietnam, we argue that this might not be the main reason not only because there were also restrictive and prolonged lockdowns in Vietnam but, more importantly, as reflected by our interviewees as well as the senior vice president at strategic advisory firm Dentons Global Advisors Paul Triolo, "COVID lockdowns will force some companies to diversify their manufacturing locations, the zero-COVID policy will not permanently damage China's status," said in an interview (Iyengar, 2022); the major escalation in Taiwan, on the other hand, "would be a much more important signpost in determining China's future as a manufacturing hub." That said, unlike Samsung, Apple has not explicitly decoupled with China as "either as a market or as a manufacturing base, Apple will not give up on China while they also need to diversify their manufacturing to other locations to handle the increasingly heightened US's protectionism," said a manager of Apple's specialized supplier (Online interview, July 2021). Hence, despite both Samsung and Apple planning to expand to Vietnam, after balancing their attributes, such as the cost capabilities, their ways of decoupling and recoupling to handle the geopolitical risk were different, warranting further exploration.

The lead firm-centered vertical and network relationships in the strategic coupling of the RRD have brought about profound implications for the cross-border production configuration. The implications could vary, according to figure 8.1, depending on the firm- and network-specific attributes since how firms react to the changing dynamics and the strategies they deploy to reorganize their networks and thus the ways of how coupling happened and the subsequent regional developmental outcomes largely differ. First, the lead firms in the mobile phone production networks may seek out new suppliers in the RRD to replace those left behind in China. This could lead to the formation of new relationships between lead firms and suppliers. Second, existing suppliers in the RRD may seek to upgrade their capabilities to meet the demands of lead firms in the networks. This could lead to a strengthening of existing relationships between lead firms and suppliers, resulting in a more robust strategic coupling and increased value captured by the actors in the host region, which is seen as ideal for the host governments. Of course, the relocation of production from China to Vietnam could on the other hand result in increased competition between suppliers in the RRD and eventually lead to a "race to bottom" situation, which could be a dark side of strategic coupling (Phelps et al., 2018; Yeung, 2021b). Indeed, in connection to coupling dynamics as well as the regional development outcomes, the current chapter discovers that the ways how these two lead firms coordinated their production networks have fundamental impacts on the multi-scalar coupling processes and in turn lead to very different relocation progresses and development outcomes.

Multi-scalar Recoupling with the RRD in the Production Shift from China

Before dissecting the embedding and coupling process of these actors with the ones in Vietnam, one should notice the differences between the relatively closed production network of Samsung and the relatively opened one of Apple (see, e.g., Yeung, 2022b) and the rising coordinating power of Foxconn as Apple's strategic partner (see, e.g., Yang, 2017). The combined effects may lead to different practices of recoupling with the RRD, reflected by different engagement in various levels of industrial parks (see table 6.4).

Drawing lessons from China, different levels of Vietnamese governments have initiated various policies to promote export-oriented development (Anh et al., 2014; Chan & Yang, 2022b). To attract the inflows of TNCs, particularly from China, the decree on the establishment of export-processing zones (EPZs) was promulgated firstly in 1991 to create a favorable business environment. Various zones, including more general industrial zones (IZs), economic development zones (EDZs), and high-tech zones (HTZs), have been established since then. During Vietnam's economic reform, the decentralization initiatives have enabled provincial and local authorities to gain certain power and "freedom" to develop their economies (Nguyen et al., 2004). And these zones have been developed and managed by various levels of the Vietnamese government, which enable the explicit multi-scalar strategic coupling, to transplant the manufacturing industries to Vietnam (Liang et al., 2021). As shown in table 6.4, in general, the financial incentives offered in EDZs and HTZs are much higher than those in IZs and EPZs. Nonetheless, they have higher thresholds, such as requirements for investment amount and investing sector. Unlike chapter 6 in which we dived in to see the detailed extra-firm deliberations between each tier of the firm, that is, LG, Foxconn, and the lower tier suppliers, and the multi-scalar host institution using the four building components of a state-firm relationship, we focus more on comparing the cases of Samsung as well as Apple and its strategic partner, Foxconn, in the following section to see how they recouple differently with the RRD's multi-scalar institution, especially under the GPN risks.

Global lead firms, such as Samsung, have been deliberately attracted to the national-level industrial zones by the Vietnamese government long before these GPN risks. China was the key assembly hub of Samsung before the 2010s. In the late 2000s, Samsung started to relocate its production to Vietnam and opened its first mobile phone plant in Vietnam in Bac Ninh Province (figure 3.5) in 2009 with a nearly 700 million USD investment. After just a decade, by employing approximately 160,000 workers in Vietnam (Hosokawa & Tomiyama, 2018), Samsung has become Vietnam's largest investor and exporter contributing roughly a quarter of Vietnam's total export value.

Apart from structural coupling to take advantage of Vietnam's regional assets, that is, low costs and preferential policies in IZs and EPZs, Samsung has started to transplant parts of its higher value-added activities to couple with Vietnam functionally, particularly by embedding into HTZs, in recent years. For example, Samsung has commenced the construction of a 220 million USD worth R&D center in Hanoi, which will focus on the 5G network technology. "The R&D center not only proves Samsung's long-term investment commitment in Vietnam but also shows the group's determination to support the country in becoming the leading manufacturing hub in Southeast Asia," said Mr. Choi, the general director of Samsung Vietnam, in a press release (VCCI, 2022). The functional coupling and a rather deep embedding of Samsung in Vietnam is indeed the result of the bargaining between Samsung and the national-level governments in Vietnam, as remarked by an interviewee, "(O)f course, we all (different levels of Vietnamese governments) want to take advantage of Samsung in setting up R&D sectors and to benefit the local firms . . . while higher-level officials have higher expectations for Samsung, the provincial ones are satisfied with Samsung just being in their province and contributing to the GDP" (Interview in Hanoi, December 2017). Yet, as admitted by a provincial government official in Bac Giang, although most provinces want to attract Samsung, they failed to do so because what they can offer is limited and restricted compared with that of the prime minister (Interview in Bac Giang, December 2017). Hence, the extra-firm bargaining in the recoupling mainly happened between the national-level governments and Samsung. On the one hand, Samsung has structurally coupled with and embedded in IZs and EPZs in Vietnam and relocated its production plants by taking advantage of the regional assets like other TNCs. On the other hand, Samsung has also functionally coupled with HTZs governed by the national-level government in Vietnam enjoying even more favorable incentives by expanding their R&D activities to Vietnam in return. That is, the Vietnamese government has satisfactorily facilitated the transplantation of the low value-added electronics manufacturing activities of Samsung from China via IZs and EPZs while also bargained with Samsung to functionally recouple with Vietnam and develop a higher value-added electronics production development path by offering national administrative-level HTZs and other preferential policies.

More interestingly, the pandemic did not prevent Samsung from relocating to Vietnam, according to our follow-up interviews. Instead, the unexpected pandemic has led to an even deeper embedding of Samsung into Vietnam. Echoing the findings by VCCI (2020), which stated that "almost 23% of foreign operations altered their supply chains by shifting purchases to new suppliers," the local suppliers thus had more chances to participate in the global production networks amid the COVID-19 due to the logistics disruption. Although the number of Vietnamese enterprises selected as the first-tier supplier of Samsung has not drastically increased under the pandemic (from four to forty-two in 2019 and fifty in 2020) as the requirements of Samsung remain high and upgrading of the local suppliers takes time, the increase of second-tier suppliers was observable; the number of Vietnamese enterprises participating in Samsung's supply chain surged rapidly to 191 (VietnamPlus, 2021). As confirmed by our interviewee working as a consultant in Vietnam (Online interview, July 2022), "particularly during the pandemic in 2020–2022, more domestic generic suppliers in Vietnam got the opportunity to work with Samsung . . . not sure if this is still the case after the COVID-19 shock." In addition, the proactive recoupling with Vietnam was not only reflected by simply including Vietnamese suppliers but also by the "domestic business improvement consulting program" implemented by Samsung even amid the pandemic to improve productivity, management capacity, and product supply capacity so that Vietnamese enterprises could update and join its supply chain (VietnamPlus, 2021).

Unlike the case of the brand-name manufacturer Samsung, the relocation progress of Foxconn—Apple's biggest contract manufacturer—has not been as smooth as according to chapter 6. Briefly speaking, the attempt to relocate to Vietnam did not come after the trade war or the pandemic but could at least date back to the mid-2000s according to our study. Even though provincial governments in general welcomed and did their best to facilitate Foxconn, what Foxconn asked could only be provided by the national-level government. Yet, Foxconn could neither commit to a deeper embedding nor establish functional coupling with Vietnam in return for enjoying the preferential policies of HTZs and EZs back then. Acting as a strategic partner of Apple in the production network, it was observed by Yang (2017) that Foxconn has played an increasingly significant role in coordinating the production relocation to inland China to leverage the lower costs and the emerging domestic market. Unlike the successful case moving within China, Foxconn faced a challenging situation relocating to Vietnam. On one hand, as a newcomer, its status in Vietnam could never compare with the one in China. On the other hand, it is more about Foxconn's network position and embeddedness as stressed in the multi-scalar framework in figure 8.1, which would greatly affect its cost-capability optimizing and risk-responding strategies. "Foxconn could not commit too much (in the late 2000s) to Vietnam's government as Apple itself has not yet made up its mind or not yet indicated precisely where to go . . . Besides Vietnam, India, Thailand, and even US are possible locations," said a long-term supplier of Foxconn (Online interview, April 2020). Unlike the relocation within China, the cross-border production relocation of Foxconn could face the uncertainties raised by both changing assets, conditions, and dynamics at the local level as well as the recently heightened global-level geopolitical risks. Not only limited by the extent and the type of investments and production activities that Foxconn can relocate to Vietnam as the higher value-added activities like R&D have been strictly controlled by the lead firm, that is, Apple, Foxconn also had no choice but to import most components at that time, which further decreased its power bargaining with the national-level governments. "They (Foxconn) dare not to use the domestic vendors in Vietnam . . . If anything happens, it would be on their own shoulders," said a specialized supplier of Foxconn (Interview in Bac Ninh, December 2017). Compared to the so-called "closed" network of Samsung that is now gradually opening to domestic suppliers in Vietnam, Foxconn would not and could not easily alter its suppliers as it needs to ensure the best quality of their products, not to mention the fact that "(T)hey do not even know whether Apple really wants to shift to Vietnam at the end of the day." Until very recently, Foxconn has been rebuilding assembly lines for Apple's iPad tablet and MacBook laptop at its plant in Bac Giang province (figure 3.5) to take some production from China (Lee, 2020). Distant from the attempt in the late 2000s, this current relocation has been requested by Apple itself to diversify the risk of the trade war. While it is out of this chapter's and this book's scope and our ability to predict the future, it would be insightful to keep updating the coupling of Foxconn's production network with Vietnam's governments at various levels with the support from Apple in the coming post-pandemic era and to compare it with that of Samsung.

On a side note, compared with the rather explicit de/recoupling engaged by lead firms, for example, Apple and Samsung, and their strategic partners, for example, Foxconn, the lower-tier suppliers have undertaken a relatively implicit way of doing so. "We are in the middle of the fight . . . and we need to dodge down and not to let the local officials (in China) know we are expanding," said a manager of a lower-tier Chinese supplier (Online interview, November 2020), "while they (the lead firms) can use leaving as a chip to bargain, we will be labelled as not loyal (to China) in this conflict (between the US and China)." According to our interviews, no matter whether these lower-tier suppliers were asked by their clients or did it self-initially, all decoupled their production with China as low-key as possible as they reckoned that their "China Plus One" strategy could raise another "geopolitical risk," albeit at a much lower scale.

CONCLUSION AND DISCUSSION

This chapter offers an updated and novel investigation of the geopolitical dynamics and risks of strategic coupling in the mobile phone production shift from China and Vietnam, amidst the Sino-US trade war and the COVID-19 pandemic. Despite the fashionable discourse of decoupling from China induced by the pandemic-caused supply chain disruption, we argue that both lead firms and supplier TNCs have increasingly engaged in the prevalent "China Plus One" strategy before the trade war and pandemic. The mobile phone production network has been reconfigured by the changing local conditions in China and Vietnam as well as the heightened geopolitical tension and pandemic-induced risks at the global level. Verified by the case studies of Samsung, Apple, Foxconn, and China-based lower-tier supplier firms, we explore why and how different tiers of TNCs in the mobile phone production networks have responded strategically to the geopolitical dynamics and risk environment. By comparing the de/recoupling process and the relocation progress from China to Vietnam mainly between Samsung and Apple (with Foxconn as its strategic partner) under the changing competitive dynamics and risks of the global production network, the updated study sheds light on the impacts of firms' own attributes, for example, cost-capability ratio, societal and territorial embeddedness, as well as of their network relationships and organizational configurations on how they perceive and respond to the GPN risks and the subsequent extra-firm bargaining and coupling results.

Echoed to chapter 6, this chapter demonstrates that the development of the RRD into an emerging mobile phone cluster has been driven by a multilevel recoupling between various tiers of TNCs and different levels of the Vietnamese government. Different from the domination by Hong Kong and Taiwanese TNCs in the coastal regions of China, the cross-border electronics production expansion to the RRD has been primarily led by the inflows of NIE TNCs. Unlike the relatively "closed" production networks of Taiwanese electronics TNCs in mainland China (Yang, 2009), we elucidated that the emergence of mobile phone cluster in the RRD has been driven by a "semi-opened" production network, because of the multi-scalar extra-firm bargaining between the lead firm, that is, Samsung (and LG as shown in chapter 6), and various tiers of the host governments shaping and molding the regional assets using different development zone policies. Whereas Foxconn, as Apple's strategic partner, would and could only structurally couple with Vietnam with a much lower power over the activities to be relocated, over the inclusion of domestic vendors in the host region, and thus over the extra-firm bargaining with Vietnamese governments for more preferential treatments. Hopefully, the multi-scalar analytical framework depicted in figure 8.1 can be used to account for the cross-border production reconfiguration engaged by TNCs of different tiers in variegated industries/sectors and examine the subsequent effects of de/recoupling on local development in different regions with various levels of institutions under the uncertainties and crises in the global economic landscape.

Another valuable lesson from this chapter is that exogenous shocks could impact the operations of and interactions among multiple production networks at various scales differently as illustrated in figure 8.1. Apart from the often-used cost-based calculation, external uncertainties and risks should be considered, together with the actor's specific attributes, as a capitalist dynamic instead of just a background for a fuller picture of the network reconfiguration. Although the friction between China and the United States has accelerated the production relocation from China to Vietnam and the reconfiguration of the electronics production network in the region, both lead firms and suppliers have shown to be increasingly engaged in the prevalent "China Plus One" strategy driven by the concerns of cost-capability ratio but more so the uncertainties under the heightened geopolitical tension with the pandemic-induced supply chain disruption. The cost-capability optimizations as well as the risk-responding strategies and thus the ways how Samsung and Apple reconfigured their networks and hence their coupling and relocation progresses diverged. In connection, as stressed earlier, seeing the response to the GPN risks as an objective and rational economic concern runs the danger of decontextualizing by disconnecting the perception of and response to the risk environments from the decision-making environment. One should notice that the notion of risk is indeed a fluid and subjective interpretation of the crisis and the tolerance by the firms and their managers who are societal, territorial, and network embedded within a relational web of social relations, place-specific contexts, and decision-making environments. In addition to the changing geopolitical environment, exploring how the pandemic has influenced the production systems at multiple levels would be imperative to study the regional development in the transition toward less globalized production in the post-COVID-19 time. Little effort has been paid to update the reconfigurations of the electronics production networks since the pandemic. Contrary to the common belief, according to our preliminary observation from the follow-up investigations, the pandemic has been predominantly treated as a rather short-term hardship and has not been perceived as impactful as the Sino-US trade war by the actors we interviewed mainly owing to the fact that the lockdowns and factory closures have been seen in both Vietnam and China with the latter having stricter anti-pandemic policies, and more importantly, they anticipated a longer-lasting effect of the trade war than the COVID-19 pandemic.

All in all, geopolitical dynamics and risks of strategic coupling in the mobile phone production shift from China to Vietnam are indeed a highly complex and dynamic topic requiring frequent revisions and a multi-scalar exploration of the impacts of changing capitalist dynamics on the actors and hence their firm-specific responses and thus the de/recoupling of the regions as well as the reconfigurations of the production networks. Drawing mainly upon the GPN 2.0 notion, figure 8.1 provides a rather intuitive and systemic framework for doing so. Although our follow-up observation lasted till early 2023, the post-pandemic situation still might not be fully captured.

The questions of how and why Samsung, Apple, and one of the largest electronics contract manufacturers in the world - Foxconn, are going to relocate from China to Vietnam or other Southeast Asian countries as well as the subsequent impacts on the global mobile phone production landscape and Vietnam's regional development warrant further study. In addition, while the mobile phone production networks are still highly globalized, whether the current GPN risks would leave a long-term impact and lead to further pushback against the cross-border organization of production for other sectors in other host regions and whether the roles and influences of the state would become more explicit and developmental in the post-pandemic era to stimulate the domestic industries deserve a spotlight in future research.

Chapter 9

Conclusion and Discussion

After going through four previous empirical chapters, that is, chapters 5–8, this chapter gives a summary of the significance of the current monograph focusing on the recent wave of production relocations in the electronics industry from China to Vietnam, including the detailed relocation patterns and the reconfiguration of the production networks at multiple scales with various actors involved. Both theoretical and empirical contributions and pragmatic empirical advice will be presented after showcasing the summary of the major research findings of our study. The limitations of the current research project and the future research arenas, particularly related to the recently emerging forces driving the restructuring of global economic activities in the late 2010s, will also be discussed at the end of this chapter.

HIGHLIGHTS ON THE CURRENT PRODUCTION RELOCATION OF ELECTRONICS MANUFACTURING TO VIETNAM

To reiterate, the main objective of this monograph is to explore how labor-intensive industry has expanded from the "World Factory" to developing Southeast Asia under the changing dynamics in global and regional production networks, using the case study of the production relocations of the consumer electronics manufacturing industry from China to Vietnam. The main focus of our study has been on the overall picture of the restructuring of electronics production networks and on Vietnam's internationalization to see its trade and FDI patterns, its changing roles and functions in the related production networks, as well as its coupling processes and subsequent regional developments. This book aims to provide a comprehensive look into the production relocations from China to developing Southeast Asia, that is, Vietnam, under the reconfigurations of the multi-scalar production network both spatially and organizationally, as well as the articulation of Vietnam into the global and regional electronics production networks. After an in-depth critical review of both theoretical and empirical literature related to the theorization of cross-border production activities coordinated by the TNCs, as well as the production relocations in the electronics manufacturing industry (along with the semiconductor sector and another labor-intensive industry—the textile and garment industry), several important research gaps were identified in chapter 2. Following a brief introduction to the research area and methodology in chapters 3 and 4, using mainly the statistical data extensively collected from different online databases and statistical yearbooks, the authors closely looked into the restructuring of the global and regional electronics production networks and Vietnam's participation in these networks to grasp an overall understanding of the changing dynamics in the "Global South" in chapter 5. In chapters 6 and 7, the conducted firm-level investigations, particularly the in-depth interviews in the RRD and the South East region, were presented to explore how the production networks have expanded and restructured among various firm and nonfirm actors in both host and home regions, providing more about the strategic coupling processes in detail and the regional development of Vietnam. Based on our updated observations amid the Sino-US trade war and the COVID-19 pandemic, chapter 8 investigated how these two recently emerged GPN risks in the late 2010s have impacted the actors and hence the production network configuration. The major findings of our study presented in this book are highlighted as follows.

The production relocation of the electronics manufacturing industry from China to Vietnam, which has been increasingly witnessed since the 2000s and accelerated since 2007 after Vietnam participated in the World Trade Organization, is not a simple relocation and/or expansion process that has been forced by the conventional lead firms from advanced economies solely to lower the cost-capability ratio, but it is a rather complicated and multi-scalar process that has been simultaneously driven by various tiers of firms from different origins out of various dynamics at different scales. Apart from the relatively "traditional" endogenous drivers, such as the pull factors: lower production costs and the abundant labor and production factor supply in the host regions and the push factors: heightening the rule of law and the rising costs in the home countries, particularly in the aftermath of the global financial crisis in 2008, the shrinking demands of the transitional customers, that is, the advanced economies in the West, as well as the rising consumption level of the emerging and developing economies, have also initiated the current wave of production relocations. Besides these endogenous factors, exogenous factors caused by the recent changing international political economy situations also bring new dynamics into the global production systems and foster the current wave of production relocations from China to Vietnam. First, the Sino-US trade war that started in 2018 between the "World Factory"—China—and the United States has pushed the firms located in China to relocate their productions, especially the final assembling works, to other low-cost developing countries nearby where there is an overall better international trade regime, such as Vietnam, to avoid the extra import tariffs imposed by the latter. Second, under China's OBOR initiative since 2013, there is the potential that the regional socioeconomic developments, such as the infrastructures of countries nearby China, including Vietnam, and hence the connections between these countries and China, will likely be improved due to this economic "diplomacy" strategy. Apart from the investments and firms originating from Japan and the NIEs, more OFDIs from China, as well as more Chinese firms and their production activities, are expected to flow in and move to Vietnam, alongside the call from the Chinese government to relocate the lower value-added manufacturing activities to achieve industrial upgrading.

Unlike previous waves of electronics manufacturing relocation from Taiwan to the PRD and the YRD, which were driven mainly by firms under the pressure of leading global players originating from the advanced economies in the "Global North," the recent wave of production relocation from China to Vietnam has been driven by various tiers of TNCs from different economies, both developed and developing, largely within Asia. Our study illustrates the increasing regionalization of the electronics production network. On the one hand, Vietnam has engaged in the global electronics production networks of different tiers of TNCs, mainly from relatively developed Asian countries, such as Japan and South Korea, as an assembly hub exporting to the markets in advanced economies. On the other hand, Vietnam has engaged in regional production networks by also acting as an emerging destination. Catalyzed by the Vietnamese government, the development of electronics manufacturing in Vietnam has been primarily driven by the expanded/relocated production activities of various tiers of TNCs. This includes not only the relatively developed Asian economies but also the ETNCs from emerging economies, such as China, in the region, particularly since the 2000s. As Vietnam has turned into a low value-added assembly hub in the region at an accelerating speed, it has also become a destination in regional production networks. Not only for the final products, but it has also served as an important end market for intermediate goods, for example, electronics parts and components, produced by nearby countries, especially China, which has accounted for more than half of the intermediate goods imported by Vietnam. Vietnam's electronics manufacturing industry so far still has to rely heavily on importing parts and components rather than producing them itself.

Unlike the dominant "triangular trade pattern" in which Japan and Asian NIEs produce the parts and components of higher value-added products while China assembles and exports the final products to external markets in the United States and Europe, the transformation of the "World Factory" in the 2000s has started to change China's role in the production network. Apart from solely acting as a global-level assembly base, China has also driven the current wave of production relocations. Different tiers of Chinese firms have actively invested and relocated to Vietnam, not only to follow their clients but also to expand their markets overseas, particularly under the Sino-US trade war. Besides becoming a main investor, China has been Vietnam's biggest importer of parts and components as aforementioned. As a result, in the case of the consumer electronics industry, particularly the mobile phone sector, one can see that the "triangular trade pattern" has been changing. Apart from China, which had been the biggest manufacturer and exporter, Vietnam has been catching up and becoming the second-largest exporter, in terms of phone manufacturing, in the world by importing intermediate goods from China, the NIEs, as well as Japan in the region and exporting the final goods primarily to external markets in advanced economies and increasingly to the "Global South." This furthers the consolidation of the Asian electronics production networks. While electronics firms from different origins have expanded their production into Vietnam, compared to southern Vietnam, the northern part seems to be more appealing to these firms due to its relatively cheap production factors, on average and, more importantly, its physical proximity to China, Vietnam's biggest electronics parts and components importer.

One of the features of Vietnam's economic zone policy is that there are different economic zones established and managed by different levels of the host governments. By focusing particularly on the extra-firm bargaining strategies, such as the deliberations and the tactics used in the bargaining processes by different tiers of electronics TNCs, that is, using the cases of LG (lead firm), Foxconn (first-tier supplier), and the lower-tier suppliers, with different levels of host governments, the multi-scalar strategic coupling process has been systematically explored. Different firm-specific strategies have been used by the firms to relocate their productions, organize their networks, and try to make the institutions conducive to their operations. Drawing on concepts from IB studies, we argue that the different degrees of firm-state relationships—based on levels of resource complementarity, political accommodation, organizational credibility, and personal relations—along with the varying positions of firms in the production networks, have led to different bargaining outcomes between LG, Foxconn, and lower-tier suppliers with multiple levels of host governments and thus the different strategic coupling results. As the lead firm, that is, LG, has a closer firm-state relationship with multiple levels of the host governments compared to Foxconn, it holds a bigger bargaining chip and has been able to benefit from the extra-firm bargaining process to include the industrial zone where it locates into the economic zone of preferential treatments, which also, in turn, led to a certain degree of functional coupling of Vietnam into the electronics production networks apart from primarily the structural coupling acting as an assembly hub.

As mentioned, apart from the firms from the relatively developed economies in the region, that is, Japan and those in the NIEs, the current wave of production relocations has also been also attributed to the emerging TNCs from the emerging economies. Apart from the lower production costs, the emerging domestic and regional markets serve as one main reason for these ETNCs, especially the OBMs we interviewed, to expand to Vietnam. More importantly, the production relocations of these Chinese ETNCs have been an escape response to the changing institutional environment for the labor-intensive and relatively low value-added manufacturing industries in coastal China. The spatial concentration of these Chinese small and medium ETNCs in the economic zones and southern Vietnam reflected their territorial and societal inertia. Compared to northern Vietnam, Chinese investments in the South have been long established with well-developed social networks. Consequently, except for the lower-tier suppliers that must follow their clients, the majority of these Chinese ETNCs have concentrated in southern Vietnam. More importantly, due to the high compatibility between the institutional legacies of these ETNCs from China and the institutional buildings of the industrial parks and export-processing zones at the zone level, almost all the interviewed ETNCs were located inside and took advantage of these economic zones in the host region. Hence, it is sound to say that the lesson learned from China to set up the economic zones was rather successful in Vietnam as the Chinese firms were also satisfied. Besides, the inherent legacies embedded in the Chinese firms, such as the centralized operation and the *guanxi* network, have also been reflected in the firm-specific strategies for organizing their cross-border production networks. These legacies embedded in these ETNCs with limited internationalization experience have impacted their ways of relocating and organizing their cross-border production networks, both spatially and organizationally.

Based on the authors' follow-up observations and online interviews from 2020 to early 2023, the final empirical chapter of this book, chapter 8, offers an updated and novel investigation of the geopolitical dynamics and risks of strategic coupling in the mobile phone production shift from China to Vietnam, during the Sino-US trade war and the COVID-19 pandemic. In fact, both lead firms and supplier TNCs have increasingly engaged in the prevalent "China Plus One" strategy before the trade war and pandemic. The friction between China and the United States has accelerated the production shift to Vietnam and the reconfiguration of the electronics production network in the region by the concerns of cost-capability ratio but more so the uncertainties under the heightened geopolitical tension with the pandemic-induced supply chain disruption. The actors anticipated a longer-lasting effect of the trade war than the COVID-19 pandemic. While it might be contrary to the common belief, we found that the pandemic has been predominantly treated as a rather short-term hardship and has not been perceived as impactful as the Sino-US trade war by the actors mainly because the lockdowns and factory closures have been seen in both Vietnam and China, with the latter having even stricter anti-pandemic policies. And through comparing Samsung with Apple and Foxconn, due to their different cost-capability optimizations as well as the risk-responding strategies, the ways Samsung and Apple reconfigured their networks and hence their coupling and relocation progress have been found to be highly divergent.

In a nutshell, the above study on the production relocations from China to Vietnam reveals some salient characteristics of the current restructuring of the global and regional production networks. Unlike previous waves of production relocations that were ordered by the conventional lead firms from advanced economies simply to lower the cost-capability ratio, the current wave of production relocations has been a rather complex and multi-scalar process that has been simultaneously driven by different tiers of firms from various origins out of multiple capitalist dynamics, including the risk environment. Under the current changing dynamics, the regionalization of global electronics production networks has been seen more clearly. Therefore, to understand the recent restructuring of the global and regional production networks, both endogenous and exogenous factors, and the changing roles of the emerging and developing economies, as well as the actors from and inside these economies, must be considered more seriously. The "Global South" certainly deserves more spotlight.

SYNOPSIS OF THE THEORETICAL AND EMPIRICAL CONTRIBUTIONS

Through previous chapters of literature reviews and empirical studies on the production relocations from China to Vietnam, six selected theoretical contributions pushing forward and enriching the economic geography literature in terms of global production systems are summarized. Additionally, the most important achievement of our project—the empirical contributions—will also be wrapped up.

In the conventional conceptualization of global production system, the industrial development in developing countries was primarily driven by the "offshoring" of the production activities coordinated by lead firms from

Western advanced economies, such as the United States and European countries, to cut down costs and to serve the consumers back in their home markets. However, this book demonstrates that the recent wave of production relocations within Asia, as well as the restructuring of production networks, has been driven by various tiers of firms from different economies mainly in the region. Apart from the lower production costs, our study shows that production relocations from China to Vietnam have been driven by different multi-scalar dynamics, including emerging markets in the host country and the region (international level) as well as the changing situations of the international political economy between China, Vietnam, and other countries, such as the United States.

Second, and in relation, the roles of the actors in and from the emerging and developing countries have been largely ignored in the previous conceptualization of the production systems that are "Northern lead-firm centric" (Horner & Nadvi, 2018). The firm actors from these countries have now played an increasing role in driving the reconfigurations of the production networks both spatially and organizationally. Nevertheless, even in the recent studies on the regionalization of global production networks, the roles of these firms have not been fully explored. While the attention has been mostly concentrated on the emerging "giants," particularly the state-owned enterprises (SOEs) from these emerging economies, the small and medium private firms have been understudied. From chapter 7, one can see that the privately owned small and medium-sized enterprises (SMEs) from China have gradually contributed to the outward FDI of China and the restructuring of production network, particularly at the regional level. Hence, this book enriches the economic geography literature by intentionally incorporating the ETNCs, particularly the ones originating from developing and emerging economies, in the GPN study.

In connection, the home and host institutional environments faced and the institutional legacies embedded in these firms, have been overlooked in the literature. Taking Chinese SMEs as an example, the institutional environments encountered by these privately owned firms have been different from the SOEs and the emerging "giants." This affects the ways these firms internationalize and organize their cross-border production networks. Unlike previous studies, which paid much attention to the institutional settings mostly at the regional level, our study showcases that the zone-level institutional building is also crucial for facilitating the institutional escape and embedding process and hence deserves more attention in the studies of production relocations. In addition, we also discovered that the inherent legacies embedded in these ETNCs impact their production relocations and their production network reconfiguration both spatially and organizationally. Thus, the unique home imprints on these firms should not be ignored, especially in studying private SMEs with limited internationalization experience.

Fourth, although the newly developed GPN 2.0 framework has placed special attention on the extra-firm bargaining process, the focus so far has been mainly on explicating the overarching outcomes while leaving the details about the deliberations and actual tactics used by the firms, as well as the causal mechanism of the process, largely unexplored. By interpreting the firm-state relations from the institutionalist perspective and by referring to the notion of multinational corporation-host government relationships in the international business (IB) literature, an analytical framework that conceptualizes the building of the firm-state relationships and the strategies adopted by the firms in the firm-state interactions has been developed to further look into the actual ways in which the TNCs could bargain with the host government and turn the institutional environment conducive. Apart from the economic geography literature, chapter 6 also contributes to the IB literature by applying the idea of the multinational corporation-host government relationship to multi-scalar qualitative network research.

Fifth, although three competitive dynamics, namely cost-capability ratios, market, and finance, within the broader risk environments, have been added as the causal drivers in the GPN 2.0 framework in shaping firm strategies, through chapters 7 and 8, we pointed out that one cannot ignore the fact that the firm-based sensemaking of reality and the strategy-making process are, in fact beyond the rational calculation. Apart from the impacts of the home imprints on the ETNCs with limited internationalization experience mentioned earlier, echoed with Völlers et al. (2023), chapter 8 explicitly unveiled that the organizational decision-making is closely connected closely to the perception of the risk from the simulative decision-making environment and the spatial-relational context where the firms and their managers stay. Hence, the risk is indeed a fluid and subjective interpretation of the crisis and the tolerance by the firms and their managers.

Last but not least, although the GPN framework embraces a multi-scalar definition of the institution, there has been insufficient analysis of the relational and scalar interactions among different levels of institutions. Furthermore, the empirical research has mainly focused on the regional-level actors and strategies for the promotion of strategic coupling, which tends to inhibit the agency of the national states (Dawley et al., 2019) as well as international organizations. However, these actors often act as important mediators in the coupling process, so they are too significant to be ignored. Therefore, in each empirical chapter of the current monograph, we have intentionally put back the "multi-scalarity" in the GPN studies by looking into the strategic coupling and the interactions between different levels of the host institutions, from the national to the regional and the zone levels, and various tiers of firms in the networks.

Apart from the theoretical contribution, this book also updates the empirical literature regarding the current wave of production relocations of labor-intensive industries from China to the developing countries nearby, that is, Vietnam. As pointed out by Yang (2016), research attention has been increasingly placed on the production relocations within the "World Factory" at the intraprovincial and interprovincial levels nowadays. While the cross-border production relocations "going out" of China have rarely been studied so far. An increasing interest in this topic has been shown by scholars in different fields since the mid-2010s. Nevertheless, the related research has been relatively preliminary as most of it pays attention to the overall production relocation/trade patterns and/or focuses only on the national level. On the other hand, research looking into Vietnam's internationalization has also been in the infant stage so far, as it has mostly focused on Vietnam's opening and integration with the global economy, as well as the impacts of FDIs, and most recently, the positions of Vietnam in different global value chains. Compared to these studies, which mainly rely on statistical data and aim to generalize the situations for policy suggestions, this book offers a rather comprehensive look into how TNCs and ETNCs of various levels from different origins have relocated to Vietnam and organized their cross-border electronics production networks. By thoroughly studying the ways different firms from various economies, mostly originating from the NIEs, Japan, and China, expanded their production activities into Vietnam, as well as the articulation of Vietnam into the production networks of different scales and hence the regional developments, this book not only renews the production relocation literature, but it also showcases the increasing regionalization of the production networks and the detailed restructuring mechanisms.

In a nutshell, our study presented in this book has hopefully pushed forward the theoretical development of the global production systems, particularly the GPN 2.0 framework, in two aspects: the framework per se and the application of the framework. Apart from the conceptual loopholes identified in this newly developed framework, that is, the GPN 2.0, the current study reflects the salient features of the changing production networks, with the rise of the actors from/in the emerging and developing economies, which must be noticed to refine the conceptualization of the "Northern lead-firm centric" GPNs before applying it to analyze the current changing global and regional production networks with the surging participation from the "Global South." Furthermore, our study has pioneered in giving a comprehensive multi-scalar look into the recent wave of production relocations from China to Vietnam. Through four chapters of in-depth empirical studies, apart from the contributions to inspecting the restructuring of global and regional electronics production networks, this monograph also generates some pragmatic implications that can assist both the firm and nonfirm actors in the network in better grasping the opportunities in the current changing global economic landscape for the better value captures in the networks and hence the regional developments.

REAL-WORLD APPLICATIONS AND POLICY IMPLICATIONS

As the increasing regionalization of the global electronics production networks and the rise of the "Global South" as well as the emergence of unprecedented uncertainties at different scales nowadays, have been witnessed, it is high time for the actors in the network, both firms and nonfirm ones, to rethink their directions and strategies under the current changing dynamics to ensure participation and the better capture and enhancement of values from the production networks. Five sets of ideas for four different parties have been generated from the findings of the current book.

First, as for the producers in emerging economies, such as China, who have hit the "glass ceiling" of upgrading in the production networks dominated by lead firms, and who have already upgraded to become OBMs but found the shrinking traditional Western market too saturated and competitive, since the emerging domestic and regional markets in the "Global South" have been witnessed, these firms may consider diversifying their markets. "The rise of Asia, in particular, has been reflected not just in productive capacity but also in terms of consumption" (Coe & Yeung, 2019: 776). Instead of solely serving the lead firms and the developed economies, they could try to couple with their emerging domestic markets and the markets nearby so that they may be able to engage in higher value-added activities, such as R&D and marketing, instead of simply being simply the manufacturers and get upgraded. Compared to the established TNCs from the developed countries, the firms from the emerging and developing countries have competitive edges built on closer connections with the end consumers in the emerging markets and thus a better understanding of the consumers' needs (Brandt & Thun, 2011). As for the OBMs originating from these economies, expanding overseas to emerging markets in other developing countries not only broadens their market base but also, through expansion, enables them to uphold their position in the network and learn how to internationalize and organize their cross-border production networks at a higher spatial scale, even with relatively limited experience, resources, and market power. This also helps them to better prepare for crises in the network so that they can diversify their risk and reorganize their network more easily in the future. Yet, although the host region government would try to reduce the institutional differences to attract foreign investors, unless with strong bargaining chips, the inherent institutional inertia might still hinder these ETNCs from adapting to the institutional buildings in the new locations.

Second, while the cultural and institutional thresholds in the host region have existed, whether the backward linkages between the suppliers and the foreign firms can be formed successfully depends more, in fact, on the former's fitness for the latter's network settings. To engage in the production networks of the TNCs and the ETNCs and to benefit from the spillover effects, the capabilities of these suppliers cannot be too low. Especially in industries with large foreign shares, for example, the electronics industry in Vietnam, the large technology gaps between the domestic firms and their foreign counterparts could constitute unsurmountable obstacles to spillovers (Kokko, 1994). Hence, to leverage the current restructuring of the electronics production networks, these suppliers in the "Global South" are encouraged to invest in upgrading their own technological capabilities and/or to participate in the training programs offered by the higher-tier firms, such as the ones provided by Samsung mentioned in the previous chapter.

Third, as for the governments hoping to push further industrial upgrading apart from the export-led growth model, the emerging domestic market and the regional markets nearby should be considered, as these "new" markets, to a large extent, could lead to the reconfigurations of the production systems, that is, shifting the end of the networks, which is likely to open up new opportunities and, more importantly, the upgrading prospects for domestic firms. Apart from upgrading the old paths, one of the common ways to transform the industry sector is to encourage the low value-added domestic firms in the labor-intensive and/or environment-polluting industries to "go out," for example, the "emptying the cage for new birds" strategy practiced in Guangdong in the late 2000s. We have shown that besides the SOEs and those relatively large TNCs, the privately owned SMEs should not be overlooked during the industrial transformation process, as they have contributed to a significant and increasing share of the OFDI. Taking the ETNCs from China as the case, although we have pointed out in chapter 7 that these firms have been increasingly internationalized, their "going out" has still been very challenging due to their limited resources, powers, and experience. To speed up the transformation and upgrading process of the home economies, besides the host institutions, the home governments might also assist these firms in getting rid of the home imprints, such as the heavy reliance on *guanxi*, to better adapt to the business environment overseas.

The fourth and the fifth sets of policy implications are for the host governments in developing countries, such as Vietnam, hoping to tie a node with the production networks. Instead of simply offering preferential policies to attract FDI inflows and production relocations, the governments should be long-sighted and carefully search for the ideal types of strategic coupling between their regions and the production networks and the ways the domestic firms could participate in the production networks of these investors. To attract foreign producers, especially the ones with limited experience, using development zones to narrow the institutional gaps between the host region and the home region where the firm originates could help. As TNCs are, in general, reluctant to nurture domestic suppliers in the host region, the host governments at different levels should assist the domestic suppliers to improve their capabilities to let them at least reach the standard of joining the network in the first place. Since pro-manufacturing preferential policies have been a central part of the motivations driving production relocations to Vietnam, therefore the governments in the host country can use these incentives as bargaining chips to persuade TNCs to include more domestic suppliers in their production networks, help them to upgrade, and relocate higher value-added production activities as well as achieve a relatively functional strategic coupling instead of locking in with the structural strategic coupling. One valuable lesson from Vietnam's case is its multi-scalar institution-building toward investment and industrial development, in which the provincial governments have certain freedoms and more preferential policies are in the hands of the national-level government. The flexibility of this multi-scalar institution-building is that, on one hand, the provincial governments can proactively attract smaller investors while the national-level governments can have more bargaining chips in deliberations with the larger investors (in terms of investment size and network position) that can help upgrade industrial development in the host region. As aforementioned, apart from the institutions at the national and regional levels, the zone-level institution-building should not be ignored as it has also been found to be critical in attracting SMEs. In addition, apart from the industrial and investment-related preferential policies, access to the surging domestic and regional market can also serve as another bargaining chip, especially in the aftermath of the global financial crisis in which consumption in the "Global North" has been shrinking.

The fifth set of suggestions is closely related to the recent uncertainty and risks in the GPN. Apart from the three capitalist dynamics in the GPN framework, one should not ignore the role of risk in driving the de/recoupling process. Under the Sino-US trade war, as we have shown in chapter 8, rather than production costs, the geopolitical characteristics of Vietnam have been the main attraction for TNCs to move in. Instead of seeing the TNC as an organization making decisions based on rational calculations, the host governments should be aware that they themselves have a significant role in constituting the place-specific contexts and decision-making environments in which the organizational decision-makers are embedded. This can alter the risk perception and interpretation and hence the risk responses of the actors. The GPN risks are multi-scalar. Besides the regional level, the COVID-19 pandemic demonstrates every possible adverse impact of a risk on global production systems and its consequence of leading to further regionalization of the systems in the future. As far as the cases of the electronics industry and Vietnam are concerned, one may see the other side of the coin in which opportunities were brought to the latter as TNCs turned to domestic suppliers to secure their component supply due to the global logistics disruptions caused by the pandemic.

Due to both exogenous and endogenous factors at different scales, the production relocations of labor-intensive industries from China to Vietnam and, more broadly speaking, the restructuring of the electronics production networks are expected to continue for at least the next few years. To better grasp the emerging opportunities, actors in the networks, both firm and the nonfirm ones, must be aware of the changing dynamics in the networks not only at the national or regional scale but also at the global and even the local or "zone" level, for example, from the changing situations of the international political economy to the power dynamics in a development zone. Instead of seeing this wave of production relocations as a simple process of another round of "spatial fix" (Harvey, 1995) just looking for cheaper production factors, actors in the production networks should realize that, behind the curtain, it is a complex process of constant de- and recoupling of the production network organization and regional development caused by various changing dynamics, which are not only limited to the economic ones, at multiple scales in the global economy nowadays.

LIMITATIONS OF THE CURRENT STUDY AND FUTURE RESEARCH AGENDA

Although the observations of this monograph were largely based on the authors' collections of data from different reliable secondary sources and more importantly the in-depth fieldwork and the interviews, both face-to-face and online, with extensive parties ranging from firms to nonfirm actors originating from different countries and regions since late 2017, limitations of this current study are however more related to data collections. First, in the original research design, we planned to combine both quantitative and qualitative analyses to understand the current wave of production relocations. Apart from conducting in-depth semi-structured interviews, we schemed to conduct a large-scale questionnaire survey to collect ideas from the TNCs and ETNCs relocated to Vietnam to better understand the questions of "why" and "how." For instance, why have they relocated to Vietnam; why have they settled in that particular region and development zones; how do they compare the strengths as well as the weaknesses of the institutional buildings in Vietnam to other countries such as China? By using the statistical models to analyze the factors and explore the causal relationships among them, we believed that one could get more detailed insights into the rationales behind the "why" and "how" questions backed up by mathematical calculations. However, the refusal to help from the economic zone operators made the survey barely possible to proceed with our limited budget. Although some nonprofit investor associations were willing to help, the neutrality of the data due to the backgrounds of those associations could be in doubt, not to mention the data might not be available within our study period. Except for chapter 5, which has extensively analyzed the international trade and investment statistics from various databases, three other chapters, that is, chapters 6–8, primarily deployed the qualitative method to collect firsthand firm-level data through face-to-face and online interviews in various cities mainly across Vietnam and China. However, given the limited time period and resources of the research project, a limited number of actors (around fifty) were reached and interviewed. Despite the fact that a significant number of additional online interviews have been carried out online to reach out to more related parties and, more importantly, for the writing of chapter 8, to keep updating the changes amid the COVID-19 pandemic when the travel restriction was in place, unlike the in-person face-to-face interviews and without the on-site investigations, apart from the chance that we could miss different nonverbal expressions of the interviewees (Lo Iacono et al., 2016), it could also be also hard for us to interpret some context-specific ideas expressed by the interviewees. Besides, given that the main objectives of chapters 6 and 7 are to understand how different tiers of TNCs from different origins have relocated and organized their production networks in Vietnam, only around thirty involved actors were interviewed, which is indeed not quite enough in terms of generalization. Even though almost all the interviewees were at the senior management grade with an average of ten or more years of experience in the field, the fact that working with bigger samples could have led to a better abstraction induction still holds true. Although it was pointed out that it is still possible for generalizations from single case analysis as long as one takes prior considerations and/or ex-post analyses of parts of the material to look for typical materials (Mayring, 2007), certain types of the interviewed firms, that is, the lead firms from Korea that relocated from China to Vietnam, have just barely reached the recommendation number suggested by Yin (2018). Therefore, the interviewed actors cannot represent the entire population. Although generalizations have been made based on our repeated interviews, and verifications by case comparisons, as GPN takes an actor-centered approach and as the characteristics of the actors largely diverge, one should also notice that our observations are, in fact, heavily context-dependent and might not be applicable under other circumstances/cases.

Whereas the current book tried to focus on the case of the production relocations of electronics firms from China to Vietnam, especially since the 2010s, in order to better understand the changing dynamics of the current restructuring and regionalization of the production networks, four future research arenas have been spotted. First, this study has focused more explicitly on the firm-specific strategies deployed by the firms to relocate their productions and reorganize their networks to couple with Vietnam, while the market strategies (the forward linkages) of the relocated firms with the buyers, distributors, and retailers for better tapping into the changing consumption landscape are also worth studying as these efforts can alter the configurations of the production chains, not only the tail section but the entire chain (since the new markets will have a completely new set of standards and/or consumer preferences), and unveal the upgrading opportunities along the chains and networks. Second, this study has paid less attention to the consequences of the current wave of production relocations on the home and host regions. More focus should be attended to the outcomes of strategic coupling between the electronics production networks and Vietnam. To push it a bit further, apart from the models such as Vietnam's Provincial Competitiveness Index (PCI) to objectively quantify the rather economic side of regional development achievements brought by the coupling with the production networks, it is as important to see how the arrival of TNCs has impacted the regions in social, cultural, and environmental aspects to grasp the whole picture. On the other hand, it is also interesting to look into the future development of coastal China after increasingly decoupling from electronics manufacturing. Continuous effort needs to be paid to see whether Vietnam will "lock in" with the low value-added production activities and fall into the "middle-income trap" (MIT), which is commonly encountered by many developing economies.

Last but most importantly, although this study has made an inroad, more detailed research projects on how firms originating from different sources with various ownership structures and institutional inertias use diverse firm-specific strategies to reorganize their production networks under changing competitive dynamics in other industries and locations are urgently needed to better understand the reality of changing production networks at different scales, as well as the changing global economic landscape entering the 2020s. Economic globalization is currently at a crossroads (Martin et al., 2018; Coe & Yeung, 2019; Gong et al., 2022). Besides the Sino-US trade war, which the authors have explored in this monograph, the recently emerged geopolitical affairs, such as Brexit, the Ukraine–Russia war, and the related

Russia-NATO tensions, are likely to affect global trade flows, for example, through rising protectionism and potential trade sanctions, and thus the production network configurations. Apart from manufacturing and assembling, countries are increasingly encouraging/asking their domestic firms to keep strategically valuable R&D activities within their home territories. Hence, TNCs are now under pressure to disintegrate from the original networks and move at least part of their production activities back home, for example, the Made in America Movement proposed by Trump. The regionalization and even nationalization of global production networks seem to be more obvious amid COVID-19. Although global production networks still dominate, as pointed out directly by Panwar et al. (2022: 14), "COVID-19 pandemic could catalyze reshoring in some regions and in some product categories." The vulnerability of GVCs and GPNs during the pandemic has questioned the just-in-time mode of production. There have been heightened debates on bringing the production of essential goods such as medicines and medical equipment back to countries instead of relying on imports. Alongside the pandemic and geopolitical uncertainties, rapid technological breakthroughs today could be another key factor in transforming the organization of production activities. Improving levels of technology of automation, 3D printing, and the metaverse in recent decades, just like the advance of communication tools in the last century, can surely impact the methods and boost the efficiency of manufacturing and thus the production organization across space and time. In addition, the recently amplified concern for "green" production and consumption, as well as environmental sustainability (e.g., Ponte, 2020; Golgeci et al., 2021), is also likely to affect how TNCs structure their chains/networks to source their raw materials, manage their inventories, and regulate their manufacturing activities. While some scholars have taken the first step to explore these newly emerged forces, more comprehensive research is imminently needed to further investigate their natures and impacts so as to update the preexisting understanding and conceptualization of global production systems. While the literature to date has primarily studied these factors separately, one should notice that they "do not stand alone but are influencing and influenced by each other in non-trivial ways" (Gong et al., 2022: 171).

References

Akamatsu, K. (1962). A historical pattern of economic growth in developing countries. *The Developing Economies*, *1*(1), 3–25.

Akinci, G., & James, C. (2008). Special economic zone: Performance, lessons learned, and implication for zone development. In *Foreign Investment Advisory Service (FIAS) occasional paper* (pp.1–83). Washington, D.C.: World Bank Group.

Alon, I., Anderson, J., Munim, Z. H., & Ho, A. (2018). A review of the internationalization of Chinese enterprises. *Asia Pacific Journal of Management*, *35*(3), 573–605.

Anh, N. T. T., Duc, L. M., & Chieu, T. D. (2014). The evolution of Vietnamese industry. *Manufacturing Transformation*, 235–256.

Anwar, S., & Nguyen, L. P. (2010). Foreign direct investment and economic growth in Vietnam. *Asia Pacific Business Review*, *16*(1–2), 183–202.

Anwar, S., & Nguyen, L. P. (2011a). Foreign direct investment and export spillovers: Evidence from Vietnam. *International Business Review*, *20*(2), 177–193.

Anwar, S., & Nguyen, L. P. (2011b). Foreign direct investment and trade: The case of Vietnam. *Research in International Business and Finance*, *25*(1), 39–52.

Arnold, D. J., & Quelch, J. A. (1998). New strategies in emerging markets. *MIT Sloan Management Review*, *40*(1), 7–20.

Asian Development Bank. (2005, November 1). *Viet Nam Private Sector Assessment*. Retrieved on 23 May, 2019, from https://www.adb.org/documents/viet-nam-private-sector-assessment

Athukorala, P. C., & Nasir, S. (2012). Global production sharing and South-South trade. *Indian Growth and Development Review*, *5*(2), 173–202.

Azmeh, S., & Nadvi, K. (2014). Asian firms and the restructuring of global value chains. *International Business Review*, *23*(4), 708–717.

Bair, J. (2008). Analysing global economic organization: Embedded networks and global chains compared. *Economy and Society*, *37*(3), 339–364.

Baldwin, R., & Lopez-Gonzalez, J. (2015). Supply-chain trade: A portrait of global patterns and several testable hypotheses. *The World Economy*, *38*(11), 1682–1721.

Barnard, H., & Luiz, J. M. (2018). Escape FDI and the dynamics of a cumulative process of institutional misalignment and contestation: Stress, strain and failure. *Journal of World Business*, *53*(5), 605–619.

Barnes, T. J., & Sheppard, E. (2010). "Nothing includes everything": Towards engaged pluralism in Anglophone economic geography. *Progress in Human Geography*, *34*(2), 193–214.

Barrientos, S., Gereffi, G., & Pickles, J. (2016). New dynamics of upgrading in global value chains: Shifting terrain for suppliers and workers in the global south. *Environment and Planning A: Economy and Space*, *48*(7), 1214–1219.

Bathelt, H. (2005). Geographies of production: Growth regimes in spatial perspective (II)-knowledge creation and growth in clusters. *Progress in Human Geography*, *29*(2), 204–216.

Bích, Ngoc, T., & Binh, D. (2019). Vietnam's electronics industry: The rise and problems of further development. *Humanities & Social Sciences Reviews*, *7*(4), 1–12.

Boddewyn, J. J. (2016). Political Aspects of MNE Theory. In J. A. Cantwell (Ed.), *The Eclectic Paradigm: A Framework for Synthesizing and Comparing Theories of International Business from Different Disciplines or Perspectives* (pp. 85–110). London: Palgrave Macmillan.

Boisot, M., & Meyer, M. W. (2008). Which way through the open door? Reflections on the internationalization of Chinese firms. *Management and Organization Review*, *4*(3), 349–365.

Borrus, M., Ernst, D., & Haggard, S. (Eds.). (2000). *International Production Networks in Asia: Rivalry or Riches*. London: Routledge.

Brandt, L., & Thun, E. (2011). Going mobile in China: Shifting value chains and upgrading in the mobile telecom sector. *International Journal of Technological Learning, Innovation and Development*, *4*(1–3), 148–180.

Brouthers, L. E., Brouthers, K. D., & Werner, S. (1999). Is Dunning's eclectic framework descriptive or normative? *Journal of International Business Studies*, *30*(4), 831–844.

Bryson, J. R., & Vanchan, V. (2020). COVID-19 and alternative conceptualisations of value and risk in GPN research. *Tijdschrift voor Economische en Sociale Geografie*, *111*(3), 530–542.

Burt, R. S. (2009). *Structural Holes: The Social Structure of Competition*. Cambridge, MA: Harvard University Press.

Butollo, F. (2015). Growing against the odds: Government agency and strategic recoupling as sources of competitiveness in the garment industry of the Pearl River Delta. *Cambridge Journal of Regions, Economy and Society*, *8*(3), 521–536.

Camagni, R. (1992). Firm networks and the hidden costs of cooperative behaviour. In *88th Annual Meeting of the Association of American Geographers*. San Diego, CA.

Chan, D. Y. T., & Yang, C. (2022a). Institutional escape and embeddedness in the cross-border production networks: Relocation of Chinese electronics small and medium-sized enterprises to Vietnam. *Journal of Contemporary China*, *31*(137), 675–692.

Chan, D. Y. T., & Yang, C. (2022b). The transformation of Asian electronics production networks: Evidence from the participation of Vietnam. In J. R. Bryson, et al.

(Eds.), *A Research Agenda for Manufacturing Industries in the Global Economy* (1st ed., pp. 157–176). Cheltenham: Edward Elgar.

Chan, E. M. H., Ho, C. K. D., Yip, T. L., Cheung, J., & Gunasekaran, A. (2020). The Belt and Road Initiative's impact on textile and clothing supply chains in Asia: Views from Hong Kong industrial stakeholders. In E. M. H. Chan & A. Gunasekaran (Eds.), *Belt and Road Initiative—Collaboration for Success* (pp. 51–61). Singapore: Springer.

Chen, S. H., Wen, P. C., & Tai, C. Y. (2013). China's good-enough innovation: Shanzhai handsets and Shanzhai economy. In P. Cooke, et al. (Eds.), *The Economic Geography of the IT Industry in the Asia Pacific Region* (pp. 195–214). London: Routledge.

Chen, W., & Li, J. (2019). *Estimating the Scale of Relocation of Labor-Intensive Manufacturing from China: Facts and Potentials.* Beijing: Peking University, Institute of New Structural Economics (INSE).

Cheong, K. C., Lee, P. P., & Lee, K. H. (2011). Learning from the China model: What is in it for Vietnam's economic development? *Issues & Studies, 47*(4), 153–176.

Child, J., & Rodrigues, S. B. (2005). The internationalization of Chinese firms: A case for theoretical extension? *Management and organization review, 1*(3), 381–410.

Christensen, P. R., Eskelinen, H., Forsstrom, B., Lindmark, L., & Vatne, E. (1990). Firms in network: Concepts, spatial impacts and policy implications. *Networks and Regional Development*, 11–58.

Christopherson, S., & Clark, J. (2007). *Remaking Regional Economies: Power, Labor, and Firm Strategies in the Knowledge Economy*. London: Routledge.

Coe, N. M. (2012). Geographies of production II: A global production network A-Z. *Progress in Human Geography, 36*(3), 389–402.

Coe, N. M. (2021). *Advanced Introduction to Global Production Networks*. Cheltenham: Edward Elgar.

Coe, N. M., & Yeung, H. W. C. (2015). *Global Production Networks: Theorizing Economic Development in an Interconnected World.* Oxford: Oxford University Press.

Coe, N. M., & Yeung, H. W. C. (2019). Global production networks: Mapping recent conceptual developments. *Journal of Economic Geography, 19*(4), 775–801.

Coe, N. M., Dicken, P., & Hess, M. (2008). Global production networks: Realizing the potential. *Journal of Economic Geography, 8*(3), 271–295.

Coe, N. M., Hess, M., Yeung, H. W. C., Dicken, P., & Henderson, J. (2004). "Globalizing" regional development: A global production networks perspective. *Transactions of the Institute of British Geographers, 29*(4), 468–484.

Dautu. (2015, September 7). *Foxconn giants promised to go on a billion-dollar project.* Retrieved on 10 July, 2018, from https://baodautu.vn/dai-gia-foxconn-hua-leo-ve-du-an-ty-do-d32257.html (In Vietnamese)

Davis, B., & Wei, L. (2022). Who won the U.S.-China trade war? *The Wall Street Journal.* Retrieved on 11 March, 2023, from https://www.wsj.com/articles/who-won-the-u-s-china-trade-war-11653059611

Dawley, S., MacKinnon, D., & Pollock, R. (2019). Creating strategic couplings in global production networks: Regional institutions and lead firm investment in the Humber region, UK. *Journal of Economic Geography*, *19*(4), 853–872.

Dawley, S., MacKinnon, D., Cumbers, A., & Pike, A. (2015). Policy activism and regional path creation: The promotion of offshore wind in North East England and Scotland. *Cambridge Journal of Regions, Economy and Society*, *8*(2), 257–272.

Deng, P. (2012). The internationalization of Chinese firms: A critical review and future research. *International Journal of Management Reviews*, *14*(4), 408–427.

Deng, P., Delios, A., & Peng, M. W. (2020). A geographic relational perspective on the internationalization of emerging market firms. *Journal of International Business Studies*, *51*(1), 50–71.

Denk, N., Kaufmann, L., & Roesch, J. F. (2012). Liabilities of foreignness revisited: A review of contemporary studies and recommendations for future research. *Journal of International Management*, *18*(4), 322–334.

Dhar, B. K., Tiep Le, T., Coffelt, T. A., & Shaturaev, J. (2023). US-China trade war and competitive advantage of Vietnam. *Thunderbird International Business Review*, *65*(2), 255–263.

Dicken, P. (1994). Local embeddedness of transnational corporations. *Globalization, Institutions, and Regional Development in Europe*, 23–45.

Dicken, P. (2007). *Global Shift: Mapping the Changing Contours of the World Economy*. London: SAGE Publications.

Dicken, P. (2011). *Global Shift: Mapping the Changing Contours of the World Economy* (6th ed.). New York, NY: Guilford.

Dicken, P., Kelly, P. F., Olds, K., & Yeung, H. W. C. (2001). Chains and networks, territories and scales: Towards a relational framework for analysing the global economy. *Global Networks*, *1*(2), 89–112.

Dohse, D., Hassink, R., & Klaerding, C. (2012). *Emerging Multinationals, International Knowledge Flows and Economic Geography: A Research Agenda* (Kiel Working Paper No. 1776). Kiel, Germany: Kiel Institute for the World Economy.

Dosch, J., & Vuving, A. (2008). *The Impact of China on Governance Structures in Vietnam*. (DIE Discussion Report, 14/2008 pp. 1–31). Deutsches Institut für Entwicklungspolitik.

Dunning, J. H. (1977). Trade, location of economic activity and the MNE: A search for an eclectic approach. In B. Ohlin, et al. (Eds.), *The International Allocation of Economic Activity* (pp. 395–418). London: Palgrave Macmillan.

Dunning, J. H. (1988). The eclectic paradigm of international production: A restatement and some possible extensions. *Journal of International Business Studies*, *19*(1), 1–31.

Dunning, J. H. (1993). *Multinational Enterprise and the Global Economy*. England: Addison-Wesley Publishers.

Dunning, J. H. (1995). Reappraising the eclectic paradigm in an age of alliance capitalism. *Journal of International Business Studies*, *26*, 461–491.

Dunning, J. H. (1999). *Governments, Globalization, and International Business*. Oxford: Oxford University Press.

Dunning, J. H. (2001). The eclectic (OLI) paradigm of international production: Past, present and future. *International Journal of the Economics of Business*, *8*(2), 173–190.

Dunning, J. H. (2003). The eclectic (OLI) paradigm of international production. In *International Business and the Eclectic Paradigm: Developing the OLI Framework*. London: Routledge.

Dunning, J. H., & Lundan, S. M. (2010). The institutional origins of dynamic capabilities in multinational enterprise. *Industrial and Corporate Change*, *19*(4), 1225–1246.

Dunning, J. H., Kim, C., & Park, D. (2008). Old wine in new bottles: A comparison of emerging-market TNCs today and developed-country TNCs thirty years ago. In K. P. Sauvant (Ed.), *The Rise of Transnational Corporations from Emerging Markets: Threat or Opportunity* (pp.158–180). Cheltenham: Edward Elgar.

Economic Daily News. (2007, December 17). *Hon Hai is becoming the Biggest Exporter of Vietnam*. Retrieved on 10 July, 2018, from http://mypaper.pchome.com.tw/1626108/post/1300435491 (In Chinese)

Economist Intelligence Unit. (2014). *Still Making It: An Analysis of Manufacturing Labour Costs in China*. Retrieved on 10 May, 2019, from http://www.truevaluemetrics.org/DBpdfs/Economics/Economist/EIU-Chinamanufacturing-labor-cost-report-2014.pdf

Economist Intelligence Unit. (2018). *Creative Disruption: Asia's Winners in the US-China Trade War*. Retrieved on 6 May, 2020, from https://pages.eiu.com/Nov-18---Creative-disruption-Asias-winners-in-the-USChina-trade-war-MKT_registration-page.html

Eden, L., & Dai, L. (2010). Rethinking the O in Dunning's OLI/eclectic paradigm. *Multinational Business Review*, *18*(2), 13–34.

Edgington, D. W., & Hayter, R. (2000). Foreign Direct Investment and the Flying Geese Model: Japanese Electronics Firms in Asia-Pacific. *Environment and Planning A*, *32*(2), 281–304.

Elia, S., Fratocchi, L., Barbieri, P., Boffelli, A., & Kalchschmidt, M. (2021). Post-pandemic reconfiguration from global to domestic and regional value chains: The role of industrial policies. *Transnational Corporations Journal*, *28*(2), 67–96.

Ernst, D. (2005). Complexity and internationalisation of innovation—why is chip design moving to Asia? *International Journal of Innovation Management*, *9*(1), 47–73.

Etnews. (2022, November 24). *Samsung phones, cutting production in Vietnam by 40%*. Retrieved on 20 July, 2023, from https://english.etnews.com/20221104200001

Euromonitor International. (2014, July 10). *Vietnam as a Potential Market and Production Site in Major Appliances*. Retrieved on 15 November, 2019, from https://www.euromonitor.com/article/vietnam-as-a-potential-market-and-production-site-in-major-appliances

Evans, P. B. (2012). *Embedded Autonomy: States and Industrial Transformation*. Princeton: Princeton University Press.

Fforde, A. (2019). *From Plan to Market: the Economic Transition in Vietnam*. London: Routledge.

Flyvbjerg, B. (2006). Five misunderstandings about case-study research. *Qualitative Inquiry*, *12*(2), 219–245.

Forbes. (2023, January 1). *Apple to Diversify Its Supply Chain by Producing MacBooks in Vietnam.* Retrieved on 11 April, 2023, from https://www.forbes.com/sites/qai/2023/01/01/apple-to-diversify-its-supply-chain-by-producing-macbooks-in-vietnam/?sh=2872fb247d75

Freeman, D. B. (1996). Doi Moi Policy and the Small-Enterprise Boom in Ho Chi Minh City, Vietnam. *Geographical Review*, *86*(2), 178–197.

Freeman, N. J. (1994). Vietnam and China: Foreign direct investment parallels. *Communist Economies and Economic Transformation*, *6*(1), 75–97.

Fuller, C. (2021). Brexit and the discursive construction of the corporation. *Journal of Economic Geography*, *21*(2), 317–338.

Fuller, C., & Phelps, N. A. (2018). Revisiting the multinational enterprise in global production networks. *Journal of Economic Geography*, *18*(1), 139–161.

Fuller, D. B. (2019). Growth, upgrading, and limited catch-up in China's semiconductor industry. In L. Brandt & T. Rawski (Eds.), *Policy, Regulation and Innovation in China's Electricity and Telecom Industries* (pp. 262–303). Cambridge: Cambridge University Press.

Fu, T. (2017). *Market Strategies of the Furniture and Garment Industries in the Pearl River Delta, China.* (Doctoral dissertation). Hong Kong Baptist University.

Fu, T., Yang, C., & Li, L. (2020). Market imperative and cluster evolution in China: Evidence from Shunde. *Regional Studies*, *54*(2), 244–255.

Fu, W., & Lim, K. F. (2022). The constitutive role of state structures in strategic coupling: On the formation and evolution of Sino-German production networks in Jieyang, China. *Economic Geography*, *98*(1), 25–48.

Gao, B., Dunford, M., Norcliffe, G., & Liu, Z. (2017). Capturing gains by relocating global production networks: The rise of Chongqing's notebook computer industry, 2008–2014. *Eurasian Geography and Economics*, *58*(2), 231–257.

Gao, B., Dunford, M., Norcliffe, G., & Liu, W. (2019). Governance capacity, state policy and the rise of the Chongqing notebook computer cluster. *Area Development and Policy*, *4*(3), 321–345.

General Statistics Office of Vietnam. (2009–2022). *Statistical yearbook of Vietnam 2009–2022.* General Statistics Office of Vietnam: Vietnam. Retrieved on 5 April, 2024, from https://www.gso.gov.vn/default_en.aspx?tabid=515&idmid=5&ItemID=10439, 11974,12576, 13762, 14079, 15197, 16052,18533, 18941,19299.

Gereffi, G. (1994). The organization of buyer-driven global commodity chains: How US retailers shape overseas production networks. In G. Gereffi & M. Korzeniewicz (Eds.), *Contributions in Economics and Economic History* (pp. 95–122). Westport, CT: Praeger.

Gereffi, G. (1995). Global production systems and third world development. In B. Stallings (Ed.), *Global Change, Regional Responses* (pp. 100–142). Cambridge: Cambridge University Press.

Gereffi, G. (1996). Commodity chains and regional divisions of labor in East Asia. *Journal of Asian Business*, *12*(1), 75–112.

Gereffi, G. (2014). Global value chains in a post-Washington Consensus world. *Review of international political economy*, *21*(1), 9–37.

Gereffi, G. (2019). Global value chains and international development policy: Bringing firms, networks and policy-engaged scholarship back in. *Journal of International Business Policy*, *2*(3), 195–210.

Gereffi, G., Humphrey, J., & Sturgeon, T. (2005). The governance of global value chains. *Review of international political economy*, *12*(1), 78–104.

Giang, H. (2023, March 20). Samsung leaving smartphone production in Vietnam. *VnEconomy*. Retrieved on 24 April, 2023, from https://en.vneconomy.vn/samsung-leaving-smartphone-production-in-vietnam.htm

Ginzburg, A., & Simonazzi, A. (2005). Patterns of industrialization and the flying geese model: The case of electronics in East Asia. *Journal of Asian Economics*, *15*(6), 1051–1078.

Golgeci, I., Makhmadshoev, D., & Demirbag, M. (2021). Global value chains and the environmental sustainability of emerging market firms: A systematic review of literature and research agenda. *International Business Review*, *30*(5), 1–29.

Gong, H., & Hassink, R. (2019). Developing the Shanghai online games industry: A multi-scalar institutional perspective. *Growth and Change*, *50*(3), 1006–1025.

Gong, H., Hassink, R., Foster, C., Hess, M., & Garretsen, H. (2022). Globalisation in reverse? Reconfiguring the geographies of value chains and production networks. *Cambridge Journal of Regions, Economy and Society*, *15*(2), 165–181.

Green, M. B. (1993). A geography of institutional stock ownership in the United States. *Annals of the Association of American Geographers*, *83*(1), 66–89.

Grimes, S., & Du, D. (2020). China's emerging role in the global semiconductor value chain. *Telecommunications Policy*, *46*(7), 1–14.

Grimes, S., & Sun, Y. (2016). China's evolving role in Apple's global value chain. *Area Development and Policy*, *1*(1), 94–112.

Ha, L. T. (2019). *Chinese FDI in Vietnam: Trends, status and challenges*. ISEAS-Yusof Ishak Institute.

Hai, N. M., Hai, D. H., & Hung, N. M. (2018). Analysing the effects of the exporting on economic growth in Vietnam. In L. H. Anh, et al. (Eds.), *Econometrics for Financial Applications* (pp. 597–610). Cham: Springer International Publishing.

Harvard Business Review. (2021). *The strategic challenges of decoupling*. Retrieved on 24 April, 2023, from https://hbr.org/2021/05/the-strategic-challenges-of-decoupling

Harvey, D. (1982). *The Limits to Capital*. Oxford: Basil Blackwell.

Harvey, D. (1995). Globalization in question. *Rethinking Marxism*, *8*(4), 1–17.

Henderson, J., and Nadvi, K. (2011). Greater China, the challenges of global production networks and the dynamics of transformation. *Global Networks, 11*(3), 285–297.

Henderson, J., Dicken, P., Hess, M., Coe, N., & Yeung, H. W. C. (2002). Global production networks and the analysis of economic development. *Review of International Political Economy*, *9*(3), 436–464.

Herr, H., Schweisshelm, E., & Truong, M. H. V. (2016a). *Vietnam in the Global Economy: Development through Integration or Middle-Income Trap?* Hanoi: Friedrich-Ebert-Stiftung Vietnam Office.

Herr, H., Schweisshelm, E., & Truong, M. H. V. (2016b). *The Integration of Vietnam in the Global Economy and its Effects for Vietnamese Economic Development* (Global Labour University Working Paper No. 44). Digital library of the Friedrich Ebert Foundation.

Hess, M. (2004). "Spatial" relationships? Towards a reconceptualization of embedded ness. *Progress in Human Geography*, *28*(2), 165–186.

Hess, M. (2018). Global production networks. In D. Richardson (Ed.), *The International Encyclopedia of Geography: People, the Earth, Environment, and Technology* (Article. 0675). Chichester: John Wiley & Sons Ltd.

Hess, M. (2021). One: Global production networks: The state, power and politics. In F. Palpacuer & A. Smith (Eds), *Rethinking Value Chains* (pp. 17–35). Bristol: Policy Press. Retrieved on 13 April, 2022, from https://bristoluniversitypressdigital.com/edcollchap-oa/book/9781447359180/ch001.xml

Hess, M., & Yeung, H. W. C. (2006). Whither global production networks in economic geography? Past, present, and future. *Environment and Planning A*, *38*(7), 1193–1204.

Hirschman, A. O. (1958). *The Strategy of Economic Development*. New Haven, CT: Yale University Press.

Hoa, D., & Lin, J. Y. (2016). Provincial governance and foreign direct investment in Vietnam: An empirical study at sub nation level. *International Journal of Business and Applied Social Science*, *2*(5), 1–11.

Hoang, L. (2022, August 6). Samsung to begin making semiconductor parts in Vietnam in 2023. *Nikkei Asia*. Retrieved on 21 February, 2023, from https://asia.nikkei.com/Business/Tech/Semiconductors/Samsung-to-begin-making-semiconductor-parts-in-Vietnam-in-2023

Hollington, A., Salverda, T., Schwarz, T., & Tappe, O. (2015). *Concepts of the Global South* (Vol. 2015). Global South Studies Center Cologne.

Hollweg, C., Smith, T., & Taglioni, D. (Eds.). (2017). *Vietnam at a Crossroads: Engaging in the Next Generation of Global Value Chains*. Washington, DC: World Bank Publications.

Hong Kong Trade Development Council. (2020). *Northern Vietnam: A Magnet for foreign investment.* Retrieved on 20 April, 2023, from https://research.hktdc.com/en/article/MzgwMjM2NTI0.

Horner, R. (2014). Strategic decoupling, recoupling and global production networks: India's pharmaceutical industry. *Journal of Economic Geography*, *14*(6), 1117–1140.

Horner, R. (2016). A new economic geography of trade and development? Governing South-South trade, value chains and production networks. *Territory, Politics, Governance*, *4*(4), 400–420.

Horner, R. (2017). Beyond facilitator? State roles in global value chains and global production networks. *Geography Compass*, *11*(2), 1–13.

Horner, R., & Murphy, J. T. (2018). South-North and South-South production networks: Diverging socio-spatial practices of Indian pharmaceutical firms. *Global Networks*, *18*(2), 326–351.

Horner, R., & Nadvi, K. (2018). Global value chains and the rise of the Global South: Unpacking twenty-first century polycentric trade. *Global Networks, 18*(2), 207–237.

Hosokawa, K., & Tomiyama, A. (2018, July 23). Samsung suppliers in Vietnam branch out to new frontiers. *Nikkei Asia*. Retrieved on 20 April, 2023, from https://asia.nikkei.com/Business/Business-trends/Samsung-suppliers-in-Vietnam-branch-out-to-new-frontiers.

Hsu, J. Y. (2017). State transformation and the evolution of economic nationalism in the East Asian developmental state: The Taiwanese semiconductor industry as case study. *Transactions of the Institute of British Geographers*, *42*(2), 166–178.

Huang, X., & Chi, R. Y. (2014). Chinese private firms' outward foreign direct investment: Does firm ownership and size matter? *Thunderbird International Business Review*, *56*(5), 393–406.

Hymer, S. (1960). *The International Operations of National Firms: A Study of Direct Foreign Investment.* (PhD thesis). Massachusetts Institute of Technology, Cambridge, MA: The MIT Press.

International Labour Organization. (2022). *Viet Nam's Electronics Supply Chain: Decent Work Challenges and Opportunities*. Geneva: International Labour Office.

Ivarsson, I., & Alvstam, C. G. (2010). Supplier upgrading in the home-furnishing value chain: An empirical study of IKEA's sourcing in China and South East Asia. *World Development*, *38*(11), 1575–1587.

Iyengar, R. (2022, July 28). Why apple can't quit China. *Cable News Network (CNN)*. Retrieved on 27 April, 2023, from https://edition.cnn.com/2022/07/28/tech/apple-china-manufacturing-sales/index.html

Jackson, P. (2002). Commercial cultures: Transcending the cultural and the economic. *Progress in Human Geography*, *26*(1), 3–18.

Jamrisko, M. (2019, June 3). *Vietnam tops list of biggest winners from U.S.-China Trade War*. Bloomberg. Retrieved on 19 June, 2021, from https://www.bloomberg.com/news/articles/2019-06-03/vietnam-tops-list-of-biggest-winners-from-u-s-china-trade-war#xj4y7vzkg

Jandl, T. (2013). *Vietnam in the Global Economy: The Dynamics of Integration, Decentralization, and Contested Politics*. Plymouth: Lexington Books.

Jenkins, R. O., & Thoburn, J. T. (2003). Can trade reform reduce global poverty? *IDS Policy Briefing 19*. Brighton: Institute of Development Studies. Retrieved on 17 April, 2020, from www.ids.ac.uk/ids/bookshop/briefs/PB19.pdf

Jessop, B. (2001). Institutional re (turns) and the strategic-relational approach. *Environment and Planning A*, *33*(7), 1213–1235.

Jones, A. (2008). Beyond embeddedness: Economic practices and the invisible dimensions to transnational business activity. *Progress in Human Geography*, *32*(1), 71–88.

Kadarusman, Y. & Nadvi, K. (2013). Competitiveness and technological upgrading in global value chains: Evidence from the Indonesian electronics and garment sectors. *European Planning Studies*, *21*(7), 1007–1028.

Kaplinsky, R., & Farooki, M. (2010). Global value chains, the crisis, and the shift of markets from north to south. In O. Cattaneo, et al. (Eds.), *Global Value Chains in a Postcrisis World: A Development Perspective* (pp. 125–154). Washington, D.C.: World Bank Publications

Kaplinsky, R., & Farooki, M. (2011). What are the Implications for Global Value Chains when the Market Shifts from the North to the South? *International Journal of Technological Learning, Innovation and Development*, *4*(1–3), 13–38.

Kasahara, S. (2004). *The Flying Geese Paradigm: a Critical Study of Its Application to East Asian Regional Development* (United Nations Conference on Trade and Development Discussion Papers No. 169). Geneva, Switzerland: United Nations Conference on Trade and Development.

Kawakami, M., & Sturgeon, T. J. (2010). *Global Value Chains in the Electronics Industry: Was the Crisis a Window of Opportunity for Developing Countries?* (Policy Research working paper No. WPS 5417). Washington, D.C.: The World Bank.

Kenney, M. (2004). Introduction. In M. Kenney & R. Florida (Eds.), *Locating Global Advantage: Industry Dynamics in the International Economy* (pp.1–20), Stanford, CA: Stanford University Press.

Knight, F. (1921). *Risk, Uncertainty, and Profit.* Boston: Houghton Mifflin.

Ko, W. W., & Liu, G. (2017). A typology of guanxi-based governance mechanisms for knowledge transfer in business networks of Chinese small and medium-sized enterprises. *Group & Organization Management*, *42*(4), 548–590.

Kokko, A. (1994). Technology, market characteristics, and spillovers. *Journal of Development Economics*, *43*(2), 279–293.

Kostova, T., Roth, K., & Dacin, M. T. (2008). Institutional theory in the study of multinational corporations: A critique and new directions. *Academy of Management Review*, *33*(4), 994–1006.

Kuchiki, A. (2007). *Industrial Policy in Asia.* (Institute of Developing Economics Discussion Papers No. 128). Chiba, Japan: Institute of Developing Economics.

Lăng, T. (2022, July 26). The journey of Samsung in Vietnam. *Viettonkin Consulting.* Retrieved on 24 April, 2023, from https://www.viettonkinconsulting.com/news/the-journey-of-samsung-in-vietnam/

Lee, A., & Zhou, C. (2019, April 23). China's belt and road may accelerate exit of manufacturing? *South China Moring Post.* Retrieved on 22 December, 2019, from https://www.scmp.com/economy/china-economy/article/3007183/chinas-belt-and-road-may-accelerate-exit-manufacturing

Lee, J. (2016). Global value chains and the changing pattern of North-South Trade: Apparel, electronics and automotive sectors in 2005–2014. *Journal of International Trade & Commerce*, *12*(6), 1–21.

Lee, J., & Gereffi, G. (2015). Global value chains, rising power firms and economic and social upgrading. *Critical Perspectives on International Business*, *11*(3/4), 319–339.

Lee, J., Kim, J. C., & Lim, J. (2016). Globalization and divergent paths of industrial development: Mobile phone manufacturing in China, Japan, South Korea and Taiwan. *Journal of Contemporary Asia*, *46*(2), 222–246.

Lee, J., & Lim, H.-C. (2018). *Mobile Asia: Capitalisms, Value Chains and Mobile Telecommunication in Asia.* Seoul: Seoul National University Press.

Lee, Y. (2020, November 26). Exclusive: Foxconn to shift some Apple production to Vietnam to minimise China risk. *Reuters*. Retrieved on 24 April, 2023, from https://www.reuters.com/article/us-foxconn-vietnam-apple-exclusive-idUSKBN2860VN

Lee, Y. S., Heo, I., & Kim, H. (2014). The role of the state as an inter-scalar mediator in globalizing liquid crystal display industry development in South Korea. *Review of International Political Economy*, *21*(1), 102–129.

Leslie, D., & Reimer, S. (1999). Spatializing commodity chains. *Progress in Human Geography*, *23*(3), 401–420.

Levy, D. L. (2008). Political contestation in global production networks. *Academy of Management Review*, *33*(4), 943–963.

Lian, C. (2018). Relocating china's manufacturing capacity and industrialization to Africa. In T. Simelane & L. Managa (Eds.), *Belt and Road Initiative: Alternative Development Path for Africa* (pp. 89–100). Pretoria: Africa Institute of South Africa.

Liang, Y., Zeng, J., Kuik, C. et al. (2021). Policy transfer and scale reconstruction of China's overseas industrial parks: A case study of the Malaysia-China Kuantan Industrial Park. *Journal of Geographical Sciences*, *31*, 733–746.

Liem, N. D. (2015). China FDI in Vietnam after Twenty Years. *Vietnam Social Sciences*, *6*(170), 20–31.

Lin, J. Y. (2012). From flying geese to leading dragons: New opportunities and strategies for structural transformation in developing countries 1. *Global Policy*, *3*(4), 397–409.

Lo Iacono, V., Symonds, P., & Brown, D. H. (2016). Skype as a tool for qualitative research interviews. *Sociological Research Online*, *21*(2), 103–117.

Luo, Y. (2001). Toward a cooperative view of MNC-host government relations: Building blocks and performance implications. *Journal of International Business Studies*, *32*(3), 401–419.

Luo, Y. (2004). A coopetition perspective of MNC–host government relations. *Journal of International Management*, *10*(4), 431–451.

MacKinnon, D. (2012). Beyond strategic coupling: Reassessing the firm-region nexus in global production networks. *Journal of Economic Geography*, *12*(1), 227–245.

MacKinnon, D., Dawley, S., Pike, A., & Cumbers, A. (2019). Rethinking path creation: A geographical political economy approach. *Economic Geography*, *95*(2), 113–135.

Mann, C., & Kirkegaard, J. (2006). *Accelerating the Globalization of America: The Next Wave of Information Technology*. Washington, D.C.: Institute for International Economics.

MarketWatch (2017, July 31). *Foxconn's History of Broken Promises Casts a Shadow on Wisconsin News*. Retrieved on 11 July, 2019, from https://baodautu.vn/dai-gia-foxconn-hua-leo-ve-du-an-ty-do-d32257.html

Martin, R., Tyler, P., Storper, M., Evenhuis, E., & Glasmeier, A. (2018). Globalization at a critical conjuncture? *Cambridge Journal of Regions, Economy and Society*, *11*(1), 3–16.

Masina, P. (2012). Vietnam between developmental state and neoliberalism: The case of the industrial sector. In K. Chang, et al. (Eds.), *Developmental Politics in Transition* (pp. 188–210). London: Palgrave Macmillan.

Mathews, J. A. (2017). Dragon multinationals powered by linkage, leverage and learning: A review and development. *Asia Pacific Journal of Management*, *34*(4), 769–775.

Mayring, P. (2007, September). On generalization in qualitatively oriented research. *Forum Qualitative Sozialforschung Forum: Qualitative Social Research*, *8*(3).

McCann, P. (2010). International business and economic geography: Knowledge, time and transactions costs. *Journal of Economic Geography*, *11*(2), 309–317.

McCarty, A., & Steley, C. (2004). *Vietnam Economic Country Update 2004*. Hanoi: Mekong Economics Ltd.

McKinsey Global Institute (2016). *Urban World: The Global Consumers to Watch*. London: McKinsey & Company.

Meyer, K. E., & Nguyen, H. V. (2005). Foreign investment strategies and subnational institutions in emerging markets: Evidence from Vietnam. *Journal of Management Studies*, *42*(1), 63–93.

Milelli, C. (1997). Asian economic integration and the role of the Japanese corporate networks: The case of the electronics industry. In S. Dzever & J. Jaussaud (Eds.), *Perspectives on Economic Integration and Business Strategy in the Asia-Pacific Region* (pp. 189–207). London: Palgrave Macmillan.

Mohammad, W., Elomri, A., & Kerbache, L. (2022). The global semiconductor chip shortage: Causes, implications, and potential remedies. *IFAC-PapersOnLine*, *55*(10), 476–483.

Murphy, J. T. (2012). Global production networks, relational proximity, and the sociospatial dynamics of market internationalization in Bolivia's wood products sector. *Annals of the Association of American Geographers*, *102*(1), 208–233.

Nadvi, K. (2014). "Rising powers" and labour and environmental standards. *Oxford Development Studies*, *42*(2), 137–150.

Nakamura, H., & Marukawa, T. (2024). How can the value added of Vietnam's export industries be increased? *The Japanese Political Economy*, 1–21.

Navas-Alemán, L. (2011). The impact of operating in multiple value chains for upgrading: The case of the Brazilian furniture and footwear industries. *World Development*, *39*(8), 1386–1397.

Neilson, J., & Pritchard, B. (2009). *Value Chain Struggles: Institutions and Governance in the Plantation Districts of South India*. Chichester: Wiley-Blackwell.

Neilson, J., Pritchard, B., & Yeung, H. W. (2014). Global value chains and global production networks in the changing international political economy: An introduction. *Review of International Political Economy*, *21*(1), 1–8.

Neilson, J., Pritchard, B., & Yeung, H. W. (Eds.). (2015). *Global Value Chains and Global Production Networks: Changes in the International Political Economy*. London: Routledge.

Neilson, J., Pritchard, B., Fold, N., & Dwiartama, A. (2018). Lead firms in the cocoa—chocolate global production network: An assessment of the deductive capabilities of GPN 2.0. *Economic Geography*, *94*(4), 400–424.

Nell, P. C., Puck, J., & Heidenreich, S. (2015). Strictly limited choice or agency? Institutional duality, legitimacy, and subsidiaries' political strategies. *Journal of World Business*, *50*(2), 302–311.

Nguyen, H. T., Nguyen, H. V., & Meyer, K. E. (2004). Foreign direct investment in Vietnam. In S. Estrin & K. E. Meyer (Eds.), *Investment Strategies in Emerging Economies* (pp. 243–268). Cheltenham: Edward Elgar.

Oh, J. H., & Mah, J. S. (2017). The patterns of Korea's foreign direct investment in Vietnam. *Open Journal of Business and Management*, *5*(2), 253–271.

Oliver, C. (1996). The institutional embeddedness of economic activity. In J. A. C. Baum & J. E. Dutton (Eds.), *Advances in Strategic Management* (pp. 163–186). Greenwich, CT: JAI Press.

Organisation for Economic Co-operation and Development. (2021). SME and entrepreneurship policy in Viet Nam. In *OECD Studies on SMEs and Entrepreneurship*. Paris, FR: Secretary-General of the OECD.

Ozawa, T. (2011). The (Japan-born) "flying-geese" theory of economic development revisited—and reformulated from a structuralist perspective. *Global Policy*, *2*(3), 272–285.

Pache, A. C., & Santos, F. (2010). When worlds collide: The internal dynamics of organizational responses to conflicting institutional demands. *Academy of Management Review*, *35*(3), 455–476.

Pan, C. (2009). What is Chinese about Chinese businesses? Locating the "rise of China" in global production networks. *Journal of Contemporary China*, *18*(58), 7–25.

Panwar, R., Pinkse, J., & De Marchi, V. (2022). The future of global supply chains in a post-COVID-19 world. *California Management Review*, *64*(2), 5–23.

Park, S. H., & Luo, Y. (2001). Guanxi and organizational dynamics: Organizational networking in Chinese firms. *Strategic Management Journal*, *22*(5), 455–477.

Peng, M. W., Wang, D. Y., & Jiang, Y. (2008). An institution-based view of international business strategy: A focus on emerging economies. *Journal of International Business Studies*, *39*, 920–936.

Phelps, N. A., Atienza, M., & Arias, M. (2018). An invitation to the dark side of economic geography. *Environment and Planning A: Economy and Space*, *50*(1), 236–244.

Pickles, J., Barrientos, S., & Knorringa, P. (2016). New end markets, supermarket expansion and shifting social standards. *Environment and Planning A: Economy and Space*, *48*(7), 1284–1301.

Pincus, J. (2015). Why doesn't Vietnam grow faster? State fragmentation and the limits of vent for surplus growth. *Journal of Southeast Asian Economies*, *32*(1), 26–51.

Piore, M. J., & Sabel, C. F. (1984). *The Second Industrial Divide: Possibilities for Prosperity*. New York, NY: Basic Books.

Ponte, S. (2020). Green capital accumulation: Business and sustainability management in a world of global value chains. *New Political Economy*, *25*(1), 72–84.

Puck, J. F., Rogers, H., & Mohr, A. T. (2013). Flying under the radar: Foreign firm visibility and the efficacy of political strategies in emerging economies. *International Business Review*, *22*(6), 1021–1033.

Ren, X., & Yang, S. (2020). Empirical study on location choice of Chinese OFDI. *China Economic Review*, *61*, 1–11.

Reuters. (2020, June 19). Samsung to relocate Chinese display production to Vietnam. *Reuters*. Retrieved on 24 April, 2023, from https://www.reuters.com/article/vietnam-samsung-idUSL4N2DW2CV

Revilla Diez, J. (2016). Vietnam 30 years after Doi Moi: Achievements and challenges. *Zeitschrift für Wirtschaftsgeographie*, *60*(3), 121–133.

Roztocki, N., & Weistroffer, H. R. (2008). Information technology investments in emerging economies. *Information Technology for Development*, *14*(1), 1–10.

Saxenian, A. L. (2006). *The New Argonauts: Regional Advantage in a Global Economy*. Cambridge, MA: Harvard University Press.

Schoenberger, E. (1988). From Fordism to flexible accumulation: Technology, competitive strategies, and international location. *Environment and Planning D: Society and Space*, *6*(3), 245–262.

Scott, A. J. (1988). Flexible production systems and regional development: The rise of new industrial spaces in North America and Western Europe. *International Journal of Urban and Regional Research*, *12*(2), 171–186.

Scott, A. J. (1992). The collective order of flexible production agglomerations: Lessons for local economic development policy and strategic choice. *Economic Geography*, *68*, 219–233.

Serič, A., Görg, H., Mösle, S., & Windisch, M. (2020, April 17). *Managing COVID-19: How the Pandemic Disrupts Global Value Chains*. Industrial Analytics Platform, United Nations Industrial Development Organization. Retrieved on 26 April, 2020, from https://iap.unido.org/articles/managing-covid-19-how-pandemic-disrupts-global-value-chains

Shin, J. S. (2017). Dynamic catch-up strategy, capability expansion and changing windows of opportunity in the memory industry. *Research Policy*, *46*(2), 404–416.

Shortell, T. (2019, September 20). *Vietnams Value in Supply Chains*. CB Richard Ellis. Retrieved on 19 May, 2020, from https://www.cbre.com/insights/articles/vietnams-value-in-supply-chains

Smith, A., Pickles, J., Buček, M., Pástor, R., & Begg, B. (2014). The political economy of global production networks: Regional industrial change and differential upgrading in the East European clothing industry. *Journal of Economic Geography*, *14*(6), 1023–1051.

Sturgeon, T. J. (2002). Modular production networks: A new American model of industrial organization. *Industrial and Corporate Change*, *11*(3), 451–496.

Sturgeon, T. J., & Kawakami, M. (2011). Global value chains in the electronics industry: Characteristics, crisis, and upgrading opportunities for firms from developing countries. *International Journal of Technological Learning, Innovation and Development*, *4*(1–3), 120–147.

Sturgeon, T. J., & Memedović, O. (2011). *Mapping Global Value Chains: Intermediate Goods Trade and Structural Change in the World Economy* (UNIDO Development Policy and Strategic Research Branch Working Paper No. 05/2010). Vienna, Austria: United Nations Industrial Development Organization.

Sturgeon, T. J., & Zylberberg, E. (2016). *The Global Information and Communications Technology Industry: Where Vietnam Fits in Global Value Chains* (World Bank Policy Research Working Paper No. 7916). Washington, D.C.: World Bank Publications.

Sturgeon, T. J., & Zylberberg, E. (2017). Vietnam's evolving role in ICT global value chains. In C. H. Hollweg, T. Smith, & D. Taglioni (Eds.), *Vietnam at a Crossroads: Engaging in the Next Generation of Global Value Chains* (pp. 133–158). Washington, D.C.: World Bank Publications.

Suchman, M. C. (1995). Managing legitimacy: Strategic and institutional approaches. *Academy of Management Review*, *20*(3), 571–610.

Sunley, P. (1992). An uncertain future: A critique of post-Keynesian economic geographies. *Progress in Human Geography*, *16*(1), 58–70.

Sunley, P. (2008). Relational economic geography: A partial understanding or a new paradigm? *Economic Geography*, *84*(1), 1–26.

Su, X. (2014). Multi-scalar regionalization, network connections and the development of Yunnan Province, China. *Regional Studies*, *48*(1), 91–104.

Sweeney, P. (2022, November 29). China decoupling takes one step forward, one back. *Reuters*. Retrieved on 24 April, 2023, from https://www.reuters.com/breakingviews/china-decoupling-takes-one-step-forward-one-back-2022-11-29/

Tang, F., Gao, X., & Li, Q. (2008). Knowledge acquisition and learning strategies in globalization of China's Enterprises. In I. Alon & J. R. McIntyre (Eds.), *The Globalization of Chinese Enterprises* (pp. 31–43). New York, NY: Palgrave Macmillan.

Taylor, M. J. (1975). Organizational growth, spatial interaction and location decision-making. *Regional Studies*, *9*(4), 313–323.

Thoburn, J. (2009). *Vietnam as a Role Model for Development* (WIDER Research Paper No. 2009/30). Helsinki, FI: The United Nations University World Institute for Development Economics Research (UNU-WIDER).

Thorbecke, W. (2016). *Understanding the Flow of Electronic Parts and Components in East Asia*. Research Institute of Economy, Trade and Industry.

Thun, E., Taglioni, D., Sturgeon, T., & Dallas, M. P. (2022). *Massive Modularity: Understanding Industry Organization in the Digital Age* (World Bank Policy Research Working Paper No.10164). Washington, D.C.: World Bank Publications.

Tibken, S. (2015, July 22). *Schooling Vietnam: How Tech Companies are Training the Next Wave of Workers*. Computer Network. Retrieved on 15 January, 2019, from https://www.cnet.com/news/

Titievskaia, J., Kononenko, V., Navarra, C., Stamegna, C., & Zumer, K. (2020). Slowing down or changing track? Understanding the dynamics of "slowbalisation". *European Parliamentary Research Service*. EU: European Parliament.

Truong, H. Q. (2022). *Vietnam's Global Value Chains Participation and Policy Implications for South Korea-Vietnam Economic Cooperation* (KIEP Research Paper No.22–37). Sejong, KR: Korea Institute for International Economic Policy.

Tung, A. (2003). Beyond flying geese: The expansion of East Asia's electronics trade. *German Economic Review*, *4*(1), 35–51.

United Nations Conference on Trade and Development. (2004). *The New Geography of International Economic Relations* (Document No. TD/B/51/6). Office of the Chairman of the Group of 77, New York.

United Nations Conference on Trade and Development. (2018). *ASEAN Investment Report 2018: Foreign Direct Investment and the Digital Economy in ASEAN*. New York, NY: United Nations.

United Nations Industrial Development Organization. (2015). *Economic Zones in the ASEAN*. UNIDO Country Office in Viet Nam.

United Nations Industrial Development Organization. (2017). *Demand for Manufacturing: Driving Inclusive and Sustainable Industrial Development* (Industrial Development Report 2018). Vienna, Austria: United Nations Industrial Development Organization.

United Nations Industrial Development Organization. (2021). *Industrial Development Report 2022. The Future of Industrialization in a Post-Pandemic World* (Industrial Development Report 2022). Vienna, Austria: United Nations Industrial Development Organization.

United States Government Accountability Office. (2006). *OFFSHORING: U.S. Semiconductor and Software Industries Increasingly Produce in China and India* (Report to Congressional Committees). Washington, D.C.: United States Government Accountability Office.

Vietnam Chamber of Commerce and Industry. (2020). *The Provincial Competitiveness Index Report 2020*. Retrieved on 16 April, 2023, from https://pcivietnam.vn/en/publications/2020-pci-full-report-ct187

Vietnam Chamber of Commerce and Industry. (2021). *The Provincial Competitiveness Index Report 2021*. Retrieved on 16 April, 2023, from https://pcivietnam.vn/en/publications/2021-pci-full-report-ct204

Vietnam Chamber of Commerce and Industry. (2022). Samsung completed parts of construction of R&D centre in Hanoi. *Vietnam Investment Review*. Retrieved on 16 April, 2023, from https://en.vcci.com.vn/samsung-completed-parts-of-construction-of-rd-centre-in-hanoi

VietnamNet. (2016, May 25). Foxconn acquires Microsoft's smartphone facility in Vietnam. *VietnamNet Global*. Retrieved on 15 November, 2019, from https://english.vietnamnet.vn/fms/business/156919/foxconn-acquires-microsoft-s-smartphone-facility-in-vietnam.html

VietNamNet Bridge. (2018, April 26). Vietnam ranks 12th globally in electronic exports. *VietnamNet Global*. Retrieved on 9 November, 2019, from https://vietnamnet.vn/en/vietnam-ranks-12th-globally-in-electronic-exports-E199406.html

VietnamPlus. (2018, June 16). Trade union set up in LG Display Vietnam-Hai Phong. Retrieved on 15 January, 2019, from https://en.vietnamplus.vn/trade-union-set-up-in-lg-display-vietnamhai-phong/132990.vnp

VietnamPlus. (2021, August 27). Samsung Vietnam helps local firms join global supply chain. Retrieved on 24 April, 2023, from https://en.vietnamplus.vn/samsung-vietnam-helps-local-firms-join-global-supply-chain/207116.vnp

Völlers, P., Neise, T., Verfürth, P., Franz, M., Bücken, F., & Schumacher, K. P. (2023). Revisiting risk in the Global Production Network approach 2.0—Towards a performative risk narrative perspective. *Environment and Planning A: Economy and Space*, *55*(8), 1833–2165.

Vo, T. T., Le, V. T., & Vu, T. T. A. (2007). *Provincial Extralegal Investment Incentives in the Context of Decentralisation in Viet Nam: Mutually Beneficial or a Race to the Bottom* (UNDP Policy Dialogue Paper No. 5088790-01). Hanoi, VNM: United Nations Development Program.

Witt, M. & Lewin, A. Y. (2007). Outward foreign direct investment as escape response to home country institutional constraints. *Journal of International Business Studies*, *38*(4), 579–594.

Womack, B. (2006). *China and Vietnam: The Politics of Asymmetry*. Cambridge: Cambridge University Press.

World Vision. (2017, June 22). New LG-funded IT library to support vocational training in Hai Phong. *World Vision International in Vietnam*. Retrieved on 15 January, 2019, from https://www.wvi.org/vietnam/pressrelease/new-lg-funded-it-library-support-vocational-training-hai-phong

Wrana, J., & Nguyen, T. X. T. (2019). "Strategic coupling" and regional development in a transition economy: What can we learn from Vietnam? *Area Development and Policy*, *4*(4), 454–465.

Wu, B., & Deng, P. (2020). Internationalization of SMEs from emerging markets: An institutional escape perspective. *Journal of Business Research*, *108*, 337–350.

Xu, Y. (2014). Chinese state-owned enterprises in Africa: Ambassadors or freebooters? *Journal of Contemporary China*, *23*(89), 822–840.

Yamakawa, Y., Peng, M. W., & Deeds, D. L. (2008). What drives new ventures to internationalize from emerging to developed economies? *Entrepreneurship theory and practice*, *32*(1), 59–82.

Yang, C. (2009). Strategic coupling of regional development in global production networks: Redistribution of Taiwanese personal computer investment from the Pearl River Delta to the Yangtze River Delta, China. *Regional Studies*, *43*(3), 385–407.

Yang, C. (2012). Restructuring the export-oriented industrialization in the Pearl River Delta, China: Institutional evolution and emerging tension. *Applied Geography*, *32*(1), 143–157.

Yang, C. (2013). From Strategic coupling to recoupling and decoupling: Restructuring of global production networks and regional evolution in China. *European Planning Studies*, *21*(7), 1046–1063.

Yang, C. (2014). Market rebalancing of global production networks in the Post-Washington Consensus globalizing era: Transformation of export-oriented development in China. *Review of International Political Economy, 21* (1), 130–156.

Yang, C. (2016). Relocating labour-intensive manufacturing firms from China to Southeast Asia: A preliminary investigation. *Bandung: Journal of the Global South*, *3*(3), 1–13.

Yang, C. (2017). The rise of strategic partner firms and reconfiguration of personal computer production networks in China: Insights from the emerging laptop cluster in Chongqing. *Geoforum*, *84*, 21–31.

Yang, C., & Chan, D. Y. T. (2023). Geopolitical risks of strategic decoupling and recoupling in the mobile phone production shift from China to Vietnam: Evidence from the Sino-US trade war and COVID-19 pandemic. *Applied Geography, 158*, 103028.

Yang, C., & Fu, T. (2017). From exports to sell in China: Transformation of the export-oriented firms in the Pearl River Delta. *Geografiska Annaler: Series B, Human Geography*, *99*(4), 380–398.

Yang, C., & He, C. (2017). Transformation of China's "world factory": Production relocation and export evolution of the electronics firms. *Tijdschrift voor Economische en Sociale Geografie*, *108*(5), 571–591.

Yang, D. Y. R., & Chen, Y. C. (2013). The ODM model and co-evolution in the global notebook PC industry: Evidence from Taiwan. *Advances in Applied Sociology*, *3*(1), 69–78.

Yang, D. Y. R., & Hsia, C. J. (2007). Spatial clustering and organizational dynamics of transborder production networks: A case study of Taiwanese information-technology companies in the Greater Suzhou Area, China. *Environment and Planning A*, *39*(6), 1346–1363.

Yang, D. Y. R., Hsu, J. Y., & Ching, C. H. (2009). Revisiting the Silicon Island? The geographically varied "strategic coupling" in the development of high-technology parks in Taiwan. *Regional Studies*, *43*(3), 369–384.

Ye, M., Shen, J. H., Golson, E., Lee, C. C., & Li, Y. (2022). The impact of Sino-US trade friction on the performance of China's textile and apparel industry. *International Finance*, *25*(2), 151–166.

Yean T. S., Yi, A. K. J., & Ann, T. B. (2019). US-China trade war: Potential trade and investment spillovers into Malaysia. *Asian Economic Papers*, *18*(3), 117–135.

Yeung, G. (2001). *Foreign Investment and Socio-economic Development in China: The Case of Dongguan*. Basingstoke: Palgrave.

Yeung, H. W. C. (1994). Critical reviews of geographical perspectives on business organizations and the organization of production: Towards a network approach. *Progress in Human Geography*, *18*(4), 460–490.

Yeung, H. W. C. (1998). The social-spatial constitution of business organizations: A geographical perspective. *Organization*, *5*(1), 101–128.

Yeung, H. W. C. (2004). *Chinese Capitalism in a Global Era: Towards Hybrid Capitalism*. London: Routledge.

Yeung, H. W. C. (2005). Organizational space: A new frontier in international business strategy? *Critical Perspective on International Business*, *1*(4), 219–240.

Yeung, H. W. C. (2006). *Situating Regional Development in the Competitive Dynamics of Global Production Networks: An East Asian Perspective* (Working Paper Series No. 2006–15). London: Plenary lecture at the Regional Studies Association Annual Conference.

Yeung, H. W. C. (2007). From followers to market leaders: Asian electronics firms in the global economy. *Asia Pacific Viewpoint*, *48*(1), 1–25.

Yeung, H. W. C. (2009a). Transnationalizing entrepreneurship: A critical agenda for economic geography. *Progress in Human Geography*, *33*(2), 210–235.

Yeung, H. W. C. (2009b). Regional development and the competitive dynamics of global production networks: An East Asian perspective. *Regional Studies*, *43*(3), 325–351.

Yeung, H. W. C. (2014). Governing the market in a globalizing era: Developmental states, global production networks, and inter-firm dynamics in East Asia. *Review of International Political Economy*, *21*(1), 70–101.

Yeung, H. W. C. (2015). Regional development in the global economy: A dynamic perspective of strategic coupling in global production networks. *Regional Science Policy & Practice*, *7*(1), 1–24.

Yeung, H. W. C. (2016). *Strategic Coupling: East Asian Industrial Transformation in the New Global Economy*. Ithaca, NY: Cornell University Press.

Yeung, H. W. C. (2017). Global production networks and foreign direct investment by small and medium enterprises in ASEAN. *Transnational corporations*, *24*(2), 1–42.

Yeung, H. W. C. (2019). *Global Production and Economic Development in Asia: A Study of Leading Electronics Firms and their Production Networks*. Global Production Networks Centre, National University of Singapore.

Yeung, H. W. C. (2021a). The trouble with global production networks. *Environment and Planning A: Economy and Space*, *53*(2), 428–438.

Yeung, H. W. C. (2021b). Regional worlds: From related variety in regional diversification to strategic coupling in global production networks. *Regional Studies*, *55*(6), 989–1010.

Yeung, H. W. C. (2022a). Explaining geographic shifts of chip making toward East Asia and market dynamics in semiconductor global production networks. *Economic Geography*, *98*(3), 272–298.

Yeung, H. W. C. (2022b). *Interconnected Worlds: Global Electronics and Production Networks in East Asia*. Stanford, CA: Stanford University Press.

Yeung, H. W. C., & Coe, N. (2015). Toward a dynamic theory of global production networks. *Economic geography*, *91*(1), 29–58.

Yeung, H. W. C., & Liu, W. (2008). Globalizing China: The rise of mainland firms in the global economy. *Eurasian Geography and Economics*, *49*(1), 57–86.

Yin, R. K. (2018). *Case Study Research and Applications* (6th ed.). Thousand Oaks, CA: SAGE.

Zhang, J. (2014). Global financial crisis and the "spatial fix" of China's world factory: The great "Long March" Inland. In Y. Atasoy (Ed.), *Global Economic Crisis and the Politics of Diversity* (pp. 132–154). London: Palgrave MacMillan.

Zhao, S. (2010). The China Model: Can it replace the Western model of modernization? *Journal of Contemporary China*, *19*(65), 419–436.

Zhu, S., & He, C. (2013). Geographical dynamics and industrial relocation: Spatial strategies of apparel firms in Ningbo, China. *Eurasian Geography and Economics*, *54*(3), 342–362.

Zhu, S., & Pickles, J. (2014). Bring in, go up, go west, go out: Upgrading, regionalisation and delocalisation in China's apparel production networks. *Journal of Contemporary Asia*, *44*(1), 36–63.

Index

About the Authors

David Yuen Tung CHAN is a research assistant professor at the School of Graduate Studies and a center fellow at the Institute of Policy Studies at Lingnan University. As an economic geographer, his main research interests cover regional economic development in China and Southeast Asia, (de) globalization/regionalization, digitalization, industrial transformation, global production networks, and global value chains. He has published papers in international journals such as *Journal of Contemporary China*, *Applied Geography*, *Current Issues in Tourism*, *Journal of Urban Affairs, Tijdschrift Voor Economische en Sociale Geografie*, as well as chapters and articles in edited books, magazines, and newspapers.

Chun YANG is a chair professor in the Department of Geography and associate dean (research) at the Faculty of Arts and Social Sciences at Hong Kong Baptist University. Her main research interests are in urban and regional development, global/cross-border production networks and transnational corporations, the geographies of innovation and technology, and industrial restructuring and local clusters in China, particularly the Pearl River Delta, Hong Kong, and the Greater Bay Area, as well as Southeast Asia. Professor Yang is currently an editor of *Cambridge Journal of Regions, Economy and Society* and an editorial/advisory board member of leading international journals, including *Applied Geography*, *Journal of Economic Geography*, *Environment and Planning A*, *Progress in Economic Geography*, *Bandung: A Journal of Global South*, and *Weizenbaum Journal of the Digital Society*. She served previously as an associate editor of *Regional Studies, Regional Science* (2014–2019). Professor Yang has published extensively in high-ranking international journals such as *Economic Geography*; *Annals of the American*

Association of Geographers; *Applied Geography*; *Regional Studies*; *Journal of Contemporary China*; *Geoforum*; *Global Networks; Urban Studies*; *Cities; Geoforum*; *Environment and Planning A*; *Environment and Planning C*; *Political Geography*; *Eurasian Geography and Economics*; *European Planning Studies*; and so on.

www.ingramcontent.com/pod-product-compliance
Lightning Source LLC
LaVergne TN
LVHW091529200926
848483LV00002B/341

* 9 7 8 1 6 6 6 9 3 1 4 6 4 *